FAMILY FIRST

Your Step-by-Step Plan for Creating a Phenomenal Family

Dr. Phil McGraw

SIMON &
SCHUSTER

New York   London   Toronto   Sydney

First published in Great Britain by Simon & Schuster UK Ltd, 2005
A Viacom Company

1 3 5 7 9 10 8 6 4 2

Simon & Schuster UK Ltd
Africa House
64–78 Kingsway
London WC2B 6AH

www.simonsays.co.uk

Simon & Schuster Australia
Sydney

A CIP catalogue record for this book is available from the British Library

ISBN 0-7432-6788-5
EAN 9780743267885

Printed and bound in Great Britain by
Mackays of Chatham Plc, Chatham, Kent

To Robin, Jay and Jordan, my family,
my base of operations,
my strength in life.

And to
My mother, who has loved and sacrificed for her family
with joy and selflessness. In memory of my father,
whose spiritual growth was inspiring.

And to
All the parents in this world who are striving to get it right, maximize their
histories and give their children a real chance at authenticity,
success and happiness.

Acknowledgments

It is an obligation to protect and care for our families, but it is a task that should be filled with joy. Likewise, creating this book has been a demanding project, but one from which I have derived a great deal of pleasure. *Family First* is one of those projects in life where lots of people do the work, but one person seems to get all the credit. I had the distinct privilege of working with an incredible "family" of tireless and dedicated people who helped me with the challenge of bringing together *Family First*.

I first thank Robin, my wife, friend and co-parent for her patience, counsel and encouragement during the two-plus years that I have worked to conceptualize and write *Family First*. Ours has truly been a partnership as we have raised our two boys, with great hope and optimism that they would one day become fine young men. Robin, you have often said that God put you on this earth to be a wife and mother. Our family, of which you are the heart, is testimony that you have risen to embrace that calling. Over the last twenty-eight years, we have loved, cried, laughed, despaired and celebrated. Through it all, your commitment as a wife and mother has never wavered and I thank you for the gift of our family, for the gift of you.

I thank my sons Jay and Jordan for supporting their dad and being such good sports about sharing our family with the cameras and the world. You boys are what make it all worthwhile as I watch each of you become the unique and authentic young man you are meant to be. You make me proud every day of my life.

I thank my mother and father, who did the best they could with what they had at the time and for never giving up on me or our family across their fifty years of marriage. I also thank my sisters Deana, Donna and

Brenda, who hung in there with me as we made our way through our family's ups and downs and who are still so active in my life today. Being part of our family helped prepare me to lead my own.

I thank Oprah for helping to create the opportunity for me to make a difference in the families of America and the world. Oprah, you are an inspiration and an example to us all by the way you live your life and give so much to so many. Thanks for being such a dear friend to me and my family.

A very special thanks to G. Frank Lawlis, Ph.D., who serves as a supervisory psychologist for the American Mensa, was awarded the Diplomate by the American Board of Professional Psychology in both Clinical and Counseling Psychology and is a fellow of the American Psychological Association. Frank, not only are you an invaluable walking encyclopedia of psychology, for almost thirty years now you have been a close and valued friend. I truly believe that you are the greatest authority in psychology today and the insight, analysis and creative thinking you have brought to this undertaking have been tremendous. I know I can continue to look to you for guidance and the occasional good argument! You are a part of my extended family!

Thanks especially to Maggie Robinson, Ph.D. You are a great editor and writer, and your diligent work on organization and flow has made this book all the more beneficial and remarkable. I've said it before and I'm saying it again, I am proud to call you my friend.

Thank you also to Wes Smith. Your staggeringly positive attitude, great sense of humor and vast energy were essential to completing this project. Your involvement and vision have made this a better book.

Thank you as well to John Chirban, Ph.D., Th.D., who serves as clinical instructor at Harvard Medical School, as psychologist at the Cambridge Health Alliance and as professor of Psychology and chairman of the Department of Human Development at Hellenic College. Your depth of knowledge in psychology and theology was incalculable in your review of the manuscript and your critique and insight truly helped this book to grow in important ways.

Thanks to Terry Wood, Carla Pennington, Gwynne Thomas, Kandi Amalon and Angie Kraus; you are a world-class team! Your dedication, feedback and expertise in creating the *Dr. Phil* show every day and help in bringing my views to so many families make a huge difference. Thanks for your commitment and for continuing to be my "feminine side."

My sincere appreciation and thanks also to Carolyn Reidy, president of Simon & Schuster, and to Dominick Anfuso, my editor, for always sharing in my vision and remaining ever-flexible. Your intimate involvement and aggressive commitment to getting this book into every home in the nation is invaluable and much appreciated.

Thanks also to Scott Madsen for always being at my side and working so tirelessly to keep our message flowing and creating and protecting a semblance of order in my life. Your commitment and support have never waned over the last thirty-five years, and I can't tell you what a difference it has made.

Thanks to Bill Dawson for always being on my team and caring so much about me and my family. Bill, your friendship, counsel and guidance over the last fifteen years have been extremely valuable. Thanks for all the late-night meetings and for so often giving up your Saturdays and Sundays.

This page is not big enough for me to properly thank my team at the Dupree Miller & Associates. When Jan Miller gets onto a project, the world just might as well surrender! Jan, you are the consummate agent and your spirit is absolutely uplifting each and every day. Thanks for believing so much. As I have said before, Shannon Miser-Marven is an absolute "secret weapon" in the world of publishing. Shannon, you are the most talented and committed professional I have ever encountered in any field. I could not have done this book without your minute-to-minute, hour-to-hour hands-on involvement. Jan, you and Shannon are the best of the best and a great combination. Thanks also to Alia Brinkman on the Dupree Miller team. Your hard work is appreciated.

Contents

Dear Parents,

I want to talk to you about family: yours and mine. I'm writing this book as an adult child of loving but sometimes ill-equipped parents, as a current father and husband, and lastly as a career mental-health professional. It is as a fellow concerned parent that I would like to talk to you now, one on one.

I know and feel that, as parents, you and I share some very important priorities. Just like you, I love my family more than anything in this world and I want us all to be safe, healthy, happy and prosperous in everything we do, both within our family and as we go out into the world. It's a day-to-day challenge, but most days it seems to be going "pretty well" at my house. (With two boys, one of them a teenager, living at home, that could have changed in the five minutes since I started writing this letter!) I hope that you are enjoying some harmony as well. However, as parents, it is our job to be aware of everything that can even potentially impact our families. We must be particularly sensitive to those things that can threaten our peaceful and joyful existence, whether those threats come from the outside world or from within our own homes, hearts and histories.

People enter our family's world from all walks of life: teachers, coaches, extended family, school bullies, the all-powerful peers and others. Some are well-intentioned and some not. These people may have priorities and values that are different from our own and they can tremendously affect how our children think, feel and behave now, as well as who they become as adults. Bombardment from a massive and slick media can undermine morals and values in even the strongest of families if purposeful care is not taken to control and counteract those messages. Television, music and movies manufacture heroes and icons with an utter disregard for what is being glamorized. It is our duty as the leaders of our families to make sure we are counteracting rather than contributing to the craziness. We must make certain that we do not threaten our own families from within due to our own lack of adjustment, poor priorities and absence of leadership or by using the negative products and techniques of our own upbringing. As parents we are certainly not the only influences in our children's lives, so we absolutely must make sure we are the best and most persuasive influence in our children's lives.

Cynics will tell you that in our fast-paced society "family" is becoming obsolete, that it is just an old-fashioned, lost concept, getting buried in a busy world of "enlightened" people. I'm here to tell you that that is not right, not even close. Family is even more important today than in generations past, and its erosion is unacceptable. This is a fight we can and must win. This is a fight we will win if we just do our homework and plug in. As a parent you have the power to set your child on a course for success. You may or may not feel powerful right now, but if you have the courage to rise to the challenge your child can and will be blessed beyond belief.

I'm here with a message of hope and optimism, because I believe that families in America, your family and mine, can thrive, survive and in fact flourish! What's more, I believe that you, specifically, can assume the noble role of leading your family through this modern maze, and turn up the volume on the values and beliefs that define what you want for your children and family. All you need is energy and a really good plan. As to the needed energy, you have only to look to the love in your heart to know that you have the power and energy to meet this challenge of creating an environment in which your children and your family can rise above the noise of a world that I sometimes think has gone absolutely mad. That love you have for your children and family is the necessary fuel for your efforts. Now comes the plan, the detailed step-by-step plan that you need to win this tug-of-war with the world and ensure that you have and maintain a PHENOMENAL family!

What I intend to do in *Family First* is tell you with great precision what you need to stop doing and what you need to start doing to lead your family with such a pure purpose and power that the competing messages and influences are drowned out. I plan to help you define success for your specific child or children and then take the steps to create and claim it for you and yours. Your children are the stars in your crown and it is time for them to shine; it is okay for them to shine and, if you do your job, shine they will.

It is time that as parents we say, "Hey, I do not surrender, I do not give up. I will not be intimidated by all the forces tugging on my children and family. I will not accept that disconnected children are just 'how it is' these days. I do not accept the epidemics of oral sex, drugs and alcohol in the middle and upper schools. I do not accept a child that appears 'deaf' when I say, 'Pick up your toys and don't hit your sister in the head anymore.' I will not continue to parent out of fear that my kids won't like me if I require more from them behaviorally, academically and spiritually as I teach them that relationship-building is important in life. I will not feel guilty and go into debt trying to keep them in designer clothes and toys from preschool on up! I am not charged with being their friend, I am charged with being their parent, their protector, their teacher and their leader. I will 'rise above my raisin',' if necessary, to break any family legacy that may be contaminating how I lead my family and deal with my children. Give me the specific tools, guidance and techniques and I will work to socialize my children in a way so that they become immune to the many seductive promises of instant gratification, false realities and provocative lifestyles of today's fast-paced world. I will not let the television or Internet 'babysit' them as I communicate only through e-mails, pagers and cell phones. I will instead plug in the old-fashioned way and prepare them to deal with the distractions that assault them and blur their vision of self. I will create the pride, unity and loyalty and 'team spirit' that is so critical to a phenomenal family."

As fellow parents, Robin and I prayed about this important challenge and made a pledge to each other, to our family and ultimately to God a number of years ago, and I now invite you to do the same through the reading and application of *Family First* and any and all of the many resources listed in the bibliographical references. What you are about to do—whether it is part of an effort to get your family out of the ditch and back up on the road of life or to strengthen and protect the wonderful family you now enjoy—is give your family the greatest advantage that you can.

So buckle up and hold on, as we do this together, hand in hand!

P.S. Your kids just got lucky!

Part One

CREATING YOUR PHENOMENAL FAMILY

1

Family Matters

What's wrong with the world . . .
People livin' like they ain't got no mamas.
—THE BLACK EYED PEAS

He lives in two worlds, this twelve-year-old boy. Every day, he troops in and out of those two worlds, in and out of the tiny paint-peeled tract house he lives in with his father, mother and three sisters. To say his is a modest neighborhood is kind. To the casual observer the houses are indistinguishable. There is kind of a peace and order to the cookie-cutter sameness, everything in its place and a place for everything. At least so it appears. Like every other neighborhood in America, suburbia or the inner city, every home is a façade, an outward face that betrays little of what lies inside. Sometimes what is inside is the opposite of peaceful. Behind the social masks, all too often lie families that are chaotic and disconnected, that threaten to disintegrate with the next crisis. The boy lives in just such a house and in just such an American family.

Outside the doors of his home, the boy finds a world that seems immeasurably more validating. He has a small group of friends and acquaintances to whom he in some ways feels closer than his own family. Yet they too seem distant and different because *he* is different, at least in his own eyes. Among them, he, like so many others, wears a social mask of "okayness," but he doesn't know theirs is a mask as well. He seems relaxed, even confident, but secretly he's always on guard, because he knows he's not like them, not really. He knows he and his family are poor and that they live differently with different problems, problems you just don't talk about. He's making one of the first and most common mistakes children make: He's comparing his private reality, his world behind the door, to the social mask of all of his friends. He assumes that what he sees is the truth, and in comparison, his image of his own family situation suffers dismally.

In the world beyond his home, the discovery of athletics has been an absolute godsend. He and his family don't have the money, the clothes or the ability to participate in any of the extracurricular activities except for sports, which are free to all students. In fact, at his young age, the boy already works two jobs, and so he embraces sports as a leveling device. On the playing field, he doesn't have to talk or be like everybody else; he doesn't have to have money or a fancy upbringing or even a stable home. He just has to be what he is—a strong and coordinated kid, able to excel at just about any sport. Through athletics, he has found not only his self-esteem but an acceptable outlet for a burning anger that he doesn't understand, but knows is always there. Even with sports as an outlet, violence and fights are an everyday occurrence in a rough testosterone-driven world. Backing down is not an option. Because of sports, the urge to win has been planted in his head like a fast-growing seed—he loves being in the thick of competition and he has learned what it takes to win and others are eager to follow. The seed has sprouted; he doesn't like being second-best.

School life is less comfortable. He is smart, though not academically motivated. He reads all of his textbooks from cover to cover the first few weeks of school and masters the material, but could care less about class or grades. Homework is turned in only if it is handy to do so. Teachers find him quietly charming but reluctant to get involved. His writing is excellent when he bothers to do it. His test average is A+.

To his twelve-year-old sensibilities, being out with his buddies, playing sports with a passion and getting through each day are what life is all about—"out there," at least, in "that world." Out there, in that world, he is his own person, but always with an undertow from the other world, the world behind the door.

Once he goes home, he enters a completely different world, and he becomes a completely different person.

Cut off from his friends, his athletics and his school life, he is withdrawn, sullen, depressed, lethargic and emotionally detached from the rest of his family. Being the only boy, he has his own small room and he stays in it the vast majority of his time. He has no television, not even a radio. He just stays quietly to himself and even comes and goes through his bedroom window to avoid walking through the house. Unbeknownst to his parents he roams the streets after the family is asleep. He sleeps little as his paper route starts at 4:30 A.M. Days and nights don't seem much different when you are alone. He yearns for the hours to pass so he can make his way out into the other world, the one in which he is more functional, engaging, successful and motivated, at least in some areas of life. There is an astonishing contrast between what he is like in that world, out there, and what he is like in this world, in here.

But why?

Before that question is answered, let me tell you that in the many years that I've worked with the parents of troubled youngsters like this one, it became quite common to hear a mother or father request that their "problem" child be fixed. "Get our child straight!" they would demand. "We just don't know what happened! He just seemed to go downhill overnight. He is so withdrawn, so down and depressed. What is wrong with him? Can't you do something to fix this problem?"

Is this right thinking? Not even almost. No matter what maladaptive behaviors a child is exhibiting, I can guarantee you that the problem is almost certainly with the entire family, and most often the child is just the sacrificial lamb dragged to the altar of the counselor because he or she happens to be making the most noise and has the least amount of power or ability to shift the focus to someone else.

Trying to understand a child's behavior without interviewing the rest of the family just won't cut it, and any therapist worth their salt knows it. I want to be sure you know it too. So let's step through the front door with the twelve-year-old boy I described earlier and observe the other five parts that would be missed if a therapist, or more importantly, you, as a defensive parent, trivialized or ignored the family aspect.

Life "in there," life with his family unit, is tumultuous, volatile and unpredictable. Here's the real cause for this boy's refusal to plug into his family: His father is a severe and chronic alcoholic. He is typically emotionally unavailable to the boy, and to the rest of the family. He and the boy have clashed violently when the alcohol takes over and while the father barely remembers the confrontations, the experiences are seared into the boy's mind and heart. Further, the father has aborted his career in sales, uprooted the family, moved to a new state and returned to school at a university in the hope of a brighter yet highly speculative future. Though nobly inspired, this decision hurtled this family of six into grinding poverty. There is little inner connection as each family member's own personal struggles drain them of energy. Hunger gnaws at times and doing without is just how it is. Life is insecure, as the children are the poor "new" kids. Life is emotionally barren, full of desperation and drama, with one crisis after another. Tired and struggling, this family is not coping well at all.

Clearly scarred by the psychological and emotional stress, the boy's two older sisters try in their own way to escape the turmoil. But this turns out to be a classic case of "out of the frying pan into the fire." Both sisters have ill-fated elopements with boyfriends before finishing high school. Tension is everywhere in the home. The boy loves his sisters and they have protected him and helped him in a number of ways, but then they were gone. When they returned home, they were strangely different. They weren't just the other kids in the family anymore. And so, the boy feels further isolated. Although loving and caring, the mother works long and grueling hours on her feet as a store clerk just to keep food on the table. She is ill-equipped to deal with or counterbalance such a dominantly patriarchal family and such disconnected kids fleeing from their father's alcoholism. Baby sister is cute but silent. God only knows what she must be thinking. She is extremely dependent, afraid to leave home even to sleep over at a friend's house. She must stay close; this deal could cave any minute. The boy stays close to her, and they talk late at night, but he realizes that the less she knows, the better.

Both the mother and father were born into poor, uneducated families, and consequently, they had very little idea that life offered anything other than what they were exposed to. Tragically, the father had suffered severe mental, emotional and physical abuse at the hands of his own mother, and this legacy crippled his relationship with his own wife and children.

This is the world in which we find this twelve-year-old boy. He is embedded in a family on the verge of imploding and to evaluate him in isolation would be an exercise in futility. There is in this world an enveloping bleakness.

Trouble runs in packs.

If you haven't figured it out already, I know every detail of this story because I lived in that house. The story is my own. I was the twelve-year-old boy who moved from one world to the next, and back again. That was how I saw and experienced my life. That doesn't mean that my perception is correct or is how the other five members of my family would describe it. Every family member's experience and perceptions are different, but you can bet that everything each member thinks, does or feels bears on every other person in the family.

Although it isn't much fun to recall, I'm telling you this story because it's one I lived, and one I can say with great confidence illustrates that *family matters*. Family matters because it is the single most outcome-determinative factor shaping one's outlook and achievement. Your family powerfully determined what you've become and how you think about yourself, and so it will be for your own children. That's why among all words in the English language, none means more to human beings than "family."

In a typical family of four, there are five distinct personalities because you must also count the collective one. Your family's collective personality is a bundle of all the personalities, subsystems, roles and rules that exist, values embraced, the togetherness (or lack of) in which you live, standards and expectations and the thoughts and beliefs you share. The collective personality of your family can affirm and build on what you have to start with or it can countermand and erode the family unit.

If you want to understand your children, you must think of your family as a system. Whether we're talking about a family with a husband, wife and children, a single-parent family, a blended family, a gay or lesbian family or a multigenerational family with grandparents living in the home, a family is a system, not just a collection of individuals. If you were to look up "system" in the dictionary, you'd see it defined as "a regularly interacting or interdependent group of items forming a unified whole." To understand this concept, think of the systems at work in everyday life—even your own body, which is made up of a number of interacting parts. For example, if you rupture a disc in your lower back, you may experience what is called referred pain in your legs, and even in the bottom of your feet. No part works in isolation; the function or dysfunction of even one part affects the whole.

The same is true of a family. In a family where the mother is diagnosed with cancer, her disease is not simply a personal problem; it's a family problem because the entire family is affected. Whenever something happens to a family member, whether it is cancer, substance abuse, an addiction, a chronic illness or failures in life's pursuits, no family member can avoid being touched by it.

These events dramatically impact a child's socialization—the ability to learn, be independent, get along with others and understand the importance of rules. Moreover, it impacts academic progress and the building of self-esteem.

Socialization is one of the most important jobs a family has. When the family fails to provide the healthy nurturing children need, the impact on their lives can be destabilizing and can cheat them out of the chance to be the best person they can be. Children who are not properly socialized have problems in the world. They do not respect the authority, hierarchy or boundaries of their parents. They have poor impulse control. They can be selfish and extremely demanding, with little regard for how their behavior hurts the family. The resultant dysfunction of unsocialized children simultaneously contaminates the very family that may well have spawned their troubles. A vicious cycle, to be sure.

Of course, who and what you have become is also dictated by your education and your relationships with your friends, neighbors and employers. And as previously pointed out, a huge influence is the massive media machine—five hundred TV channels, the Internet, the radio, the newspapers. If you don't think so, just consider the now-unequivocal evidence that violent television and films, video games and music increase aggressive and violent behavior in children, teenagers and even adults.

Yet for all that, the family—your family—remains the most powerful influencing factor. Your past experiences may make you want your family to not be such a powerful influence on who you are or who you become, but it is, whether you like it or not. Bottom line: We need to get it right, right now.

THE NOBILITY OF PARENTING

As a parent, you're the head of your family, and therefore you occupy an unbelievably powerful role in shaping the tone, texture, mood and quality of this interconnected and vitally important unit. You're a system manager. By successfully managing this system, you can parent your way to a phenomenal family—and avoid the problems and erosion seen in so many of the families in your very own neighborhood.

But let me ask you:

- What kind of family manager have you been up until now?
- Are you working on a day-to-day basis at managing your family, treating it as a project, giving it the priority it deserves?

- Are you creating a family environment that brings out the best in your child?
- Do you have the skills necessary to give your child his or her best chance at succeeding in this world?
- Have you overcome any "family legacy" that has contaminated the way in which you define and parent your family?
- If the other parent is in the home or active in the children's lives post-divorce, do the two of you have a parenting plan that provides guidance based on consistent values?
- Do you have a plan and an objective in mind for what success-ful parenting is and will yield in your child's life?
- Have you created an environment that generates feelings of safety, security, belongingness, self-confidence and strength for the child or children in your charge?
- Is your family nurturing your child's individuality and acting to ensure that he or she will become the unique and authentic person God intended?

I know you just answered those questions, but I ask you to go back and read them over again, and this time answer them keeping in mind that you are writing your children's future with your answers. Those questions are just a beginning of the self-examination you must be willing to do if you're going to strengthen the foundation on which your children are basing their lives. Frankly, I know that some of you reading this book right now are making choices and decisions that are setting your children up for disastrous failure. You may not know it, and you may not see the effects today, but trust me, you'll see them in the future if you're making the same mistakes so many well-intending parents unwittingly make. Are you one of those parents? Are you setting up your child to turn to drugs, violence, promiscuity, alcohol or withdrawal from life and all it has to offer? I intend to make it very clear to you whether your parenting prac-tices are likely to yield unfortunate results, and if so, how to change them, starting right now this very day.

If you want a healthy and nurturing family, and successful and pro-ductive children, you must commit yourself to acquiring the insight and skills necessary to live the values that you know in your heart are so im-portant. You didn't pick this book up because you wanted to study up on a bunch of child development theories. You bought this book because you care about your children and want action-oriented information about how to give them their best chance for success. You picked it up because you care about your family life.

I've so often heard parents say, "I would die for my children." Well, I don't want you to die for your children, but I do want you to *live* for your children.

Your role as a parent is the highest, noblest calling you will ever have in your life. What's more, I believe that you can and will rise to that challenge if given the proper knowledge and tools for this important task. I know that you already possess the most powerful and important ingredient to succeeding. That critical factor is an unconditional and heartfelt love and devotion you have for your child. But it takes much, much more than love and good intentions because you aren't the only influence in your child's life.

You must become highly aware, deeply committed and pointedly proactive. Parents everywhere are in a major tug-of-war with a slick, false-promising, glittery, well-marketed world to determine who is going to write the script of their children's lives. Given the current state of the world, I intend to hang on to my end of the rope with both hands and play a key role in writing that script. Solid values and morality seem to have stopped being a way of life and have simply become a punch line for the jokes of the fast-laners. Gone are the days when cheating in school was just some isolated case of some lazy kid copying off of the smart kid; today over half of students admit to cheating. Some kids are even using high-tech electronic pagers during tests and plagiarizing term papers off the Internet. Where once a kid could buy illegal drugs on a street corner in the bad part of town, today he can do it on the Internet from the kitchen table while you sit not ten feet away. In a phenomenon called "friends with benefits," children as young as twelve and thirteen are engaging in oral sex with no more thought or consideration than you once gave to holding hands or a peck on the cheek. No relationship, no emotion, just sex. One hundred percent of the children with access to a computer can view pornography with the click of a mouse. Our kids today are what I call an All-Access-Pass Generation.

It would be Pollyannaish for me to suggest that it is possible to shield your child completely from all of the negativity and temptation in today's world. I can't do that and I don't think anybody else can either.

But what I can do is help you add to the plus side of your child's ledger. Since you can't eliminate the bad influences, you must create deep, meaningful and consistently positive and well-grounded experiences, values and beliefs to counterbalance the negative. You must do it even though your children may roll their eyes and seem resistant. You must do it even though you're being pulled in a million different directions every minute of every day. That it is difficult makes it no less important and no less necessary.

Bad results don't just happen in the lives of other people's kids, and that is why there is all the more reason to vow to protect your own. Raising your family is not a dress rehearsal, and it can be a 24/7 job that will last for twenty-plus years, so you ought to know how to do it and do it well.

As I've pointed out, what you need in addition to the love in your heart is a very specific, step-by-step plan of action for leading your family and parenting with purpose. What you need is a really good guidance system so you know that you are tracking the target of success from one day to the next. You need to know how to create a phenomenal family and acquire the tools that will make that happen. Your family is worthy of everything you want for them; what you will learn here will help you.

All your children will ever be, they are now becoming. Let's be honest: If you're like any parent I have ever met you want your child to be the star in his or her own life—the soloist in the choir, the quarterback on the football team, the lead in the play, the beauty queen, the honor roll student or the one in the best schools. Not only that, you also want your children to be happy, secure, self-assured and confident. You want to protect your child from getting shoved in the playground, picked on by bullies or molested by sickos, safe from failure and adversity and from social and interpersonal pain in general. On top of it all, you want your children to love you, accept you, respect and admire you.

What you do with them today, when they are two, three, four, five, six or sixteen years of age, will determine what they will do at age twenty-four, thirty-four or forty-four. *You are raising adults.* Right now, they are under construction, like a new house being built from the ground up. Once that house gets completed, it is subjected to the forces of nature and the wear and tear of life. Will its foundation crack, or its roof leak? Will it hold up or cave in?

Will your children withstand the pressures of their lives and worlds, or crack when the going gets tough? Is theirs a strong foundation for what is to come? The answers to those questions depend largely on how you mold and shape your children, their values, their behavior, their ability to make sound decisions on their own, and how well you honor their individuality and nurture their unique gifts and talents. In short, it depends on what you do today to help them become responsible adults tomorrow. Do you know the saying, "Children are messages we deliver to a future we may never see"? You are preparing future adults and you are preparing future families. You're in hot pursuit of what's best for your children and your family, but you may not know which way to go or how to reach for it. That's what a "really good plan" is all about.

I'm sure it's no surprise coming from me, but the key to that plan is you. As in most things in life, the challenge of raising a successful family cannot and will not happen until you decide to clean house inside yourself first. The journey begins with you. You can't be one kind of person and another kind of parent. If you don't scrape away all the layers of your past pain and disappointment and self-destructive legacies and bad spirit, then no matter what else you learn about successful parenting, you'll have such low standards and poor values that you'll continue to sabotage your, your children's and your family's opportunities for a joyful life.

I believe we all have something I call "personal truth." Your personal truth is what you really believe about yourself when you're not "performing" and not wearing your social mask and trying to put your best foot forward. It's what you really believe about yourself when nobody is looking and nobody is listening. This personal truth is so important, because I believe that we generate for ourselves and our families the results that we believe we deserve. If we do not believe that we, our family, are worthy of a phenomenal life, we will never have a phenomenal life. If you believe you're some second-class citizen, some undeserving individual, then you'll generate results that are consistent with that belief. That's why it's so important that you look first to yourself to make sure that there is not some compromised sense of worth or value that is limiting what you can create for your family.

Your personal truth will be clearly reflected in what I call your "attitude of approach." You probably inherited most or all of your approach and that may not be a good thing. If, for example, you were abused, emotionally neglected or just overindulged, those life experiences may have powerfully and boldly written on the slate of who you are, causing you to carry forward a compromised personal truth that can and will infect your children with the same things you learned. As a result you may have a much more challenging time raising a joyful child and creating a joyful family, the very two things that should be uppermost in your priorities. Joyful children don't come to be because they were born with a "joyful gene." Joyful children are taught how to live, think, interact, control their emotions, express themselves, discipline themselves the same way they learn how to ride a bike or tie their shoes. They're *taught* how to be joyful. That is one of your challenges, since the ability to raise joyful children is a learned skill.

When it comes to raising a family and parenting children, nobody ever really taught you the rules, let alone how to play the game. Think about it: Why are our kids turning to drugs, alcohol and sex at younger and younger ages? Because nobody has ever taught people how to parent their children in a way that keeps them from needing to turn to those escape mechanisms to feel the way they want to feel.

Since you didn't get any formal child-rearing training from society, you've probably relied on role models. Yet because our own parents were never trained to be effective mothers and fathers, what kind of role models could they be? In fact, I submit to you that if you've been fortunate to have parents who were positive role models, you—and they—can thank blind luck or even trial and error that they got it right, because it's a safe bet training had little to do with it. Simply put, this means not only that you may lack crucial information, but that the information you do have may be wrong. Sometimes, the hardest part in learning new and better skills is unlearning the old ways of doing.

I've designed this book to meet you at whatever point you find yourself. I did not want to guess at where that was. I did not want to assume that I knew what to include in this to ensure it was absolutely, bull's-eye responsive to your needs. Accordingly, I spent over a year designing and conducting a massive research project examining the family and parenting issues facing all of us raising children in today's world. The research project included over 17,000 respondents who generated over 1.5 million pieces of data. That data was then subjected to vigorous clinical and statistical analysis.

The analysis examines such issues as the most critical problems faced by parents, parents' greatest fears, children's levels of responsivity to different parenting approaches, parents' greatest needs for assistance and information and an overall assessment of attitudes and outlook for the future. (As you read *Family First*, pay attention to the "Survey Facts" that appear throughout the book. Each block of information contains eye-opening data about how mothers and fathers feel about their job as parents. You'll find more information about my National Parenting Survey in the Appendix.)

It doesn't matter whether you have good, well-adjusted kids whom you want to see do better and become better, or alternatively, defiant, misbehaving kids who seem headed for jail rather than college. Or maybe you have kids in crisis, a child on drugs or a teenager who is depressed. The tools are the same, whether your child is on the honor roll or the police blotter.

> **Survey Fact:**
> One-third of parents responding to the survey said if they had to do it all again, they would not start a family.

No matter how crazy things get or how stressed you feel, you know in your heart how fortunate you are to be given the precious, priceless treasure of children. I encourage you then to see this job of parenting as noble, as a privilege with which you've been entrusted and to take from that responsibility a feeling of meaning and significance.

Reading this book is not intended to be a passive experience. As you progress through it, you'll see that it's a hands-on, action-oriented book. Every chapter calls on you to play an active role. You'll learn, and put into play, skills in example-setting, discipline, negotiation, communications, intelligence-building, strengthening self-worth and self-confidence, behavior control and family lifestyle management, useful not only in raising your children, but also in structuring the content of your family life so that it supports and uplifts your efforts. Get these skills right and the rest of your life as a parent will be easy.

If you can bring up your children to be the confident, competent people they deserve to be, you'll have successfully fulfilled your purpose as a parent and given your children the greatest of all gifts. That's what I want for my children, and I know it is what you want for yours.

It is not too late. Isn't today the day to begin? If you have a great family with great kids, then let's build on that strength. If you feel you have blown it so far, then it is time to "re-parent" your children. Re-parenting means going back to the basics and setting new goals, rules, guidelines and boundaries. It means becoming the parent God intended when he blessed you with the gift of your children. Start by waking up every morning and asking yourself: What can I do today to make my family better? What can I do today to introduce something positive into my children's lives? What can I find that is good in each child and how can I acknowledge it?

Game on. My plan is for you and your family to be the winners.

2

Special Strategies for Divorced and Blended Families

Courage is not defined by those who fought and did not fall,
but by those who fought, fell and rose again.
— UNKNOWN

For my readers who are divorced, living as a single parent, or in a blended family: I recognize that there are a lot of you out there who need a lot of answers, and you need them now. How do I play both mother and father? How much do I push and require from my child during the divorce transition? What role do I play with my stepchildren? And many more questions. The divorce rate in the United States is estimated by some statisticians to be close to 50 percent. What this means is that millions of parents in America and their children are wrestling with significant problems and needs.

Before I address the challenges your children will face if one of their biological parents is outside the home—or if you've introduced a new spouse into the family unit—I want to caution you that the majority of hurdles faced by parents in a nontraditional structure are the same as those faced by parents in a traditional structure. Kids are kids, and you shouldn't assume that because you're soloing the parenting process or parenting with a partner who's just come onboard, the tools of parenting and family life are somehow different. That said, you clearly have some extra challenges to contend with, and extra challenges require extra tools.

That's what this chapter is all about. I'm going to tell you what I believe is the truth about what you can and must do to create a phenomenal family, even if yours is a divorced family or a blended one. I'm going to give you a separate list of action items here because your situation expressly calls for it. Your job will be to jump into this chapter with a willingness to give it your full attention and focus consciously on the tasks presented. But you can't stop here. The actions I'll give you must ultimately fit into a bigger plan, a plan that works for all families, divorced, blended, or with both biological parents in the home. That plan is what you will find on every single page of this book. You must commit to folding into your family life all the tools, actions, and strategies I'm going to give you as we progress through this book. Immerse yourself in this work with a commitment of both heart and soul, and you too will emerge a winner.

Even before a divorce, children have internalized parental conflict and may already be exhibiting behavior problems. So let's talk about the conditions you're likely to find in a home touched by divorce or separation. If you're a single or a blended family parent, your child's life has been shaken to the core. While children respond to these kinds of events differently, watching a divorce unfold is likely to be traumatizing. Your son or daughter may experience great fear regarding the future. They may worry that the parent who's been awarded primary custody may "abandon" them as well. They may react with a predictable clinginess or with anger-based aggression. You must understand that if your child's mother or father has in their view been ripped from the home, the child may blame *you* for that departure. His anger will be very real, even if it's nothing more than an outward expression of hurt, fear, or frustration. Anger is often a way of coping with vulnerability. It can be a protective mechanism because if you're on the attack, getting rejected is no longer an issue. Unconsciously, the child's attitude becomes "get them before they get me." You must not personalize these reactions, but instead look past the surface and compassionately see what lies beneath.

Whatever your child's outward reaction, you can bet that the departure of a parent and/or the addition of a stepparent to the family environment will provoke a major mental and emotional response. Some children will mask it; others will not. Either way, it is there. There is now and will continue to be a reaction, and your job is to manage that reaction in as constructive and as rehabilitative a way as possible.

Both research and my own clinical experience have taught me that your child's psychological needs are greatly increased during and after a divorce. The trauma of a fractured family leaves a residue well beyond the shorter term. That residual reaction can be emotional, logistical or both. For example, when a marriage unravels, financial problems are often not far behind. Money problems can create grinding hardships. There's often an unexpected, unsettling inequity between the standard of living for a divorced husband and that of his wife, a contrast that can be very confusing to a child. Statistically, more women than men are named the custodial parent, and usually it's the women who suffer the most significant drop in income. After a divorce approximately half of all children do not see their fathers. And here's what's sad to me: Children live in the middle of this economic and emotional roller coaster and experience guilt and fear in addition to the confusion.

What's more, if you're a single parent who fought hard for primary custody, you may now be faced with supervising and disciplining your children largely on your own. And it's tough. There's a natural tendency to let the discipline slide. All too frequently, you're stretched too thin and your child suffers.

Remarriage also brings with it an explosion of stress-inducing newness, with new stepbrothers and stepsisters, new rules, new demands and new religious practices. The loss of a role model can be particularly devastating, as children faced with accelerating daily challenges and choices find that a custodial parent's compass is not always reliable. (This is a crucial topic that we will discuss in depth in Chapter 13.)

Each of these demands and countless others too numerous to mention are part of the reality that is divorce in today's world. Each requires a specific coping strategy. What remains constant, however, are the needs that these demands and stressors accentuate. Whatever your particular challenges may be, they all boil down to disruption for your child and can blunt their very important needs. These challenges could not come at a worse time for you, since you are in emotionally rough waters yourself. You'll feel overwhelmed at times trying to deal with them. Nonetheless, you *must* dial into the needs of your child. According to the American Academy of Pediatrics, up to half of all children exhibit a symptomatic response during the first year after a divorce. These symptoms include irritability, increased crying, fearfulness, decreased school performance, substance abuse, depression and aggressive and delinquent behavior. If you are consciously focused on and sensitive to your child's needs during this difficult period, you can and will do a better job of meeting them.

Their most profound needs (which may last for an extended period of time, especially if ignored or mishandled) will include:

Acceptance. This will be your children's greatest need because their self-concept is very likely in a fragile and formative stage, especially if they are at a young age. They will urgently try to gain approval and "membership," since their sense of belongingness to your family has been shattered.

Assurance of safety. You'll need to go beyond normal efforts to assure your children that though their family has fragmented, the protection it always provided remains solid. They must experience that their cocoon in life is intact and that you are on patrol. Actions speak louder than words, so the key will be maintaining a normal pace, boundaries and routines in your home, preserving the same involvement in school affairs, and giving your child the same access to interactions with friends.

Freedom from guilt or blame for the divorce. Children often shoulder the blame for the dissolution of marriage. This feeling arises from the many accusations that erupt through the divorce and its proceedings and stems from the fact that children are the central glue that hold families together. Children personalize their part in the divorce, because they know they misbehaved, and they feel that they're somehow being punished for it by the breakup of their parents. Remember that when children, alone or among their peers, experience pain, they feel singled out. And in their minds, the line between pain and punishment blurs. Be conscious of this and assure your children they're blameless.

Need for structure. With the loss of a family leader from the home (either the mother or the father), your children will check and test for structure. Give it to them in spades. This is the worst time to break patterns, even to indulge. Enforce discipline consistently, and with the right currency for good behavior (you'll learn exactly how to do this in Chapter 10). Now more than ever, your children need sameness in all aspects of their young lives. They need to see that the world keeps spinning around, and they're still an integral part of what's going on.

Need for a stable parent who has the strength to conduct business. Whether or not you feel brave and strong, you have to appear to be the best for your children. They're worried about you and about your partner, especially if there's an apparent crisis. They know you better than you know yourself, brave front or not, so they'll pick up on the heavy emotional drain you've experienced. Still, you should do everything possible to assure them of your strength—your capacity to take care of business. In doing so, you make it possible for them to relax again. So show yourself to be a person of strength and resilience.

Need to let kids be kids. Your children should not be given the job of healing your pain. Too often, children serve either as armor or as saviors for parents in crisis. Think about it: Don't children have a tough enough time in this world without being given the job of fixing your life? That said, there are two primary rules you must follow, especially in crisis and during times of instability in your family.

1. Do not burden your children with situations they cannot control. No one, least of all a child, should bear such a responsibility. It will promote feelings of helplessness and insecurity, causing them to question their own strengths and abilities.
2. Do not ask your children to deal with adult issues. Children are not equipped to understand adult problems. Their focus should be on navigating the various child development stages they go through.

Obviously, your overall goal should be to meet all of these needs and to minimize the price your child has to pay for you and your ex being unable to sustain your relationship. I say that because it's the truth, and not because I want to induce guilt. I'm not being judgmental. Only you know whether or not breaking up was the best thing for you and your children. Either way, it is what it is. The divorce has happened, and you, your ex, and your child or children are going to have to make the best of it.

I'm a strong believer that any child would rather be *from* a broken home than *live in* one. Research tells us that quite obviously, children do better in a well-adjusted two-parent home than in a single-parent home. However, that same research tells us that children do better in a well-adjusted single-parent home than in a hostile, emotionally barren, or chaotic two-parent home. If children do better when they're exposed to both parents and when there's a healthy relationship among everyone involved, then post-divorce, your goal further becomes to create that situation, regardless of the geography of the living arrangements. Even though you and your ex have terminated your romantic and committed relationship and taken up separate residences, you can still commit to having a mutually supportive relationship as co-parents of your children. If the two of you are willing to prioritize your children's interests, it will be easy to focus on what you need to do to minimize divorce-related trauma.

What you and your former spouse must resolve to do is form an alliance recognizing that you have not ended your relationship but instead changed it from an intimate, emotional, and romantic day-to-day affiliation to a relationship that's held together by common goals for your children. Joining with your ex, unselfishly putting hurt feelings aside and leaving behind the pain of betrayal and a dysfunctional history are tremendous gifts to your children.

To be cold, sabotaging, hurtful, or exclusionary with your former spouse is, in some sense, to do the same to your children. If you haven't ever thought about it that way, then let me tell you why you should: Children have a powerful genetic, emotional, and historical bond with *both* of their parents, and they need a healthy relationship with both of them. If you, by pursuing your own agenda of seeking payback for hurt feelings, resentment, and anger, alienate your child from your ex-spouse, you're attacking and hurting your child's ability to become well-adjusted. If your child seems to side with you, you may tell yourself you're winning, but I can assure you, you're not. If you undermine your ex, I promise you that your children will ultimately turn on you and resent you for it. It's sweet poison. It may feel good today to know your children are loyal to you, love you more and would rather be with you than with your ex, but in the long run, your children will recognize that what you did was selfish and hurtful to them. That's a fact you can't and won't escape. So, even if you don't work to create a healthy relationship between you and your ex and between your ex and your children, because it's the right thing to do, do it for selfish reasons. You'll pay a high price with your children, if you don't.

Is it possible there are circumstances such as mental illness, alcoholism, drug addiction, or other self-destructive lifestyles that preclude a healthy parent from supporting the relationship between their ex and their children? Absolutely. If that's the case, you shouldn't lie about the realities, and you certainly shouldn't subject your child to that kind of influence. But make sure your assessment of your ex is objective and not colored by anger, and make sure that you're not using these issues to gain a selfish advantage with your children. If it's less damning to characterize your ex's issues as illness, then do so. Preserve the relationship for their future in the hope that your ex comes around to better behavior.

Although it probably sounds illogical, the best way to know you're "ready" to get a divorce and therefore ready to form a new co-parent relationship is when you can walk out the door with no anger, resentment, bitterness, or unfinished emotional business. You're probably thinking, "If it's possible to feel such acceptance about the relationship, why break up?" Let me clarify: The time to get a divorce is when you can look at yourself in the mirror and honestly say that you've done everything possible to rehabilitate and save your marriage. You should call it quits only when you know in your heart that you've turned over every stone, investigated every potential avenue of rehabilitation, and still come up short. If you still harbor powerful and strong ill feelings, you still have work to do. I bring this up not to coax you into a guilt-driven effort to reconcile with your ex, but rather to make it clear that you must get past hurt feelings so you can have a cooperative working relationship with your child's other parent. If you were not in this state of mind when the marriage ended, commit to getting there now. Your child shouldn't pick up the tab for his parents' inability to get along.

You have a high calling here, and that calling is to nurture and prepare your children for life, despite your ill-fated union. You must put your own emotional agenda to rest. If doing so requires professional help, then get it. Even if you are financially strapped, there are resources in your community and at your church or house of worship that I know will step up and help a parent in need. Whatever it takes to create a healthier working relationship with your child's other parent, then you must do it.

Understand that post-divorce parenting is fraught with danger, danger that you will inadvertently do damage on top of what the divorce has already done. To help you recognize mistakes you may be making and to avoid mistakes you're prone to make, I want to list some of the biggest and most frequent mistakes those in your situation typically make:

- Sabotaging your child's relationship with the other parent.
- Using your child as a pawn to "get back at" or hurt your ex.
- Using your child to gain information or to manipulate and influence your ex.
- Transferring hurt feelings and frustrations toward your ex onto your child. (You may be particularly prone to this if your child bears physical or behavioral resemblances to your ex.)

- Forcing your child to choose a side when there's a conflict in scheduling or another planning challenge.
- Turning family events attended by both divorced parents into pressure cookers. Events that call for sensitivity include birthdays, holidays, school programs, extracurricular activities, and performances.
- Depending too much on your children for companionship and support because you're hurt and lonely and have adopted a siege mentality: "It's us against the world." This isn't a healthy position for either you or your child to adopt.
- Treating your child like an adult because you're lonely or just want help. It is inappropriate to give your child an adult job.
- Becoming so emotionally needy that your child develops feelings of guilt if he or she spends time or even wants to spend time with your ex, friends, grandparents or others.
- Converting guilt over the divorce into overindulgence when it comes to satisfying your child's material desires.

Besides making a commitment to avoid these mistakes, you should affirmatively commit to a family and parenting strategy that will help your child flourish in a divorced home. Key components of such a strategy include:

- Commit to learn, adopt and apply all the principles set forth in *Family First*. The philosophies, tools and strategies described in this book are critical to having a healthy, happy family and raising successful, authentic children, whether or not both parents live in the home.
- Sit down with your ex and make an affirmative plan that sets aside any differences you may have and focuses instead on meeting the needs of your children. If you must agree to disagree about what did or didn't happen in your marriage, put the focus on what *needs* to happen *now* to make sure your children don't have to pay the price for your marital misfire.
- Agree with your ex that you absolutely won't disparage each other to your children. Further, forbid your children to speak disrespectfully about the other parent, even though it may be music to your ears.
- Negotiate and agree on how you can best handle such things as handing off the children for visitation, holidays, or events. Although the

court probably set parameters for such things in terms of timing, in the interest of your children's peace and security, it's up to you to act maturely and without selfishness.

• Agree on boundaries and behavioral guidelines for raising your children so that there's consistency in their lives, regardless of which parent they're with at any given time. This should include such things as bedtime, television and computer access, socializing and other daily behavioral situations and circumstances.

• With regard to extended family members, negotiate and agree on the role they'll play and the access they'll be granted while your child is in each other's charge. I strongly believe that extended family plays a very important role in the lives of children, and particularly, that the role of both sets of grandparents should be active and free-flowing, so long as the grandparents acknowledge and agree to the same standards the divorced couple has agreed on. Your parents disparaging your ex to your children is as unacceptable as you disparaging your ex to your children.

• Communicate actively with your ex about all aspects of your child's development. Both parents should know about any and all positive or negative events in the child's developmental journey. If there are problems at school or with friends or even wonderful achievements, both parents should be fully up to speed so consistent responses can be given. If need be do so in writing or via e-mail, but do it.

• Recognize that children are prone to testing a situation and manipulating boundaries and guidelines, especially if there's a chance to get something they may not ordinarily be able to obtain. It's important that you and your ex compare notes before jumping to conclusions or condemning one another about what may have happened.

• Although it may be emotionally painful, make sure that you and your ex keep each other informed about changes in your life circumstances so that the child is never, ever the primary source of information. If you're dating someone, changing jobs or contemplating a move, be mature enough to inform your ex so he or she doesn't hear it from the child, who may then have to suffer the reaction.

• Commit to conducting yourself with emotional integrity. If you and your ex have agreed to a plan, stick to it. Say what you mean; mean what you say. Absolutely do not secretly curry favor with your child by giving more or allowing more than the other parent. Doing so is nothing less than passive-aggressive sabotage, and it will ultimately hurt your child.

Embracing these dos and don'ts will help considerably to normalize your children's lives. The key is for you and your ex to take the high road and truly make sacrifices for your children. It isn't only self-indulgent, but self-destructive for you to thrust your children in the middle of emotional cross fire. What's more, they simply don't want to hear it. I've talked to so many children in divorced homes who tell me they are so sick to death of listening to their parents complain and whine about each other that they could just scream. So don't be a tedious, immature bore. You wanted children, and now you have them. The fact that your relationship didn't work out is unfortunate, but it's not their fault.

If your spouse simply won't get in the game and adhere to the guidelines I've set forth, you must do so anyway. The only person you control is you. Let me appeal to your greed by saying that, if you do take the high road, in the long run your children will admire you for it. The day will come when they'll look back and say: "My mother [or father] behaved with such class, dignity and respect that I can see how much he or she loved me and wanted peace and tranquillity in my life. I'm so grateful for that gift. I only wish my other parent had been so selfless."

> **Survey Fact:**
> **The top three problems for blended families are discipline, resolving conflict and division of responsibility.**

If in addition to divorcing, you've also made the decision to remarry, you have a whole new set of challenges before you. In addition to the challenges of traditional and divorced families, you must follow the guidelines and actions I've just presented or will be presenting, and you must also have a strategy in place for folding a new person into the preexisting family unit. Whether or not your new spouse will be bringing children into the relationship, the family will have at least one new member, and that will create challenges for you, especially if you're the one being brought into a preexisting family. Definitely include your children in the wedding ceremony. If they have a special role and you can make it a positive experience, you will advance a lot closer to a harmonious home.

It's important to recognize from the outset of a second marriage that if one or both of you have children, whether or not you're the custodial parent with whom the children primarily reside, there are strong emotions associated with those relationships. In addition to the strong ties that exist between any biologically connected parent and child there may be additional emotional energy created by the parent and child's having been in the same "divorce foxhole" prior to the new marriage. This increased emotion will very likely take the form of protectiveness on the part of the parent. That parent may be thinking that the child has already been hurt, and the parent will be on edge about how the child is treated in the new family setup. For the new spouse, the experience can be one of walking on eggshells, trying not to make a parenting move that is regarded as out-of-bounds or that creates unfortunate echoes of the past. These are things that you and your new spouse should discuss *before* your marriage takes place, but of course it's never too late.

I'm going to discuss what I believe are the most important aspects of having a stepparent in a relationship with your children, and of being the stepparent that has to form a workable relationship with someone else's children. Quite frankly, much of the challenge here is the same as the challenge that would be facing any couple getting ready to have a child. I would tell any couple that's about to have a baby that they should sit down and discuss, and where necessary negotiate, a plan that includes such topics as:

- The role each parent would play in parenting and facilitating the development of the child.
- The division of labor concerning the child, such as feeding, bathing, supervising, doctor visits, homework, discipline, and so forth.
- Expectations as to how much space there will be in the relationship for the couple to be a couple, occasionally doing things without the child.
- What kind of access grandparents and other extended family members would have.
- Long-term goals and priorities concerning education and other developmental opportunities.
- Financial planning and priorities.

These global topics should certainly be discussed within families that have or are about to be merged, or if a stepparent is about to be added. Whether you're about to embark on this journey or are already well down the road, I recommend working through the above checklist early and often to ensure everyone's compasses are aligned. It's particularly important that I cover here the role of the stepparent and how to make that role as positive as possible.

First, let's talk about how the stepparent should relate to the children. We've all heard about such stereotypes as the wicked stepmother and such phenomena as the Oedipus complex, where children's competition for their parents' love, commitment and loyalty leads to all manner of pain and discontent. We've all seen the grade B movies where the put-upon child screams the seemingly obligatory line "You're not my mother!" There's no doubt that being a stepparent is one of the most difficult roles any adult will ever assume. So much pain can be avoided if you can agree on some very basic definitions of that role, and be alert to sensitivities associated with it.

To handle this situation with the utmost efficiency, both the biological parent and the stepparent should begin with an open and candid discussion about the fears and expectations regarding the relationship with the children. Each should know what the other expects concerning the stepparent's involvement in guiding, supervising and disciplining the children. If both partners are in the stepparent as well as biological parent role, because both have primary or even partial custody of their children, expectations of each other may differ. In other words, you may trust yourself to discipline his children, but not him to discipline yours. That's okay. What's important is that you each have an understanding and hopefully a negotiated agreement about how the stepparent role will be defined. Once you understand what each other's expectations are, you have a place to start shaping what the stepparent role will be. I always think it's important to first identify what you can agree on and thereby narrow your differences. How you ultimately define the stepparent role will, of course, be up to you. The following are my recommendations based on what I've seen work, what I've seen fail and how I think it's best to set up and define the stepparent role:

1. It's my strong belief that unless you as the stepparent are added to the family when the children are very young, it will most likely be very difficult for you to discipline your spouse's children. Every situation is different, but in most situations, disciplining your nonbiological children is fraught with danger, since it's likely to create resentment on the part of your spouse. Again, this isn't always the case, and if that's not the circum-

stance in your family, that's great, because it can give the biological parent an additional resource for handling discipline issues. While I don't believe it's very likely a workable situation for a stepparent to be a direct disciplinarian, it's extremely important that the stepparent be an active supporter of the biological parent's disciplinary efforts. The stepparent can help with enforcement and with monitoring for compliance, even if it's not their role to initiate the discipline. Both biological parents and stepparents should discuss the rules of the house and negotiate an agreement for what standards the children will be held to. This element of family life should be subject to the same negotiation and joint ownership as any other family situation.

2. The stepparent, although not actively initiating direct discipline, should certainly work to maintain the normal boundaries that exist between an adult and a child. Although it may be the biological parent who delivers an initial consequence for misbehavior, it's important that the stepparent be active in support of that decision, and care should be taken that proper respect and acknowledgment of the stepparent be given. In other words, a stepfather is not simply one's mother's husband. He is in fact an adult and an authority figure in the home.

3. In relating to all the children, the stepparent should seek to define his or her relationship as that of an ally and supporter. Whether the stepparent is the same or opposite-sexed parent, their presence can play an important balancing role in terms of modeling and information-giving about life from the male or female point of view. The role of ally and supporter is in no way to be construed as an attempt to replace the biological parent.

4. It's important that the stepparent not have unrealistic expectations about their level of closeness or intimacy with the stepchildren. Relationships are built, and it takes time and shared experiences to create a meaningful one. The stepparent should also be aware that the child may be experiencing a fair amount of emotional confusion—and may in fact feel guilty that they're betraying their biological mother or father by having a close and caring relationship with their stepmother or -father. Great care and patience should be taken to allow the child an opportunity to work through those feelings.

5. The stepmother or -father should actively support the child's relationship with the biological mother or father no longer in the home. If you are in the role of stepfather, you should make it a priority to nurture a relationship between you and the biological father and to find every possible way you can to support a relationship between him and his children. By taking the high road of facilitation, you'll find it easier to overcome feelings of resentment both on the part of the biological father *and* the children he no longer has daily access to. This may require some real internal commitment on your part, because supporting your stepchildren's relationship with their biological but absent parent may seem tantamount to also supporting that parent's relationship with your spouse. Don't let jealousy or envy of the bond they share with their children or the working relationship and history with your current mate cause you to be less than supportive of that relationship.

6. If you're the stepparent in a truly blended family, where both you and your spouse have children being merged into a "yours, mine and ours" scenario, you must take great care not to be perceived as playing favorites through a double standard in which your children enjoy a better standard of treatment than your stepchildren. The truth is, however unpopular or politically incorrect it may be to say, you'll very likely have decidedly stronger positive emotional feelings for your biological children than for your stepchildren, at least in the beginning. You'll need to cloak this difference in emotional intensity. As time goes on and you share life experiences with your stepchildren, there will be a leveling of emotions toward all of the children. In the meantime, you should be hypersensitive to the need to deal with each in a like fashion. It can be very helpful in the early stages to actually quantify and balance the time, activities and money spent on biological and nonbiological children.

7. If you as the biological parent are having frustrations with the stepparent and what they're doing in relation to your children, I encourage you at a very early point to stop complaining and start specifically asking for what you want and need. If, for example, you feel they're spending more time playing games with *their* children, ask them specifically, for example, to play three board games per week with *your* child. If he or she took his or her biological children to a fun fast-food restaurant—perhaps innocently so because he just happened to be passing by one after picking the

kids up from the Y—he may not consciously realize that your biological child was left out. Specifically ask for what you specifically want.

In summary, let me say it's true that it's difficult to see things through someone else's eyes if you haven't walked in their shoes. Whether you're the stepparent or it's your spouse who's in that role, talk frequently about how it's going and what the experience is from the other's point of view. If both of you have good intentions and a loving heart, this can be worked out. A biological parent can be given what he needs to protect his children. A stepparent can be given the time she requires to travel the relation-building learning curve. The key is to remember that the children are passengers on this train. They didn't get an opportunity to choose whether they wanted a new family member, so great care and patience should be taken to help them adapt to the situation.

As you go forward through *Family First*, remember that all of the philosophies, evaluations and tools apply to your situation as a single or blended-family parent. You have the same challenges before you that every other parent must deal with to create a phenomenal family. I've addressed some of the specific challenges you face by being in this particular situation. I do not presume to suggest that I have covered the whole gamut of challenges you are facing or will face. Hopefully you'll find and embrace my additional recommendations as you move forward through the rest of the book.

3

The Five Factors
for a Phenomenal Family

Train up a child in the way he should go and
when he is old he will not depart from it.
—PROVERBS 22:6

Starting right now, you can begin to make choices and take day-to-day actions that will create nothing short of a phenomenal family. Whether your family functions well and you want to make it better, or it's a dysfunctional mess, it didn't get that way by accident or by some outsider's doing. Whatever its state, you and your family members collectively own it. You as the parent and leader of the family have particular ownership. Whatever is happening, good or bad, is happening on your watch. My dad used to say that the world is made up of the haves and the have-nots, and that it was up to me to choose by my thoughts and actions which I wanted to be, mentally, emotionally, spiritually, financially and in every other way. I think he was right: If you want different, you have to *choose* different. Having a phenomenal family doesn't require that you had a great upbringing with positive role models, nor does it require that your kids say, "Wow, great ideas, Mom! I'm pumped, let's do it!" You can choose to have a phenomenal family if you just resolve to do it and know where to put your focus. That's where the Five Factors for a Phenomenal Family come in. These factors aren't inherited, but they're not particularly difficult to implement. Creating these factors in your family begins with you, which is why I addressed your personal truth introduced in Chapter 1. You must start by believing in yourself and your family's right to be phenomenal.

When I say "phenomenal family," I'm talking about a family where each member is a star in their own right. Each gets to use their gifts, skills and talents, and feel good about who they are and how they fit in. They get to live with hope, passion and energy. Theirs is an experience of being loved, nurtured, valued and given everything they need to go out into the world, as capable, healthy and self-confident individuals. A phenomenal family is a healthy family too, in which each person's well-being is advanced and protected, for the benefit of the entire family.

At the same time there is an interconnectedness among members that bonds the family, much like mountain climbers who rope themselves together when climbing a mountain, so that if someone should slip or need support, he's held up by the others until he regains his footing. Understand too, that this interconnectedness has a glue, a feeling of "all of us are in this together." *We all get painted with one another's brush when we are in a family.* This chapter is about saying, "My family can enjoy a closer, more connected life together, sharing strength, with each person feeling affirmed and uplifted in life-changing ways. Mine can be a family that attains new levels of caring, encouragement and acceptance. My family will have opportunities to reach for the best and have the best. And most important, we leave no one behind."

Being phenomenal is no fantasy. This can be done. The Five Factors for a Phenomenal Family that you are about to learn here will give you the power to take your family to a higher level of functioning, if you are willing to let them become the new foundation for your family life. It's these factors that will help you lead your family in the direction of greater happiness, fulfillment and love. You must decide that your family is worthy of everything you want for them. You must decide that peace, joy and abundance in a family are not just for the people next door or down the street. It's for *your* family.

Part of the solution is exactly this: having a new mind-set, a new philosophy and personal truth as well as a plan of action. In taking up these challenges, you're going to be operating from a position of strength rather than weakness because you'll be wielding valuable knowledge and clarity instead of confusion. Knowledge is power and knowing these five factors and having a very specific action plan for their implementation will enable you to step up and claim good things for your family. It's time for you to become a "have" instead of a "have-not."

Let today mark for you and your family a fresh start and a new commitment. Your family doesn't have to live with the same old patterns and mind-sets. You have the ability and the power to choose how your family lives, and the more you exercise your power to choose, the more phenomenal your family will be. So start now and go into this with the attitude that you are going to reparent your family. Resolve to get your mind right and your behavior on track. Here are the five factors, with action-oriented recommendations for change.

Factor #1: Create a Nurturing and Accepting Family System

The number one need in all people is the need for acceptance, the need to experience a sense of belonging to something and someone. The need for acceptance is more powerful in your family than anywhere else. Let me ask you: Have you ever stopped to consider why some kids pledge such undying loyalty to a team, a clique, a peer group or even the "wrong crowd"? It's because those groups, good or bad, meet their need for emotional security, expression and belongingness. If that need is not met by your family, trust me, your kids will go elsewhere to seek it in order to find approval and acceptance. There is a lot at stake here because you want those powerful affiliations to be devoted to your family. When you meet these needs in your own family, your children are less likely to turn to inappropriate outside groups. A child's pride in a school team or choir or group of friends is great. What I'm talking about runs much deeper. If your children experience in your family the spirit of acceptance, then they will find you approachable, and they will turn to you, because they know that their family is a loving place on which to fall.

Since this factor is such a core requirement for building a phenomenal family, here is what I would wish for you to be thinking, saying and folding into your personal truth now, during and after you read Factor #1:

I want and claim the right for my children to feel appreciated and valued by me and by everyone in our family. I do not want them to ever feel alone or doubt their place in a loving and committed family. I want my kids to know and feel that they are loved for who they are, that I am proud of them and that I will always be there for them. I may not endorse everything they do, but I will never reject them. If any member of my family feels like their contributions are not being recognized or acknowledged by others in the family, that's not okay—not now, not ever. I believe that children live what they learn, and I want to teach them by example that relationships in our family are sacred, to be honored and to be cherished. I know that family life has its ups and downs, its arguments, problems, conflicts and differences of opinion. There has never been a family that was free of rough spots. But I want our family relationships to be so strong that they transcend the in-

evitable daily strife of family living. I want everyone in my family to be true to themselves, loving themselves, feeling fulfilled and living with peace, joy and excitement about each new day.

Right now maybe you're thinking that these objectives are out of your reach, that they represent some kind of pipe dream fantasy, Beaver Cleaver, goody two-shoes family where everyone walks around with a plastic smile. If that type of family ever existed, it certainly doesn't now. I am not telling you to pretend that there are not problems, or that they will go away. There are good times and bad in every family. So please don't be intimidated by the lofty sound of the qualities of an accepting, nurturing family; don't be deceived into thinking you are restricted from them. Let me assure you that they are accessible to you, if you desire them for your family. Anyone can create an accepting and nurturing environment. That is an important truth for you to claim and live. Take a quiet moment and reflect on the love in your heart for each member of your family. You need to look no further for your fuel, your strength and your power.

Now let's talk about how you can bring the spirit of acceptance into affirmative, interactive action in your family. The following is a specific to-do list:

1. Put your family on Project Status. For you to create a nurturing, accepting family, you must, starting right now, put your family life on what I call Project Status. This means that you must consciously decide to actively, purposefully work on improving your family situation each and every day. I don't mean that you "need to," want to or intend to work on it. I mean you "do it," every single day. In very specific, real-life actions. Putting your family on Project Status may require significant sacrifices. In fact, as radical as it may seem, you may need to do such things as:

• **Reschedule or forgo work or business activities in order to make time to spend with your children.** Life is a series of choices and money cannot win every time.

• **Change your normal routine so that you can spend more time with your children.** This may include reading to your children at bedtime, doing hobbies together or having a family movie night each week.

• **Make an appointment with your family and keep it.** Set aside an hour a day for the family every day. Sometimes this is the hardest requirement because it means that you have to prioritize your activities. I realize that there are a lot of other important things to do, but this is something you do not put off. Do it today.

• **Help your children set and achieve goals.** A family on Project Status is a goal-oriented family. Your kids need direction in their lives. When my son Jay was researching his book *Life Strategies for Teens*, he interviewed a lot of kids on whether they used drugs and alcohol or not. The kids who did drugs and drank alcohol said they did it because they didn't have any reason not to; they were doing it to have fun. On the other hand, the kids who chose not to use these substances had a completely different answer. They told Jay: "We don't do drugs or alcohol because it doesn't fit our plan." These teens were saving money for a car, working toward tryouts for sports teams, debate squads or concentrating on getting scholarships to college. In other words, they had goals, and doing drugs was an impediment to those goals; it wouldn't get them what they wanted. It wasn't just a higher morality, they "selfishly" refused drugs and alcohol. They asked themselves the age-old question: "What's in it for me?" As a parent, you can be an influential person in helping your kids set goals, either by setting an example yourself or actually giving them milestones to work for. As they say: Idle hands are the devil's workshop.

• **Passionately adopt a mind-set that you will be committed for the long haul.** A tried-and-true formula fits the bill here: Be-Do-Have. Be committed, do what it takes and you will have what you want. Don't decide to work on your family life for just a week, a month or some preset period of time. You must parent your children *until* . . .

2. Commit at a Project Status level to discover and bring out the authenticity of every family member. Each child in your family came into this world with a core set of unique skills, abilities, interests and talents—all of which make up their genuine identity, their "authentic self." It is all of their strengths and gifts that are uniquely theirs and need expression. This self is not who you want them to be; it is who they're uniquely skilled, gifted and predisposed to be. This journey can be amazingly exciting as you discover or rediscover your very own child.

"Authentic" is a word we don't use much in our day-to-day conversations, so let me define it as I think it applies to children. Authentic children have a sense of hope, a feeling that today is as fun and exciting as yesterday and that tomorrow will be as fun and exciting as today. These children have a passion and excitement about what's happening in their lives and what's going to happen next. They feel good about themselves. They have found interests or qualities that just "light them up." They're self-assured and self-accepting. Their young lives are filled with vivid colors like a box of crayons. And they go about each day doing or discovering what they absolutely, unequivocally, passionately love. An authentic child is a joyful child, and because they have such a positive spirit, they're seldom oppositional. They have self-respect, as well as respect for others. They're responsible and they're accountable in age-appropriate ways.

The problem is that your child's authentic self may have started out clean, solid and brand new, like the last pair of new sneakers you bought them. They were unmarked and well constructed—not a scuff on them. If you left those sneakers in the shoebox, sitting on the shelf in the closet, they would stay in pristine condition. But life is not about sitting on the sidelines. Once your kids wear those sneakers out into the world, they're subjected to the forces, dirt and the demands of hard play. They start to show scuffs, the wear and tear that comes from being out in the world. It becomes hard to look at those sneakers and imagine that they were once brand-new. But they were.

Like those sneakers, your child's authentic self gets scuffed up because the world—including you—begins to write on the slate of who they are. And these life experiences, these "writings," begin changing who they are. Maybe it is the tension and fighting in your household, your divorce, being picked on at school or negative modeling from you and other adult authority figures that begin to obscure that bright light, that joyous and authentic spirit.

Life can be hard, and that's why it's so important that the family environment be your child's oasis. It's through all of these life experiences that kids start getting programmed to believe what they're expected to be and do, rather than what they are *meant* to do. But there's an authentic child in there. It shined brightly before the pains of growing up and experiencing life marked it up. There's an authentic self within each one of your children (and within you as well), and it's your job to create a family environment that will bring it out.

The following suggestions will help you get started on ways to discover and bring to the surface the authenticity and hidden talents and interests of each of your children. This may mean that you have to plow some new ground!

• **Open the door to different experiences for your children— music, art, drama, literature, science, leadership, travel, sports and so forth.** With your encouragement, expose your children to different experiences, letting them color outside the lines, to see what catches hold. Allow them to pursue activities so that they might discover an interest that they might not even know they have—whether you enjoy those activities or not. This means that you will have to be open-minded, and kiss a lot of frogs along the way. Take careful note of the activities and experiences your children naturally gravitate toward. Again, do not just choose things that you like or think they will like. Take a risk; have some fun!

• **Begin to recognize and observe in your children particular talents or a streak of intelligence and inspire them to develop it.** If your child likes to plunk the keys on the piano, take her to a recital or suggest piano lessons. Verbally gifted children usually speak or read at a young age. You can nurture this gift by giving them books, finding opportunities for writing or giving them a computer for writing. If you see that your child is good in math or enjoys puzzles, he may be mathematically gifted or skilled in science—aptitudes that can be encouraged by taking them to science fairs or computer exhibitions, providing them with a computer or doing science experiments together. Visually oriented children like to draw or build things. You can encourage this gift with art supplies, construction kits or visits to art museums.

Ron's story is a typical example of how you can discover gifts in your children, even if the details of the story are unique to him. Ron has a nine-year-old son, Stephen, who received a digital camera for Christmas and quickly mastered its intricacies. Stephen asked permission to take his new camera on a field trip to the Bronx Zoo. Ron and his wife, Stephanie, were reluctant, since it was Stephen's nature to lose things, but they acquiesced. Imagine their surprise and delight when Stephen and two friends, along with their teacher's help, incorporated the best of their 267 zoo photographs into a digital video narrative of the trip and screened it for the class, as well as for an audience of parents. It was amazing to Ron and Stephanie that these kids had so beautifully mastered this technology and put it to such creative use. Ron recognized the technical wizardry as part of his son's authenticity and is now encouraging more of the same.

As Ron did, you'll want to find these gifts in your children so you can build on them and then encourage your kids in their pursuits.

• **Respect and encourage your child's uniqueness.** Every person's particular likes, dislikes, interests and talents, no matter how different from one another they may be, are respected and "room" is made for those idiosyncrasies as long as that uniqueness is not destructive to themselves or others. In fact, everyone is encouraged to be uniquely and authentically who they are.

• **Catch your children doing something right.** Far too often, kids hear about what they've done wrong. Constant faultfinding can and will shoot down a child's sense of self-worth and initiative. If you're criticizing, you're not praising. You must start praising your children for positive behavior. Not only do you want to praise, you also want to encourage the positive behavior you observe. Tell your children things like "You're doing a great job of getting your homework done," "I'm pleased to see that you did such a fine job of cleaning your room," "I appreciate you sharing your toys with your little brother," and "Thank you for helping your mother with the dishes." Acknowledgments like these go a long way toward building character and self-esteem in your children.

• **Look for the best intentions in your children.** Too often we think that our children misbehave willfully and on purpose. Instead of being quick to blame, choose the high road and assume your child has positive intentions. If your child has drawn a mural on your wall with his crayons, for example, maybe he is just trying to provide stimulation for himself and lacks judgment; he is not necessarily being bad or naughty. And if you label his behavior as such, your child will take it to heart and often come to believe it himself. Then you have real problems. In addition to looking for the best intentions, redirect your child's energy to more appropriate behavior—drawing on an easel rather than on your walls, for example.

• **Never, ever overprogram or overschedule your child's time with too many activities.** This has the potential of backfiring in a big way by making your child dislike the activity and ultimately give it up.

By creating a family environment that gives your children room to explore their unique gifts, talents, and interests—at their own pace and with your encouragement and support—you have constructed a nurturing atmosphere where they begin to live and radiate an authentically directed childhood.

3. Create a sense of security and peace in your home. Your children look to you and your spouse as a solid and safe base of operations, and your home should be a place where, whenever your children walk through that door and pull it closed behind them, they don't have to watch their backs or question the loyalties of those within the family. They need to know that they don't have to have their antennae out. Yet when they're subjected to a conflict-ridden home, with behaviors such as open hostility, fighting and other gusts of fury between the two people they rely on for their personal security and safety, their base is shaken to the core. They begin to experience insecurity and have fears about the disintegration of the family unit.

Where your relationship standards are concerned, commit to yourself that you and your partner will not yell and scream at each other in front of your children. Children also tend to blame themselves for the ugly arguments, the kind that devolve into personal attacks, however illogical that blame might appear to an outsider looking in. They tend to tell themselves, "Somehow, this must be my fault." Kids also think that it's their job to fix things. Can you imagine how terrible it is for them to hold themselves responsible for something over which they have absolutely no control? Moreover, your children are typically not around for the peace-making. Sadly, they get exposed to all of the trials and tribulations without the benefit of participating in the peacemaking. It shakes them to the core, eroding their self-esteem and confidence in their own social situations. In particularly volatile homes, children are afraid even to bring their friends home for fear they'll be embarrassed by the open and uncontrolled hostilities.

If you argue and have disagreements, do it with dignity and respect for your partner's sense of self and be mindful of the quarrel's impact on others. It's not necessarily toxic to argue or disagree in front of your children, as long as you do it without yelling, screaming and name-calling. Let's face it: Family members do disagree. Honest disagreements can actually provide a good lesson in that family members can learn that people who love each other can disagree and express their own views without fear of losing each other or their base of operations. Children who never see an appropriate argument might become naïve and vulnerable to the realities of relationships later in life. It's only when the arguments deteriorate into yelling and screaming and character assassination that the security of individuals and the strength of the family are threatened. It's then that children become insecure.

So how can you ensure that your family becomes, and remains, a secure, stable base for your children and not a war zone? To help you answer that question, here are some actions that you will want to take now.

• **Take it private and keep it private.** Fighting unfairly—with yelling and character assassination—in front of your children is nothing short of child abuse. It can and will scar them emotionally—all because you don't have the self-control to contain yourself until you can talk privately. If you simply can't control your temper, and you allow your disagreements to deteriorate into personal attacks rather than problem-solving sessions, at least confront your spouse behind closed doors, and don't make your innocent children pick up the tab.

• **Stop being a "right-fighter,"** arguing over who is right and who is wrong. Your kids don't care who's right. They just want you to stop fighting.

• **Don't say you can't control your temper.** That's not true. It's that you *don't* control your temper. Have you had fights at your boss's house? At church? At a restaurant with friends? You don't do it when you can't. The only person you control is you. Choose to control your impulses. Find a different outlet for your frustration. Don't take it out on your children. Children learn what they live. Stop and think about what you're teaching them when you demonstrate poor impulse control yourself.

• **If you do have an honest disagreement, let your children see the resolution.** Share a moment of peace to reaffirm your bond once a resolution or decision has been reached. This might be, for example, a silent sixty-second hug, or looking into each other's eyes for a minute.

• **Eliminate patterns of verbal abuse.** You are a pivotal person in your child's life. When you yell, criticize or embarrass your child, you're leaving a permanent mark on him or her. When you fail to point out what makes you proud, why a child is special or that you love him, you also write on the slate of that child. The chart on page 40 lists steps you can take to condition yourself to stop verbal abuse (the same steps can be used if you are emotionally or physically abusive).

• **Actively support one another every today.** Make it a family policy to give one another at least one supportive remark a day—more is better—but a minimum of one per day. This can be as easy as saying: "I am thinking of you when you take that test today," or "I know that life seems strange sometimes, but I want you to know that we are in it together." These statements can become the most powerful in a child's life sometimes, and we may never know it. In addition, ask your family members how they are doing, and don't take "fine" as a final answer. Look them in

HOW TO ELIMINATE VERBAL ABUSE

1. *Identify the first sign of meltdown.* To begin to cope with your behavior, you have to identify the first sign that indicates you're beginning to spin out of control. It may be dry mouth, red ears, a flushed face, butterflies in your stomach or heart palpitations. What signals the start of your meltdown? It is imperative to identify this sign, because it is part of a chain of behavior to which you've become accustomed. Your first sign can lead to the second link in the chain, which is where you can make an important decision.

2. *Consciously choose to cope.* You can use your first sign of meltdown as a cue to cope, rather than as a cue for meltdown. When you feel the sign you've identified in step one coming on, you can make a conscious decision to use it to begin your coping sequence.

3. *Make an incompatible response.* You need to get past your impulse moment. In order to do so, you must make it impossible to abuse your child. What should you do? Leave the room. Go outside. Do whatever it takes to guarantee you will not abuse your child.

4. *Tell your accountability person.* You are abusive because you can be—you have no accountability. In order to stop, you have to take responsibility. Choose a friend, a family member or someone else to be your "accountability person." You will be morally accountable to this person. Every time you write down a destructive thought or avoid an abusive situation, call this person. Read him or her what you wrote in your coping journal, and talk about how you feel.

5. *Engage in positive interaction.* When you're through the impulse stage, go back into the room with your child. Give your child a hug, pat him or her on the back, do something positive.

6. *Long-term: Get counseling.* You need to see somebody on a regular basis to deal with what's happening inside of you. You can go to a counselor, a pastor or a social worker, somebody who will listen and continue to guide you in the right direction. Make sure that you are taking care of yourself.

---

the eyes, really ask and be prepared to listen in order to generate an honest reply. Take an interest in the route of your children's lives.

• **Deal forthrightly with destructive behavior.** Acceptance of family members does not mean acceptance of *every* attitude or behavior. It does mean valuing the human being and looking for what is worthy, vulnerable and good. If there's a situation where someone is behaving destructively or outrageously—being disrespectful, misbehaving, drinking or using drugs—you can deal with him or her in a way that clearly communicates that the behavior is unacceptable, yet in a way that ultimately promotes his or her self-esteem. You can say, for instance, "I can't and won't tolerate or endorse your behavior, because I know you're a better person than this. I'm not judging you, because I know you have good qualities and traits and characteristics. I know you can respond in a healthier, more positive way. And I won't let you be less than who you are. I'm going to require you to be that better person."

4. Respect and overtly acknowledge the roles and contributions of each family member. In a healthy, interconnected family, everybody has a role, and everybody has a purpose. In fact, everyone should feel and know that they have a contribution to make to that family, that it would matter terribly if they weren't there.

As I mentioned earlier, during my junior high and high school years, I was very much into athletics. Frequently my family would come to my games and watch me play football under the bright lights of our school's stadium or play basketball in an emotionally charged field house or wrestle in a jam-packed gymnasium. For a family that was poor, with no money for entertainment and no prospects of any, going to my athletic events was a real bright spot. If I scored a touchdown or made a big play, there was great family pride. People would come up to my father, slap him on the back and say, "Great game, Joe," just as if he'd played the game himself. I was the family entertainment and a source of pride. As withdrawn as I was, that was one of my roles. It was "currency" for me and served a needed purpose for the family. I felt good about it because what I did mattered.

> **Survey Fact:**
> Fifty-three percent of the parents indicated significant resentment in making sacrifices as a parent.

Some families have a "court jester," the designated family cutup. Usually, the mother in a family is the "glue," the adhesive that binds that family together. Mothers also typically fulfill the role of nurturer, particularly in making sure everyone is nourished (forcing food on everyone, if necessary). I encountered such a mom recently, Gail, the mother of Anna, one of my staff members. Gail had to undergo a triple bypass and was recovering in the hospital when Anna came into the room to see her mother for the first time after her surgery. Looking barely alive, her body sprouting intravenous lines in all directions, Gail looked up, dimly realizing her daughter had traveled hundreds of miles to see her, and called over to her husband. "Ed," she said in a barely audible voice, "you need to get your daughter something to eat."

Although roles are flexible and subject to change, there is no blurring of roles between parents and children in a healthy family. There is a hierarchy within the family, a pecking order that is very clear. Establishing clear roles in your family requires that you:

• **Be a clear authority figure.** In a phenomenal family, you as a parent are not really your child's "friend," nor are you their equal. You can be friendly and should be, but you never blur the boundary. Your children need you to be an authority figure who lets them know where the boundaries of acceptable behavior lie. Trying to be their friend will only undermine your authority. When you inevitably must shift from the role of friend to the role of parent in order to discipline your child, it can be very confusing and leave them feeling betrayed. "I thought you were my friend and now you ground me [or take away my toys]!" It just doesn't work. You're either a parent or a friend; you cannot be both.

• **Make the decisions for your family.** When all is said and done, the final decisions rest with you. My own family is very democratic; we take into consideration everyone's opinion. But when it comes time to make a decision, we don't manage by committee. Robin and I always make the final call.

• **Never play favorites.** No child stands above another, and as a parent, you should never play favorites. Children sense favoritism, and they often interpret it as a lack of love. It leaves a residue that can show up later as low self-esteem.

So the message should be obvious: A spirit of acceptance is a core requirement for nurturing and building a phenomenal family. When you exhibit a spirit that says you accept your children, you're saying that even though you may not always rubber-stamp things your kids are doing, you love them. You're saying that despite all the things you sometimes wish they would do or wouldn't do, the bottom line is that you accept who they are, and you will always be there for them. When children live with acceptance, approval and praise, they learn to like themselves, they learn to have faith in themselves and they learn to love.

Factor #2: Promote Rhythm in Your Family Life

One of the major themes you'll hear me repeat throughout this book is that the phenomenal family has a certain rhythm—a beat that communicates, "This is where we're from, this is what we stand for and this is what we do together." Life begins with this rhythm. An unborn child senses the tympanic sounds of his mother's heartbeat in the womb—a calming and comforting sound that continues after birth when she holds her infant instinctively over her heart, an example of the natural order of the universe. It's this beat of life that provides the comfort, the surety and the security that nurtures us and helps us grow, and then connects us to a deeper rhythm of life within our family. Children need this rhythm in their lives, and it is unsettling to them when they don't have it. This factor is absolutely critical to the well-being of your family.

Every family has a uniquely different rhythm. The family with six children has a very different rhythm than the family with one child. If you compared the family living at #6 Elm Street USA to the family living at #7 Elm Street USA, you would hear a different rhythm, just as you would hear a different rhythm while listening to two different songs. Although they both may be wonderful songs, each is distinctly different. In some families, the rhythm might be heavy metal, whereas in others it might be the rhythm of smooth jazz. But not all rhythms are good rhythms; they can be defined by chaos, pain, stress, hurt, discord, paranoia, lack of trust, dissension or deteriorating relationship standards. They are dark rhythms. That could be the rhythm of your family.

I have, through a private practice of psychology, and now through the television medium, sought to educate literally millions of parents and families, helping them create and maintain a rhythm in their family life that, although not pitch-perfect—because there is no such thing as a perfect parent or a perfect family—is meaningful for every person in the family. If you can't find your rhythm or you don't like the rhythm, how do you change it or create a new one? Let the following notes help define for you the rhythm in your family and how to restore it.

1. Create a predictable pace of family life. I know it is difficult to schedule the events of the day or the week, but your family does need a pace—a rate of progress throughout the day built around key activities.

For example, set specific times for when meals are served, have regular bedtimes, establish a specific list of chores, have certain times for homework, television, Internet use and so forth. The constancy of these things provides a cohesive dimension of family life that everyone can depend on. That predictability can have a very settling and calming effect.

• **Play games and do activities as a family.** Children are naturally inventive and enjoy family games. By having a regular game or puzzle night each week, you give your family a positive structure, something everyone begins to look forward to, and you create opportunities for connection and communication. By the way, simply watching TV or a movie is not a family activity because it requires no interaction.

• **Develop volunteer projects together.** Another way to build rhythm is to encourage your entire family to do volunteer work together and help the less fortunate. Get your family involved in church, at a shelter or in some other charitable activity on a regular basis. Whatever you do, turn the concept of giving into a proactive behavior. When you do, this will give your children a tremendous sense of accomplishment, and the value of giving will become so woven into the fabric of your family life that it will define who your family is and what it stands for.

2. Reinforce your family's values. These are foundational convictions for which your family stands, convictions that you live by, not some of the time, but all of the time. By acknowledging and living your values, you bring this much-needed rhythm into your life. One way to do this is to give a voice to your values through an ongoing dialogue, in order to reinforce what your family embraces and holds dear. For example, Robin and I have always defined for our sons what it means to be a McGraw. We say such things as, "The McGraws don't lie, steal, cheat, call people names, make racist comments or be mean to other people. The McGraws don't make fun of people who are physically challenged, and we don't talk about or be disrespectful to neighbors or elderly people." You should explain to your children why your family does not do those things—why they are unacceptable. You can explain it by saying that it isn't fair or right. It isn't something that you can be proud of or that maybe it is not productive.

3. Create a sense of your family's identity. One way to do this is to research your family tree. Too often great family stories are forgotten, and people cease to exist in our memories as a result. Make it a project to learn about previous generations, including those who have passed away. Who knows? You might be related to someone famous or even infamous. Understanding your family history strengthens the bonds among family members.

In addition, get your family involved in creating a family symbol, just as ancient cultures used to do when they designed family crests for their homes, clans and battle shields. This is a worthwhile family project that has value for learning about family roots and for building teamwork among family members.

4. Establish standards of conduct. There are probably some things that your family consistently embraces and repeats, and these are a part of your standards of conduct. Many of these standards should be pretty fixed and not open for constant discussion. For example, from the time I was three years old, my father always told me: "Son, when you meet somebody, you step up, call them by name, look them in the eye and give them a firm handshake." So if someone came to our house or met us on the street, I knew exactly what I was supposed to do. I wasn't lost, I wasn't intimidated or confused. I knew exactly what I was supposed to do and it took the pressure off me.

As children, we learned early about the importance of being considerate of another person. We were taught lessons in manners and self-restraint. We had a rhythm in our family of always saying "please" and "thank you." We never went into the kitchen without a shirt on, then and now. Respecting one another's privacy, asking permission to go into someone's room and showing respect for one another were all standards of conduct that we lived. I didn't go into my sister's room, rummaging around to look for something. I would ask her if it was in there and if I could go look. She didn't come into my room and borrow my sweat socks to go jogging; she had to ask to do it. There was a rhythm that felt like we all had some space within our home. We didn't have to lock our stuff up. We didn't have to guard our things, because we knew no one would be messing with them. A family with standards of conduct is a well-functioning family.

5. Be accountable for your choices. You and everyone else in your family are fully accountable for the choices all of you make. The choices you made and continue to make are 100 percent your responsibility, and there is a cost to those choices, good or bad, to those with whom you share your life, because your choices affect everyone else. Remember my earlier point about how we all get painted with one another's brush? You choose the attitudes you bring into your family relationships. You choose the emotions and feelings that will control your behavior in the family. And you choose how you act and how you react to everyone else in the family. Your choices affect your interactions with everyone else in your family.

Whenever I think about this, I can't help but remember my junior high school friend Tom, and how we used to catch and collect snakes. At one time we had thirty snakes, including eight or ten rattlers that were huge. My dad, my mom and my three sisters were absolutely snakephobic, so horrified of snakes that I was not allowed to bring them anywhere near the house. But Tom's father had no problem with snakes, so we kept the snakes in cages in his garage. That way, we could get them out and play with them whenever we wanted to. I wasn't allowed to do those things at my house because it affected my family. I had accountability for what I did.

Genuinely acknowledging your accountability, and how your choices affect other members of your family, means that you should be willing to ask yourself questions like the following:

- Are there certain behaviors or bad habits I need to stop? If so, what are they?
- Do I spend more money than I can afford, possibly jeopardizing the financial condition of my family?
- Do I choose to live recklessly and without regard for my personal safety?
- Am I having trouble at work, brought on by my own attitudes or behavior or by compromising my principles?
- Do I consider the consequences, positive or negative, of a career change on my family?
- Have I taken unnecessary risks?
- Have I in any way treated my children unfairly?
- Am I failing to take care of my health by simply not requiring enough of myself?
- Have I failed to take my marriage vows seriously, being emotionally unavailable or even unfaithful? Have I considered how this behavior may affect my family?
- Do I choose to put work over the priority of family?

Answer these questions, and any others that may come to mind, so as to see how your choices have the power to impact your family. Let your answers identify for you what must become priorities for repair.

6. Stand up for your family and everyone in it. In a phenomenal family, family comes first; therefore loyalty is critical in establishing rhythm in a family. You don't forsake your family because of your boyfriend, your girlfriend or your friends. There's no them-versus-us scenario. It's just us. Certainly, you should support the team your children play on, the friends they have, the choir in which they're members—and all those subgroups to which you have loyalty. But it is a different degree of loyalty than that which you have for your family. Your primary sense of belonging comes from your family. You cannot serve two masters; you cannot have divided loyalties.

Family members stand up for and champion one another. When my son Jay was nine years old, a friend of his came over to our house to play. This particular friend was from a large family that was highly combative, physically and verbally. When my younger son Jordan came into the room, wanting to participate in the activities, Jay's friend became agitated and teased Jordan. Before long, Jordan went to get some cookies for everyone. When he was gone, Jay's friend suggested that they both run out the back door and hide so that Jordan couldn't find them. Jay refused, saying, "We're not mean to each other in our family." Jay was being loyal to his little brother.

I once worked with a troubled family in which the son became heavily involved in drugs, got busted for dealing and was sent to prison. The family was embarrassed by his criminal acts, particularly his sister. My message to her was: Be loyal to your brother; don't be ashamed that he's your brother. If someone says to you, "Isn't your brother in prison?" respond by saying, "Yes he is; he made some really bad choices. Now he's paying for it, and I'm really pulling for him to turn his life around."

Loyalty begins at home. Family members make sacrifices for one another. They stick up for one another in front of others. They stand by their family. Friends come and go, but you have only one family, and it will be yours forever.

Suppose there is a "flat note" in the rhythm of your family—a workaholic father, a partner who doesn't support your desire to create a healthy family or a parent with a darker side? Creating the right rhythm does not require both parents' participation. In a perfect world, absolutely, but don't wait for your partner. The change begins with you as you decide what to do with your family. By breaking the stalemate of sitting around and waiting to see who's going to make a move first, you create the energy and the newness. Your constructive thinking will be infectious to everyone around you, especially your partner. What you hope for is that through your discussions, through your examples and through your choices, you'll be an inspiration for everyone else in your family.

You need to reclaim and find the rhythm for your own family, one in which there are positive patterns, such as discipline that establishes order and not oppression, an atmosphere that motivates and inspires change, and values that uphold and define who you are as a family and what you believe in. Most important, a family with rhythm is one where you as parents live the love you say you feel.

Factor #3: Establish Meaningful Rituals and Traditions

Whether it was the traditional holiday dinners you enjoyed at your grandparents' or the vacations you took every year with your parents, we all remember events and celebrations that define who we are as a family and how we are connected to one another. What I am talking about here are predictable activities and patterns in your family life that serve as psychological and behavioral anchors for your values and beliefs, provide your family with a sense of stability and identity, reinforce your family's heritage, give your family meaning and continue to create rhythm in your family's life. For example, your family may celebrate rite-of-passage rituals such as baptism or bar mitzvahs, bedtime rituals of a bath followed by story time, or milestone rituals such as special ways of celebrating birthdays and wedding anniversaries. There are also affiliation rituals, in which we identify with institutions, groups and things larger than ourselves. Rooting for your favorite sports team, or standing shoulder to shoulder with other members of the community and watching Fourth of July fireworks are examples of what I'm talking about.

By definition, family rituals are activities that are repeated, deliberate and coordinated and have meaning. You make a commitment to do these activities. You don't do them only when they're convenient and blow them off when they're not. The power of rituals and traditions is found in their repetition. Without these defining characteristics, a ritual falls to the level of being just a routine and loses its power.

To help frame this concept more clearly, allow me to share with you some rituals from my own family life. When I used to put my sons Jay and Jordan to bed at night (after Robin had done the hard work all day long), I'd tell them a fictional story that always starred them and made them the conquering heroes of the tale. "Once upon a time, there was a huge mountain," I'd begin, "and at the top of that mountain lived a little boy whose name was Jordan." My story would slowly unravel, telling of their adventures, their bravery and other qualities to inspire my young sons. Then, after the storytelling was over, I'd ask the question, "How do you suppose, out of all the boys in the world, I got the best ones?" Jay and Jordan would always giggle, saying, "I don't know, Dad." To this very day, these bedtime rituals remain crystal clear in my sons' memories. For the three of us, these were rituals of connection.

Now here's my point: Rituals like these help your children acquire a sense of continuity, security and love, particularly in today's world where there's so much family brokenness and emotional distance, and a pace that's, literally, a blur of hyperactivity, diversion and distraction, and what I call living in the laser lane.

Holidays, vacations, family reunions or other special events that bring families together are examples of traditions. Traditions aren't meaningless habits or ways of doing things; like rituals, they create a sense of identity and a sense of belonging among family members.

One of the earliest and most memorable holiday traditions celebrated in our family began when our older son Jay was four years old. Every year, we'd travel to Kansas City, where I grew up during my high school years, for one of the most spectacular and breathtaking Christmas lighting displays in the entire country. With one switch, the entire fourteen-square-block area of Country Club Plaza in downtown Kansas City was illuminated with thousands of jewel-colored lights outlining every tower, dome, balcony, courtyard and building. That first year, we ripped a dollar bill in half and hid it in a fountain in the plaza. The next year, we pulled out the dollar bill and matched it up. And so we'd celebrate the start of the holiday season with that tradition. We pulled that same bill out twelve years in a row. About a year ago, I visited Kansas City, and Jay wanted to know if I was going to check on the dollar bill. If that boy lives to be 110 years old, he'll never forget our trips to Kansas City!

Ever since our sons were old enough to have even a small vocabulary, Robin and I have had the tradition of making a Christmas Eve videotape about the impending visit of Santa Claus, highlights of the previous year and what each boy hopes and expects to get for Christmas. We always had a little rocking chair that we'd put the boys in, we'd place a Christmas hat on their heads, and we'd interview them on camera. Often, they'd dance or hop around, sing or dodge the camera. That was their personality at the time. As they got older, they'd roll their eyes and give smart-aleck answers on camera, but they still loved this family tradition. Our family rituals and traditions are one of the ways we've created a warm, loving and nurturing environment for our family.

So important in family life are rituals and traditions that social scientists tell us that without them, a family may be lacking in crucial ways. Your children are more likely to develop behavioral problems, you'll experience more conflict in your home and, in general, you'll create less family stability. What's more, rituals have been found to produce positive changes in the physical body, in the form of stronger immunity, lower levels of stress hormones and reduced blood pressure.

Don't think that there's some etched-in-stone way to do rituals and traditions. There isn't, and it isn't brain surgery. There can be as many different ways to create rituals and traditions as there are different families who observe them. One way is not better than another. Here are some ways to establish rituals and traditions in your own family:

• *Plan purposeful celebrations.* Birthdays, Father's Day, Mother's Day, July Fourth and other events are all opportunities to create a tradition or even a ritual (see the box on page 52 for how to create meaningful rituals). These are times that have specific meaning that pertain directly to your family members. Don't shortchange them; invest your time and effort in a meaningful celebration. During the holidays, create traditions by baking an apple pie every year or decorating the tree with the same ornaments. Play the same music at birthday parties. Make sure your children either buy or make their own gifts. If you do it for them, you cheat them out of being an active participant in the ritual. You don't even have to wait for those annual events. Create a monthly celebration, such as an "I'm glad we made it to the end of the month" party or "project wrap-up" party.

• *Hold naming rituals.* In most native cultures, young people undergo a coming-of-age ritual that often includes choosing a new name.

Naming a baby blesses that child and welcomes him or her into a family and a community. Renaming rituals allow the individual to connect with and express what is at the heart of who he or she is. You can still do something like this with your children today. When a child gets older and wants to be called by a more mature name, for example, it is perfectly okay to say, "You can be called Kathleen now, instead of Kathy," or "Robert, instead of Bobby."

• *Tell family stories.* Whether they are about the family events or some related events, family stories are a vehicle through which each generation learns to care about the previous ones. Build into family get-togethers special times for the retelling of these stories, complete with slides, pictures and mementos. Bring out picture albums or old films to enhance the storytelling experience.

• *Create special dinnertime rituals.* To increase communication at the dinner table, make time for each person in the family to share two good things that happened to them that day and two things that were not so good. This is an excellent way for family members to open themselves up to one another, and it serves to bring everyone closer together.

• *Worship together.* For many families, attending a worship service is a major family ritual. Religious services connect families with a special community of belief and support, as well as with a higher power, and they provide an experience to be together. Family participation in worship services is an excellent way to enact a family's faith through rituals and lay a spiritual foundation for children.

What is important is that you find ways of being together that work for your family. Whether or not it meets some standard that you read in a book or conforms to what your neighbors do should not matter. The litmus test should be whether or not what you're doing as a family generates the results of togetherness, communication, continuity and bonding. It's not important that you follow particular principles. It *is* important that the principles work, and that you write your own rules. Focus on what works for your family. You'll find other guidelines for creating rituals in the box on page 52.

HOW TO CREATE MEANINGFUL RITUALS
IN YOUR FAMILY LIFE

From the simple to the complex, all rituals have four key characteristics that work together so that the ritual takes on special meaning and significance for everyone involved:

1. *Celebration of self:* Usually, a ritual focuses on a person or persons to express how special they are or to help someone identify his or her unique strengths and qualities. You have a bedtime ritual of storytelling with your children, for example, to bond emotionally with them, or your daughter participates in her grade-school graduation as a step toward her future.

2. *Separation to a sacred or special place:* Because rituals are meant to celebrate change, they need to take place in a special setting, outside of your regular life. You can do this at your place of worship, a special outdoor setting or a quiet place or you can simply transform your home environment with candles, music or special toys your children might enjoy playing with.

3. *Transition:* This part of the ritual acknowledges the person's new role or ushers in a new life stage—your baby is baptized and sprinkled with water, your daughter turns twelve and is acknowledged with gifts or your family gathers to celebrate your grandparents' fiftieth wedding anniversary. Often there's some sort of symbolic component to this part of a ritual.

4. *Personal application to a better life:* For a ritual to have meaning, it must allow the individual to connect with and appreciate more than ever what is at the heart of who he or she is: Your child who is given adult status can now have more privileges and more responsibility; or your teenager who has earned an achievement can know he or she has been honored by the family.

Factor #4: Be Active in Your Communication

The greatest things you can give your children are your ears and your voice. When my son Jay asked teens across the country what they wanted most from their parents, the number one answer was to have their parents more involved in their lives. They don't want to be interrogated—just talked to! That is why at the heart of a phenomenal family there is active communication. What I'm talking about is meaningful dialogue that takes into account each family member's need for acceptance, self-respect, encouragement and security and seeks to serve those needs as part of a daily practice. When you actively communicate, you listen with the goal of understanding, respond in a nonjudgmental way, share information openly and honestly and do so in a way that keeps your family relationships on solid, loving ground.

Unfortunately, though, the agenda of the vast majority of family communication these days has become problem-driven. Even in the strongest of families, too often people talk about nothing but problems in an effort to communicate. If all you ever talk about are problems, all you'll ever have are problem relationships. Don't just communicate when there's trouble or when you're upset with one another or disappointed with something that's taken place.

Some families fail to talk or even communicate at all, something that causes far more problems than you might imagine. My clinical research shows that the amount of trouble kids get into is inversely proportional to the number of words spoken in the home. What that means is, the less you talk at home, the more trouble your kids will get into outside the home. Therefore, we need to encourage active communication in our families. Here are several strategies for doing so in your own family:

1. Talk about things that don't matter. This is a useful expression for saying talk about the little things, such as what went on in your day or in your child's day. This approach has the value of keeping the lines of communication open, especially when there's trouble or an emergency. There's a useful analogy in medicine to illustrate what I'm talking about: If you have ever been taken to the emergency room, hospitalized or been with someone who has, maybe you've noticed that one of the very first procedures administered is the insertion of an IV line. This is done quickly so that there's already an IV in in case the patient has something like a grand mal seizure. The channel—the line to the vein—is already open, and medicine can be injected directly into the bloodstream. They've got a flow going. In a similar way, when it's time to talk about something really serious with your child, the lines of communication are already open. How do you ever expect to talk to them about things that do matter if you haven't practiced by talking about things that don't? The more you talk to each other, the stronger your bond becomes. You meet on a completely different plane that does nothing but help your relationship.

2. Change the backdrop or the context in which communication occurs. You'll find that your children are much more comfortable, more receptive and tend to open up in safe environments, rather than if you sit them down in a chair or at the table to talk. Suffice it to say, this serves only to make them defensive and suspicious, and they'll disconnect from you. Under these circumstances, what is real never gets voiced, and what gets voiced is never real.

Let me give you an example of how active communication is enhanced when you're in an environment in which your child feels comfortable. My son Jordan and I frequently play video football, a game at which I start slow and taper off. I don't have a clue how to generate extra points, and half the time I'm holding the controller upside down. I don't have to tell you that he pummels me every single time and gets a big kick out of administering each whupping. However, the game has become the backdrop for some very important conversations in which he has shared some of his innermost thoughts. Listening to CDs with your children, going with them to get their car gassed, playing games together—these modes of relating break down walls, giving both of you a much more rewarding outcome than trying to force communication would. You'll get more information and greater bonding, as long as you don't interrogate or give your child the third degree.

Make time to talk—in the car, while playing games or before bedtime. The point is to make a conscious effort to look for times when you can talk to your child alone.

3. Tune into your child's world. When there's something your child is doing that at first you may not understand, your very first step should not be to judge or criticize. Your first step should be to tune in. If your fourteen-year-old son likes rap music, for instance, and it's music that's not banned from the radio, you meet him where he is. If my son buys some new CDs, I want to talk about that. It's not the music that's important to me. What's important to me is that it is important to him.

Tune in not only to his musical tastes and purchases, but also to everything in which he's involved and interested: favorite subject at school, favorite website, friends and so forth. Know what is going on in your children's lives and in their hearts and minds. Then make a commitment to be actively interested in one another's lives. If you want to have mutual interests, you have to be mutually available.

4. Discuss sensitive subjects such as politics or religion. These discussions are for the sole purpose of teaching children how to express their opinions and how to communicate. It is not a debate, but rather an opportunity for children to feel free to articulate opinions without criticism. Providing a forum for your child's self-expression is one of the ways you can bolster their self-confidence and enhance their communication skills.

5. Do some "quilting." This is actually a term I use to describe family interactions involving a common activity. Originally, quilting was a project, usually done by a group of women or members of the family as part of a quilting bee, where patches were sewn together to make a quilt. The object of quilting is to begin a group project together, not necessarily quilting but in the general spirit of the quilting bee. Examples of quilting projects include painting a room, cleaning the house, washing the car, making a dollhouse, building a playhouse or a treehouse or tending a garden. Quilting is an excellent way to create opportunities for communication and bring the family together for a project.

We'll go into more detail—and I mean much more detail—when we talk about communication as a parenting tool in Chapter 8. Begin right now to prioritize active, ongoing communication in your family life, even if you're the one who must initiate it. It will strengthen family relationships, build bridges between you and other family members and help nurture the authenticity of every child in your family.

Factor #5: Learn How to Manage Crisis

When it comes to family life, it's not a question of whether or not a crisis will hit. It is a question of when. No matter how smoothly your life goes, no matter how well you parent with a purpose, you'll encounter some crisis, and it will impact your life together as a family. Maybe you discover that your child is addicted to drugs or alcohol. Or your family must adjust to life with a chronically ill child or parent. Perhaps your family is dealing with your divorce, or you find evidence that your child is identifying with some counterculture like Goth. Maybe your son is on a failure track at school. There are endless challenges that can and will pop up because life is not a success-only journey. An important hallmark of phenomenal families is that they don't panic or turn on one another when the pressure is on. Phenomenal families are loyal to one another and emerge from the other side of the crisis stronger and more bonded than ever.

Some crises are of our own making; others intrude on families from the world. No matter what the origin, a crisis is a wake-up call that something is wrong in your family and can threaten its viability. And remember that certain events may not seem like a crisis to you as a parent but may be of monumental enormity in the eyes of a child.

There are some families who, when confronted by a crisis, are prone to panic, decompensate or fall apart. When facing challenges, these families are handicapped by self-limiting beliefs. Those beliefs are extremely important because I believe that people create the results in life that they believe they deserve. If you're a parent who believes peace and tranquillity and all good things in life are meant for other people, people who deserve the good things, then your family is doomed to a painful existence. This type of parent simply holds on to the belief that any crisis is too overwhelming and impossible to handle. They surrender to a negative result with no fight or resistance.

On the other hand, I'm sure you've seen other families who deal with a shattering crisis in a constructive manner. They view the crisis as a manageable challenge, sharing the conviction, "We believe we deserve to survive intact and we will find a way." As a result, they are better equipped to find workable solutions and less likely to overlook alternatives that can be incredibly powerful. These families have the skills to move through the crisis and come out stronger than ever—with greater attention to what matters, a renewed focus on priorities, a clearer moral compass and heightened sense of purpose in their lives or family relationships that are more loving than they might have otherwise been. Know this: You *do* have a choice about whether the crisis will be your family's absolute undoing, or whether it will become a time for your family to rally, emerge strengthened and create value from adversity. The worst of times can bring out your family's best.

Your best chance to navigate the rough waters of a crisis is to have a consciously designed crisis management plan in place for overcoming the tough stuff—before it hits. Earlier in my career, I had the privilege of being professionally involved in aviation—a love of mine from an early age—as a human factors consultant for various airlines, reconstructing psychological circumstances leading to airline disasters.

As a matter of crisis management, the aviation industry adopted what was referred to as a Cockpit Resource Management plan, which included a very specific emergency procedure. The key was that the emergency plan was decided upon well in advance of a flight crew ever getting into an emergency. The reason for this should be obvious: The time to decide what to do when you have an engine fire is not when you have an engine fire. The time to decide that is ahead of time. Pilots have access to a thick, two-thousand-page manual that describes what to do in any kind of emergency. But as you might suspect, they don't have time to thumb through a manual to find out how to climb out of trouble; they don't even rely on memory. Instead they have a very few lines of emergency instructions, in boldface, attached to the instrument panel. This tells them exactly what to do in a crisis; they can therefore react to problems in a timely fashion.

I'm convinced that families should have a similar crisis management plan—bullet-point lines stating exactly what your family will do when things get out of control, every time something goes wrong in the family, written down so that you do not even have to think. The time to do this is now. Your "boldface" plan might include any number of the following:

• *Be prepared before a crisis strikes.* The crucial thing about crisis is preparation. The accompanying chart on pages 60–61 listing Hot Warning Signs can provide clues that you may have a crisis on your hands, or whether one is brewing. As a parent, stay alert to these early warning signs. Ignoring these warning signs could mean a tragic outcome for your child or your family.

• *Stay calm.* No matter how you feel when a crisis hits, you must remain calm. Stay in charge of yourself, and this will inspire confidence and reassurance in the rest of your family. Do deep-breathing exercises if you have to, since these will fuel your brain with more oxygen for clearer thinking and better decision-making.

• *Remove danger.* This might mean calling the police yourself, confiscating dangerous things, keeping your child from having contact with certain people or removing him from a dangerous place (physically or emotionally) or a dangerous person.

• *Work the problem, not the person.* One of the most powerful tools you have at your disposal to manage and overcome the crisis is to work the problem, not the person. Never attack or blame the family member in crisis. When you're upset with a child, it can be terribly tempting to blame and criticize him. But when you choose to blame a child in trouble, that child learns to cover his tracks the next time he gets into trouble. And trust me, he'll get into trouble again, since crisis-prone behavior that goes unresolved does nothing but compound.

By aiming your energies at solving the problem instead, you ensure that you're not just spinning your wheels and that you're working the crisis from a solution standpoint, rather than indicting the person with blame and isolated punishment. Just by putting that simple control on your family life—working the problem and the crisis, not the person— you've made another gigantic step toward building a phenomenal family.

• **Close ranks.** When a crisis erupts, family members tend to turn on one another, blaming or ripping into someone with personal attacks. Once this spirit takes over, relating stops and the destruction of family relationships starts. There's little peaceful or supportive coexistence of people who are supposed to accept and believe in themselves and in one another. Never, ever, turn on one another, put family relationships on the line or cave into pressure. Instead, close ranks and support one another. You must resolve that your relationships will exist on a level above blame and personal attacks. If family members are unable to turn to one another, a crisis will shatter family unity and make it practically impossible to get through troubled times together.

• **Communicate.** For a family in crisis, communication is vital. Be honest and encourage an environment of openness. The best way to accomplish this is simply to stop talking and start listening. Give your child your undivided attention. Listen to your child and his or her story, or listen to the authorities and their viewpoint. Let your children freely ask questions, and reward their questions with words such as: "I'm glad you came to me with that question." Tell them too: "I'm here for you, to answer your questions and your concerns." When you do speak, the actual words you use are less important than the attitude you convey. The attitude you should adopt is one of hope for the resolution of the crisis and love for your child, no matter what.

• **Reassure the family member in crisis that the home environment is a safe place, where the family cares about him or her.** You may not like what that child did—you certainly don't endorse failing grades, drug abuse, promiscuity or whatever the crisis is, and you do hold your child accountable for his or her behavior—but he knows you are going to help him damage-control the situation. In fact, in a healthy family, no one should tolerate any overtly maladaptive behavior, such as physical violence, mental or emotional abuse and certainly no substance abuse. If the wheels come off, they will come off, but you're going to stand by your child during the crisis and help him get through it. You're a resource for your children. Tell your child: "You are cared for, you are my first priority and you will be protected." In addition, convey to your family: "Life will not be like this forever. Our family *will* heal."

• **Maintain a degree of normalcy.** You may not be able to do everything you used to do, but try to keep up your normal daily routines and familiar rituals as much as possible. This will have a calming, stabilizing effect on the rest of your family.

• **Contact and use the resources you have.** Your family does not have to go through a crisis alone. Draw on resources such as a pastor, minister, rabbi or other spiritual leader; other family members; your child's teachers; a school psychologist or counselor; your child's pediatrician; local support groups; or your state or county mental health association. These resources will assist you in identifying and implementing constructive solutions. Let them help you.

• **Be open to all solutions, even things you might initially want to dismiss.** Just because you don't agree wholeheartedly with an avenue of approach doesn't mean it might not work in your family. Don't slam the door on certain alternatives, or even coping tools such as tension-reducing activities, without exploring them completely first. Maybe you think they won't help or that they won't work. But what if something like this is exactly what you need when a crisis strikes? What if it is? Please understand: Now is not the time to be judgmental, resisting some tools and resources that may genuinely help you. If you downplay this now, you may be cheating your family later.

• **Don't worry about the future.** Stop asking yourself, "What if something else happens again?" Remember that something traumatic happened and you got through it. If something else happens, you'll get through that too.

Hot Warning Signs

Here are some telltale warning signs that you can use to determine whether or not a family member is possibly headed for a crisis.

Endangering Self or Others	Depression	High Stress	Drug Abuse	Gangs and Violence
• Talks about committing a criminal, hostile act, especially toward her/himself, with a plan	• Loss of interest in all activities, especially the ones previously interested in	• Trouble focusing because of a significant traumatic event	• Change of friends, new best friend uses drugs	• Admits they are in a gang
• Begins to take action toward a plan, such as stockpiling guns, poison or sleeping pills	• Appetite disturbance with change in weight, either increase or decrease	• Intense fear, helplessness or horror	• Careless about personal appearance	• Is obsessed with particular clothing attire
• Gives away prized possessions	• Difficulty sleeping	• Withdrawal of emotional response to everything (detachment, numbing)	• Decline in participation at home	• Adopts an unusual desire for secrecy
• Begins to take impulsive risks with himself or others	• Agitation and restlessness	• Reduction of awareness of environment ("being in a daze")	• Diminished interest in hobbies, sports or favorite activities	• Exhibits a change in behavior and conduct, withdraws from family
• Begins to neglect his appearance	• Low energy	• Memory losses, especially about a traumatic event	• Irritability, extreme shifts in mood	• Is frequently deceitful about activities
• Abuses drugs or alcohol	• High feelings of worthlessness or guilt	• Nightmares and recurrent images of fearful thoughts	• Eating and sleeping habits change	• Declining grades in school
• Isolates her/himself (running away, dropping out of school, etc.)	• Difficulty in concentrating or thinking through solutions		• Lack of appreciation for family values	• Truancy/tardy records
			• Lying	• Begins breaking rules frequently

- Shows dramatic changes in behaviors and mood

- Has a close friend or relative who commits a hostile act or suicide

- Loses or gains weight

- Has trouble sleeping (sleeps excessively or has insomnia)

- Shows consistently poor judgment

- Thoughts of suicide
- Hallucinations, delusions or becoming extremely suspicious of others

- Poor concentration
- Irritability and restlessness
- Sleeping problems

- Changes in school performance, tardiness, truancy
- Missing money, personal belongings, prescription drugs
- Using street or drug language
- Eyes are red or glassy or nose is runny with no allergies to blame
- Family history of alcoholism or drug abuse
- Discovery of pipes, rolling papers, medicine bottles, butane lighters or other suspect paraphernalia

- Obsessed with gang music or videos
- Shows evidence of physical injuries but lies about causes
- Produces unexplained cash, clothing, music CDs
- Exhibits use of drugs and alcohol

• *Find meaning in your suffering.* Don't allow yourself to be dev-astated for no reason, no meaning and no purpose. You've got to create some value to the pain that you experience in your life. I'm not suggest-ing that one of your choices is to decide that anything that may happen in your life is positive. Obviously, that's not always a rational reaction. Should some injury or tragedy befall one of your children or another fam-ily member, you may choose to learn from the event, and thereby protect him or her and your other children more effectively in the future. You may choose to see that your child learns to deal with and overcome adversity. You may choose to help those who are further back down the trail than you are. You may choose to take some social action in order to create meaning out of suffering and to change the situation in which the crisis took place, thereby protecting other families. If you use your pain and what you've been through in your life, you create value from adversity.

As you begin to fold these Five Factors for a Phenomenal Family into your home life, let's have some fun and also signal to the other family members that things are different. Sometimes even the simplest things can get your family's attention and make them aware that they are in fact entering a new day and a new time. Here are a few simple but tried-and-proven suggestions for signaling change in your day-to-day family life. These admittedly superficial changes are of no particular consequence other than that they get everyone else's attention and let everyone know that your family is doing things differently, starting today. Start with this short list of suggestions, and feel free to have some fun and add some of your own. For example:

- Have your kids switch rooms.
- Serve dinner in the dining room instead of at the kitchen table or bar.
- Paint your living room or den a new color.
- Get a different haircut.
- Play music in your house instead of watching constant tele-vision.
- Rearrange the furniture in your house.

If you commit to and are able to bring these factors to life in your own family, you will see amazing progress in the quality of your home life and interconnectedness. If, despite your best efforts, you simply can't get traction to create the change that you want—be patient.

You may think that you're changing your behavior, as well as the characteristics and nuances of your family environment, when in fact you're really not. For example, you may feel you've become emotionally available and that you've changed your interactions with your family for the better. Others may disagree, however. So please stay patient; you must work hard to incorporate these factors into your family. It is a process that takes commitment and persistence. Be honest with yourself and if you're still struggling, go on alert to the fact that you, or some other family member, may be experiencing more than just a lack of knowledge about how to create healthy family behavior. You may be suffering from deeply entrenched, serious conflicts or pain from your life that are blocking your ability to implement these five factors. You cannot give away what you don't have and these five factors are all about giving. If such is the case with you or one of your children, this too is under your control. Even though such barriers may exist outside your conscious awareness, your inability to bring about meaningful change in a timely fashion should be a clue. Your accountability extends to reaching out for additional help. As the leader of the family, it is your job to do what it takes to create what you want. A well-chosen psychologist, psychiatrist, social worker or pastoral counselor could be just the spark plug you need to create these five factors as realities in your home. You can do this!

My goal in this chapter has been to provide you with factors made up of thoughts, feelings and behaviors that can be created by you for your family from the inside out. In the next chapter, we will be talking about some important aspects of your learning history that may be contributing to or contaminating your family life. The truth is there may be internal barriers, but the first place I would look is your family legacy. Approach the next chapter with an open mind and a willingness to consider both the pros and cons of your upbringing. As you take a close look at your family legacy, we'll identify the gifts you received from your parents, as well as possible contaminants they may have visited upon you.

Getting familiar with these aspects of your family life will be action-filled, and will make your journey through this book exciting, eye-opening and infinitely rewarding for you as a parent. Keep this in mind: Let the destination we're headed for always be the creation of *your* phenomenal family.

4

Your Family Legacy

Parents often talk about the younger generation
as if they didn't have anything to do with it.
— HAIM GINOTT

You now know that there are five factors for a phenomenal family, each with a clear series of actions designed to bring these factors alive in your deserving family. The next logical step is to assess whether aspects of your upbringing sabotages or facilitates your ability to implement them.

A particularly wise poet (and obviously a highly observant parent) once wrote, "Children learn what they live." No truer words have ever been put down on paper. You are who you are today in large part due to the impact your parents had (and still have) on your life. How many times have you said jokingly or otherwise, "Lord, please don't let me become my MOTHER!!" (We all say it, even if we love our mothers deeply.) The truth is, we are prone to reflecting in our current lives the very values, thoughts, actions and beliefs that were so consistently modeled for us by our parents. Some of what they modeled was good and worthy of embracing, but some of it was not. Our parents' impact ranged from the powerfully overt to the profoundly subtle, from the solid and sound to the sick and destructive. Perhaps surprisingly, it is the subtle, the less obvious, parental influences that are most likely to have seeped undetected into your thoughts, feelings, beliefs and behaviors. I strongly suspect that you'll find evidence of those subtle influences even in your physical mannerisms, such as hand gestures, the way you walk, the way you tilt your head or your voice intonation. Similarly, I'll bet there are certain words or phrases that you say exactly the way your mother or father said them. You may find yourself in certain events or circumstances that are so reminiscent of your childhood you can almost see and hear your mother or father as you speak or react in the here and now.

So many of your behaviors, as a parent and otherwise, can be traced back to your growing-up years, when you lived with your parents. Is *this* some great revelation? Of course it isn't. Everyone knows that our parents have an impact on who and what we become. You *know* you're like your mother or your father. You have probably said, over and over again: "I'm doing exactly what my parents did, and I hate that!"

The reason I am including this discussion, here and now, is because I want you to take that commonsense awareness to the next level of specificity and understanding. I want to bring your upbringing to the center stage of your consciousness so that you can actively deal with it and not parent with blinders on. I don't want you just to acknowledge that your parents probably shaped who you have become in general, and who you have become as a parent in particular, and leave it at that. I'm challenging you to identify with great detail exactly what values, beliefs, characteristics, traits and behaviors have been passed on to you as a function of your experiences with your own parents. I don't want this to be a philosophical exercise; I want this to be an action-oriented plan for specific and lasting change. Only when you identify and isolate the elements of your family legacy can you create an action-oriented to-do list for positive change. The trick is to zero in on and separate the negative influences from the positive ones so you can nurture some and eradicate others.

As I said earlier, I was greatly frustrated by my father's alcoholism and the personality traits that he exhibited when he was drinking. I hated every second of it and at times hated him for what he was doing to me and to our family. When he was drinking he was selfish, rude, insensitive and at times plain mean-spirited. I was humiliated by his conduct and lived in constant fear that he would further embarrass us all. I responded by being withdrawn, guarded and cynical. I don't want to carry those traits, attitudes or fears on to my family now. I've had to single out those experiences and guard against their influence on me in the here and now. But, and this is a big "but," he also modeled for me an amazing work ethic and an unwavering devotion to protecting our family from dangerous people, places and events. He would never say something couldn't be done and was intimidated by no man or challenge. He was an absolute romantic with my mother and often made sacrifices for us all that he probably thought went unnoticed. They did not. He taught me to lead my family and to cherish my wife, even though he sometimes failed in all of the above. His striving was inspirational, and I am a better man for having been exposed to his good qualities, and even more so for being aware of and eliminating his negative ones.

Although many childhood experiences may have been of short duration, they could have very well had powerful lasting effects, and certain here-and-now experiences can take us back to those lost memories in a flash. Sometimes these events we thought were gone forever resurrect themselves, often with very vivid and powerful emotions. Dr. Joe Miller, a great and lifelong friend and the physician who delivered both of our boys, once wrote a compelling article about just such a phenomenon. He pointed out that even something as simple as certain smells or aromas can take us back instantly, causing us to recall and reexperience in a powerful way the feelings connected with a particular scent we encountered as a child. When I read his article, chills went up my spine because I've experienced exactly that phenomenon a number of times.

For many years during my childhood, my father, much to my chagrin, smoked pungently aromatic cigars. The smell stuck to him like glue, even when he wasn't smoking. It permeated his skin, hair, clothes, car, even his favorite chair. To this very day, I can walk past a cigar smoker on the street, pick up the scent of that tobacco and instantly experience a powerful recollection of my father. In that moment, I see his face, the expression in his eyes, the slope of his shoulders, and I hear his voice in my head. No, I'm not crazy, and I'm not hallucinating. I'm just experiencing a powerful recollection that fortunately for me is now mostly pleasant, as time and maturity have gently polished my memories of that imperfect but devoted man. I now see a certain symmetry in having a father with imperfections since I was anything but a perfect child.

So how about you? Are you parenting on autopilot? Think about it: If a simple smell experienced more than forty years ago, whether pleasant or haunting, can exert such a powerful effect, what is the potency of a parent's actions and words?

Let's talk specifics. Your parents raised you a certain way, and you're likely reflecting those experiences in one of two ways. The first and most common reaction is to do exactly what your parents modeled as they raised you. If they were yellers and screamers, odds are you are as well. If they were cold, withdrawn and totally absorbed in other aspects of their own lives, neglecting yours, you probably do the same thing. If they lived vicariously through you and your activities, viewing them as a "second time around," you probably prowl on the sidelines at every Little League game, screaming like a loudmouth idiot (can you tell that really bugs me?) or act the role of stage mom at the local yokel beauty contest. Not good!

The second common response is to react *against* the experience and behave in a radically different way. In reaction to being raised with yelling and screaming, you may be the nicest, sweetest and most lenient parent you could ever imagine. Sounds perfect, but nothing extreme ever is. This opposite reaction may have led you to being overindulgent, spoiling your children, a behavior that often leads to poor impulse control in kids, misbehavior and even low academic performance.

Both extremes can leave permanent scars on your children. The point is that good or bad, right or wrong, your family in general and your parents in particularly powerful ways wrote on the blank slate that is you. The way you parent your children today is clearly influenced by your own parents, and to some extent, you may have, before now, involuntarily accepted it and are parenting on autopilot today.

I've seen this truth lived out time and time again during the nearly thirty years I've been working with people. Marisa was abandoned by her mother as a toddler and in the absence of maternal bonding, she grew up with a lack of self-confidence to the point where she rarely ventured outside her home. Clearly, this horrible desertion had scarred her for life. Timid in the extreme, Marisa was terrified of any new experience that would place her in the midst of unpredictable challenges. Like a contagious disease, Marisa's fear of the unknown was passed on to three of her children. One of her daughters never found real employment, and two of her sons remained in marginal jobs for decades because the known was infinitely preferable to the unknown.

Eva works hard all week as a responsible career woman, yet turns her home into a drunken battleground every single weekend. By dinnertime Friday night, she is into her second bottle of wine. Her husband might as well have a bull's-eye drawn on his chest. He is the target as a knockdown, drag-out fight ensues in front of their seven-year-old daughter. The war ends with Eva slamming her bedroom door and retreating there until morning, when she wakes up and acts as if nothing ever happened. Same song, second verse. She grew up with exactly the same deal; she lived it every weekend as a child.

Daniel's dream is to someday see his nine-year-old son Bobby make it to the big leagues. Every practice, Daniel pushes Bobby. He screams at him when he bats, when he's in the field. "Do better! Push harder! What's wrong with you? Hustle, hustle, hustle! You want to be a loser?" Bobby has grown to hate baseball. Every time he isn't good enough for his dad, he feels like a failure. He tries to hide the tears, but even when he fights them back they just fall "inside" instead of out. What Daniel doesn't seem to remember is that twenty years ago, it was his own cheeks that the tears rolled down when his father pushed him in exactly the same way.

What I'm talking about with these stories is your family legacy, the powerful programming your upbringing has had on your choices and behavior as an adult and as a parent. It's impossible to overemphasize the power of this legacy on your life. Only when you realize this can you start to make some conscious, here-and-now choices about how you raise your children, rather than being mindlessly controlled by your past. I intend to show you how to take back your power and make your own decisions about how you want to raise your own children.

You probably have many good qualities as a parent, and you probably have some bad ones as well. You do what you know because you can't do what you don't know. What you know, and what you have learned, may be defective information, but you can't know that unless you know its source and evaluate its real impact on you when you were on the receiving end.

Before moving on, I want to emphasize that this is not about blaming your parents, or anyone else for that matter, for the way you raise your children. Please don't do that. It's so much easier to tell yourself that any problems with your kids are someone else's fault—their teachers' fault, their peer group's fault, your parents' fault, their absent father's fault, the coach's fault or even the kid's fault (as in the so-called bad seed theory, that a child can be born bad).

You don't want things to be your responsibility, so you'll go to any extreme of rationalization and justification to explain why they aren't, to the point of transferring blame elsewhere. But the reality is that you'll never, ever fix your problems blaming someone else. The sooner you accept that, the sooner your life gets better.

You had no choice about how your parents did or didn't raise you, and you had no choice about how it may have programmed you to parent

your own children. I certainly don't want to trivialize what you may have had to endure as a child. Not at all. I realize that certain realities, some of them horribly sick realities, may have been visited on you when you were a child. I'm not suggesting that, as children, we choose any or all of the events and circumstances in our lives. We don't pick our parents. We're neither responsible nor accountable for tragedies such as being raped, abused or molested. That's not what I'm saying. What I'm saying to you is that while as a child you may not have had the knowledge or power to make certain choices, and are therefore not accountable for those events, as an adult you do have the ability to choose your reaction to those childhood events and circumstances. You must accept the premise that the only time is now. The past is over, and the future hasn't happened yet. You can continue to passively be a product of your family legacy, or you can make a conscious choice to take a different path and learn different skills and abilities be-ginning right here, right now. This isn't about blame, it is about change.

> **Survey Fact:**
> Forty-eight percent of parents said that their own parents had too high expectations and feel that this caused high anxiety for them as adults

You may think your family life and your parenting skills have failed, you may feel like you've tried everything, you may feel tired, deflated and defeated and you're blaming yourself for how your kids are turning out. In reading this book so far, you may already recognize mistakes you've made, but cut yourself some slack here. If you did it wrong, I'm betting you didn't know any better. You did it *inadvertently*. If that's true, then you shouldn't *blame* yourself. Self-blame can create a paralyzing guilt, and we don't have time for you to be kicking yourself. I need you fully in the process we're em-barking on. The National Parenting Survey I conducted of thousands of parents reveals that a significant number of mothers and fathers are guiltily *blaming* themselves for their poor parenting practices. Let me hit the pause button here and explain that there's a huge and important dif-ference between blame and responsibility, and you need to understand the distinction.

To deserve blame, you must have *intended* your actions or recklessly disregarded the possible consequences. By contrast, responsibility simply means that you were involved and took actions that generated consequences but there was no malicious intent. Responsibility, or accountability, does not imply intent or recklessness; it says only that you did or allowed something to be done, whatever led to the final outcome. I'm not just playing semantics to make you feel better. This is an important point.

If I'm roughhousing with my friends, jump on a chair with both feet and break it, I've at least shown a reckless disregard for that property. I'm responsible for the damage, and I can be justly *blamed* for it. Now suppose I simply sit down on the chair and it breaks. I'm responsible for the damage. But I was using the chair properly and had no intent to destroy it, so I'm not to be blamed as though I had maliciously destroyed it. I am still responsible, and I am accountable, but *blame* is inappropriate.

Poet Maya Angelou's comment on past behaviors says it best: "You did what you knew how to do, and when you knew better, you did better." Whatever you have done in the past to raise your family, you did what you knew how to do. You did it, you're accountable for it and you are responsible for it. I hope that as we work together through this book, you will know better and you will do better—a whole lot better.

From this day forward, I'd like you to make yourself accountable for making intelligent and informed choices about how you lead your family and parent your children. Whatever you did or didn't do, felt or didn't feel, gave or didn't give, shared or didn't share, it's done. What's important is that, by reading this book, by doing the work within it, by opening your mind and heart to the possibility of a difference in your family life and in your role as a parent, you've started on the right path.

You may not have all the tools you need yet, but that's where this book comes in. But again, you do have the most important element for success: You have that unconditional love for your children that only a parent can have. As I said at this book's beginning: "You may have to rise above your raisin'." There's no time like the present, and change starts with that acknowledgment I mentioned above. You have to ask yourself some hard questions.

- When one of my children misbehaves, do I respond in the way one of my parents responded, perhaps with anger, yelling or screaming?
- Do I live other hand-me-down patterns of parenting I've duplicated from my childhood?

• If I'm repeating "patterns of abuse" handed down from my own upbringing, can I admit them, own them and change them?

Research tells us that you may be prewired neurologically and psychologically to respond in a certain way. Studies show that childhood traumatic events, even events significant in their absence, whether we remember them or not, can leave scars that last a lifetime. For example, if as a child you were seldom comforted, you may have no conscious recall of this memory—but then later as a parent, you discover you're mysteriously distressed or anxious over showing or expressing affection to your child. Your child may then pick up on these signals and believe that he's in some way unworthy. This is a heavy burden for a child to wrongly bear and all because you're living a legacy. The trouble is, no one has ever taught you how to kill the infection so you don't pass it on. You'll learn how to do that here.

You'll want to account for the significant events, and your memories of them, that have been seared on your heart and mind. You'll go through a journaling process aimed at identifying past events and experiences that shape your present parenting behavior. Finally, you'll have to understand what you have been told by your parents so persistently and sometimes destructively, and how you may be echoing those same messages to your own children. The key to identifying these important influences is knowing precisely which questions to ask.

You may find that a significant part of your family legacy is what your parents *didn't* teach you. Erin had such a legacy. She was raised by two very loving parents. But her father was like a lot of parents—he didn't really seek active participation in Erin's life. Not once during her school years did he look at her homework, tests or assignments. He'd regularly miss important sports events in which she competed. At no time did he ever read her bedtime stories. From Erin's earliest years, her father opted out of virtually everything in which she was involved. When Erin became a parent herself, she walked out of this history and created an entirely different way of parenting. She and her husband John became involved parents, active in every aspect of their children's lives. There are many parents like Erin who've had the courage and the wisdom to rise above their raisin'.

I predict that before you're through with this chapter, you'll very probably step back from your own family life and wonder how in the world you could have been thinking what you were thinking, not seeing what you were not seeing and choosing the behaviors you were choosing. Answering questions about yourself and your family—the right questions—can help you get honest with yourself and start you thinking about how and where you can change. You can't afford to be naïve or gullible in assessing what's going on in your family life. We're going to deal constructively with a few key issues that will help you get a clearer view of the legacy you've inherited. If you care about your family—and I know you do—you'll give this series of challenges your full commitment.

Important: Stay open to the *positive* parts of your family legacy so that you can pass them on to your children as you move through the days and years of your life.

FAMILY LEGACY PROFILE

This exercise will require you to perform an "autopsy" on your childhood relationship with your parents. If your parents are still living, you'll have to lay aside the present relationship to thoroughly recall your impressions and emotions, as a child or as a teenager literally in their grip. In other words, your relationship with your mom or dad may have now matured into a healthy one that may have a different character altogether from when you were younger. Be honest about the way it was. You must ignore any present good feelings for the moment. Using a confidential, for-your-eyes-only journal, answer the following questions about your mother and father as thoroughly as you can. As you work through this exercise, you'll see that some questions call for a few words, while still others need a short paragraph in order to be answered properly. In deciding how much detail to give a particular answer, please keep the following in mind: The more thorough you are in rooting out your past family life experiences, the more effective you are going to be at changing the way you interact with your present-day family. Consider having one of your siblings answer these questions too. Doing so will give you accountability in being honest about your past. You can then compare notes to use in later planning.

1. The best qualities of my mother were:
2. The best qualities of my father were:
3. The worst qualities of my mother were:

4. The worst qualities of my father were:
5. What I loved most about my mother:
6. What I loved most about my father:
7. My mother showed her love for me by:
8. My father showed his love for me by:
9. When I was afraid, my mother/father would:
10. When my family celebrated an event (Christmas, an achievement, etc.), we would:
11. I often felt most secure when my mother/father would:
12. My favorite memories of me and my family were:
13. The times I would like to forget about my family were:
14. The affection displayed by my mother/father toward me was:
15. The most destructive times in my family were:
16. When my parents got into conflict, they would:
17. What I got from my mother I did not want was:
18. What I got from my father I did not want was:
19. What I resented most from my mother was:
20. What I resented most from my father was:
21. My relationship with my mother has contaminated my present relationship with my family by:
22. My relationship with my father has contaminated my present relationship with my family by:
23. If I had only one last minute left to tell my mother something, I would tell her:
24. If I had only one last minute left to tell my father something, I would tell him:
25. I would describe my mother's style of parenting as (strict, moderate, democratic, lenient, permissive, uninvolved, etc.):
26. I would describe my father's style of parenting as (strict, moderate, democratic, lenient, permissive, uninvolved, etc.):
27. Other people who were significant in my childhood and adolescence as parental figures were:
28. These other significant parental figures shaped my development by:
29. The characteristics I saw in my mother's parenting behaviors that I see in my own are:
30. The characteristics I saw in my father's parenting behaviors that I see in my own are:

31. The kinds of parenting behaviors of my mother that I want to avoid in my own are:
32. The kinds of parenting behaviors of my father that I want to avoid in my own are:

As I have said, a real key is knowing what questions will lead you to the important answers. You have just answered some very focused questions about your parents, their behaviors and the way they raised you. Let's expand on this. I'm now going to ask you to create a miniprofile, or sketch, of your parents. To do that, it will be helpful for you to summon up a mental picture of them and of your family life as you were growing up, using the following series of penetrating questions to flesh out that picture and make it as detailed as possible. Answer these questions in a free-flowing essay form. Be careful to address each subpart of each item. The more you write, the more you will learn. If one or both of your parents or stepparents are now deceased, it may be difficult to visualize their earlier lives, but do your best.

1. Was your relationship with your parents characterized by lots of warmth and affection, or was it more standoffish? Did you ever feel emotionally deprived or neglected? How did they express their affection toward you? Did they withhold affection? Did they use particular physical gestures such as hugs to communicate affection for you? Did they reserve for you favorite expressions or pet phrases?

2. When you misbehaved, were disobedient or got into trouble, how were you disciplined? Did your parents use physical punishment such as spanking or restrictions such as grounding or sending you to your room? Did they try to make you feel guilty about what you did or withdraw their love? Or were your parents lenient, often letting you off the hook? Try to recall and record specific instances that speak to these questions.

3. Now I want you to dig up some buried emotional issues, positive and negative, from your past that may have seeped into your present family interactions. Require of yourself the most detailed and thorough memory you can muster. Think of childhood and adolescent experiences that involved your parents when you felt very loved, fearful, lonely, joyful, peaceful, sad, victorious, safe, secure or any other powerful emotion you can recall. You've learned from and been changed by these experiences.

Describe these emotions and the circumstances tied to them as clearly as possible so you'll come away with the depth of information you need. Things that emotionally affected you in the fourth grade can still affect you at age forty-two. What are you telling yourself about these events or circumstances today?

4. Your parents may have labeled you in some way. Labels are self-descriptions that reflect certain conclusions you've reached about yourself. Many of these labels came from your parents, from a cruel peer group, from teachers and coaches, or they came from within you when you observed yourself messing up in life. But whatever their source, you tend to internalize these labels, believe your labels and live up to your labels. They can become the definition of you if you let them. List the labels that were given to you by your parents (dummy, smart one, lazy, good boy, pretty and so forth). Put a check mark beside the ones you can sense are a part of you today. Circle those you may have given to your own children.

5. Everyone has tapes that play in their heads. Tapes are a type of internal dialogue based on past experiences, generated from particular moments or self-observations in your past history. They've become encoded in your memory and are a part of your internal dialogue, the inner conversation you have with yourself all day long. They predict and therefore control your thinking and your behavior and thus the outcome you have. For example, if your internal dialogue goes like this: "My father was a loser; I will be a loser, regardless of what happens," then that tape is likely to program you for failure in life. In this exercise, I'd like you to start thinking about the negative tapes your family legacy may have recorded in your mind. Write them down in your journal. To get you thinking, here are some additional examples.

I will never have a good experience; my family was so dysfunctional that we never learned how to have fun.

My future will be like my past, unlucky and unproductive. I should never expect to be successful, because it is not my destiny.

I was abused as a child. People will use me for what they want and be insensitive to how I feel.

*My family was low-class. I will be low-class. There is nothing I can do
to change that.*

6. Now try to remember when conflict erupted in your home. Did disagreements escalate into an all-out war, waged in front of you and your siblings? Alternatively, did your parents treat any kind of conflict as embarrassing and unacceptable, such that even minor disagreements were quickly suppressed? What did your parents fight about—finances, responsibilities, parenting habits or family activities? How would you characterize your parents' style of conflict? What strategies did they use for resolving a dispute? Did they make compromises? Offer apologies? Take a stand and freely communicate their positions? Retreat behind a slammed-shut door, refusing to negotiate? Never resolve the conflict, but let it fester?

7. What kind of family environment did your parents create? Was there tension in the air? Were you and your siblings allowed to express your opinions, or were they suppressed? Were problems brought out into the open and discussed, or were they swept under the rug? Did your parents participate, and stay involved, in your school activities? How interested were they in your schoolwork, your academic performance, your friends, your activities and your life in general?

8. What behavioral shortcomings, psychological problems or maladaptive behaviors did you grow up with that your parents also displayed? These might be depression; alcoholism, drug abuse or other addiction; absence from the home; favoritism toward certain siblings; divorce or separation; conflicts with stepparents; verbal or physical abuse; open conflict; or a passionless relationship with a spouse. Are any of these dysfunctional patterns or circumstances wreaking havoc or devastation in your life or your partner's life today? Think about these situations from your past and how they might be infecting your own family today.

PUTTING IT ALL TOGETHER

Before you go on, look back over everything you've written about your family legacy—the questions you've answered, the paragraphs you've recorded in your journal. If you've done an honest and thorough job with these exercises, you've turned the floodlights on some very important items of focus. You have identified legacies, good or bad, helpful or harmful, that are playing out in your own family today. Now it's time to bring these legacies into even sharper focus. Using the work you've just detailed, complete the following statements. Let these statements provide a structured approach to getting a stronger handle on your family legacy and what must take precedence for change.

1. My relationship behaviors with my spouse or partner differ from my parents' in the following ways:
2. My relationship behaviors with my spouse or partner are very similar to my parents' in the following ways:
3. The results of behaving and reacting in these ways have been:
4. My parenting behaviors with my children differ from my parenting in the following ways:
5. My parenting behaviors with my children are similar to my parents' in the following ways:
6. The results of behaving and reacting in these ways have been:
7. Based on the responses I've given above, my existing relationship with my spouse in the future will be:
8. Based on the responses I've given above, the results in my children's futures will be:
9. This exercise suggests that the behaviors I need to eliminate are:
10. This exercise underscores the importance of continuing to emphasize change and improvement in the following behaviors:

CONNECTING THE DOTS

By completing the above inventory of your legacy, you've identified the behaviors, attitudes and beliefs that have stuck with you. Your parents may no longer be standing there criticizing you, but trust me, if you're living your legacy, you have taken over for your parents. But be encouraged. You have found the bottom; here comes the power. You can't change your legacy. But you can change what you do in response to that legacy, so that your past does not become your future. What you're about to learn in the following multistep process will give you the power to eliminate those negative influences from your current family life and create lasting change.

Step #1: Acknowledge and Identify Parts of Your Legacy That Must Change

Based on your answers to the above questions, you now have in your hands some valuable information about change-worthy behavior in your life. Review your answers to these last ten questions. What are the legacies you most need to change? What actions do you need to take to change them? What is currently contaminating the way you parent today?

In your journal, make two columns. At the top of the first column, write "changes"; at the top of the second column write "actions." Then list the changes and the actions you need to take to repair these hand-me-down behaviors. Let your actions be goals for change. To jump-start your thinking, I've provided some examples.

Changes	Actions
More emotional support in my child's crisis	Speak out to my child's needs instead of catastrophizing and worrying about material things
More affection	More touching and less criticism
Less loud talk and yelling	More listening and checking my voice
More humor	More laughing at myself
More consistent care	A daily plan to tell my family, "I love you"

If you discovered through doing the work of this chapter that you are disciplining your child as you were disciplined, and you see that this leads to the wrong outcomes, attitudes or reactions, it is time to do something different. I will go into discipline in greater detail in the behavioral change chapter, but for now, it is important to make a list of discipline issues you've inherited from your own upbringing. As you did in the previous exercise, make two side-by-side columns in your journal—one named "instead of" and the other "use." In the first column, list ineffective forms of discipline; in the second column, list alternatives you can use. I've given you some examples below.

Instead of:	Use:
Yelling	Address the issue with a calm, affirmative voice.
Hitting	Use the steps for eliminating abuse listed in Chapter 3.
Getting mad	Admit frustration, but approach issue with intention to change behavior instead of angry spite.
Labeling with words	Direct my attention to the behavior instead of to the hostile child.

Step #2: Identify Self-Defeating Internal Responses

In this step, I'd like you to audit your internal dialogue to tune into what it is telling you about how you parent. What labels has your legacy generated? What tapes has your legacy generated or contributed to? What are the beliefs you have constructed about yourself as a parent as a result of your legacy?

Review what you've written in your journal so far to root out your internal responses. Write down as many responses as you can, so you can see exactly where you need to make adjustments.

Step #3: Test Your Internal Responses for Authenticity

Next, I want you to make an honest self-appraisal of what you believe about yourself as a parent. In what I call a "litmus test for logic," I would like you to evaluate several of your internal responses—labels, tapes, beliefs and so forth—against the following criteria:

- **Is it true?**

- **Does holding on to the thought or attitude serve your best interests?**

- **Are your thoughts and attitudes advancing and protecting your health?**

- **Does this attitude or belief get me more of what I want, need and deserve, particularly in regard to my family life?**

Thoughts and labels that do not measure up to all four of the criteria in the litmus test for logic should be rejected. To keep from habitually gravitating back to those long held negative thoughts you should generate a new thought that meets the four criteria for the litmus test for logic. I call these thoughts Authentically Accurate Alternate Responses or AAA Thinking.

Here are a few examples:

Unacceptable Internal Dialogue	New AAA Response
I will never have a good experience; my family was so dysfunctional that we never learned how to have fun.	*My family is worthy and deserves to live with dignity and respect.*
	I am living for the present, where I can decide for my family, instead of being a prisoner of the past and its memories and pain.

Whatever you've clung to from the past carries great significance for you as a parent today. You've just completed the necessary process of reviewing your family legacy. You've revisited the profound influence your own parents have had on you, and you've reviewed the raisin' you need to rise above. And you've targeted specific behaviors for change. This very focused look at your family legacy should give you the insight and the power to make some positive changes. When you do, you'll be amazed at what you get back, and how much stronger and more loving your relationship with your family will be. Embrace your new thinking and the future that lies before you with a spirit of forgiveness for that which now lies behind you. Harboring bitterness and resentment is like wearing an anvil around your neck. You deserve better, and it's time that you gave yourself permission to have it.

5

Your Parenting Style

Raising kids is part joy and part guerrilla warfare.
—ED ASNER

Bonnie's head throbs, signaling the onset of a debilitating migraine. The veins in her neck bulge from the yelling and the screaming. This always happens in the aftermath of one of those bitter confrontations with Tammy, her sixteen-year-old daughter. Bonnie had let loose a stream of ultimatums that ignited Tammy like a match. There was broken glass strewn all over the kitchen floor, "flack" from the window that had shattered when Tammy slammed the door after storming out of the house. This battle, like so many others, had been waged over Tammy's boyfriend, of whom Bonnie does not approve. Whenever the talk turns in that direction, and to details about their relationship, Bonnie demands that they break up. Can't Tammy see that he's no good? Can't she see that he's just out for what he can get? Can't she see that he's a scumbag? It's the same battle, only now it's in the seventh or eighth round.

Knowing Tammy is headed for sure heartache, Bonnie has been trying to spare her daughter unnecessary pain. She cannot, and will not, sit idly by and let her daughter experience an emotional crash. It's all about efficiency with Bonnie. She knows the answer; she gives it. She doesn't mince words; she gets to the point and often she tries to force her daughter to comply with her way of thinking. Openly hostile, Tammy resents Bonnie's desire to manage everything about her life. Tammy sees her mother as controlling and dictating—someone who just won't give it a rest. Their interactions are confrontational, and neither is willing to compromise. Unfortunately, their experience of family is one of frustration—an unending power struggle.

Although this mother and daughter are constantly at odds, both are very much alike. Tammy's behavior bears a strong resemblance to her mother's.

From what you've read so far, is the situation as unstable as it appears? It depends on how you look at it. Is Bonnie wrong to deliver clear and straightforward thoughts and instructions if she is confident that she has the answers? The answer is no. Is Tammy wrong to be confident, self-reliant and secure that she can make informed and intelligent decisions? Absolutely not.

The real problem here is not the situation with either of the individuals; the problem here lies in a clash of styles. Bonnie is what is termed an Authoritarian parent. She rules with an iron hand, although she is very loving and very caring. Tammy doesn't want conflict, but she feels it is forced upon her when her mother tries to dominate. Both of them have specific qualities in their personalities and should not necessarily change them. What Bonnie needs to understand is the old saying, "Different strokes for different folks." You have to approach people differently, and her daughter is no exception.

Tammy's younger brother, Bobby, is the absolute antithesis. He is about as passive and as unmotivated as a kid can be. This kid wouldn't yell "fire" if he was on fire. Bonnie has the same attitude and takes the same approach with Bobby as she does with Tammy—setting limits, stating and enforcing rules and being directive—and, quite differently, it works like a charm with Bobby. He likes direction about as much as Bonnie likes to give it. It's a good fit between the two, and they seldom engage in conflict. It is important to note that in both cases, there is a difference in personality styles and that Bonnie's own style works for one child, but it does not work for the other. Two different children. Two very different response patterns to their mother.

Every parent and every child, without exception, has a way of interacting with each other. Sometimes those interactions are highly positive and affirming; at other times they are volatile and counterproductive. Your style—and whether it meshes or clashes with your child's—strongly influences the relational dynamics in your family and how successful you'll be as a parent and as a family in general. With this in mind, let this chapter help you identify and understand your own parenting style, and your child's type, as another crucial step toward becoming a phenomenal family. What you will learn here builds on what you discovered about your family legacy in the previous chapter.

Think about something with me for a moment: Suppose you've been trying to get one of your children to buckle down, start studying more and focus on grades—yet nothing you do to solve these problems ever works. In fact, "discussions" always escalate into frustrating, no-win confrontations, in which you both wind up mad and upset. Sound familiar? Then suddenly, you understand how to change that pattern. You push the right buttons—and bingo—your lazy son or daughter starts doing his or her homework, making much better grades and getting more confident at school. You've solved the problem, and with it, you've motivated your kids to do what you want them or need them to do. There is a sense of peace within your home, a sense of accomplishment in your children and a sense of connectedness in your family that hasn't been there in a long time. Their lives, your life, your family's life, is different right away.

Having read this, you may be thinking, "Phil, what's the secret, what's the magic formula? I want to solve these problems, but I don't know how. I'm tired of butting heads with my kids all the time!"

The ability to problem-solve effectively in your family is not restricted to some magic formula, nor is it accessible to a chosen few. It is a matter of understanding something called your *parenting style*, and adapting that style to match your child's behavior to create compatibility. This is a foundational necessity if you want to start working for real change in your family.

As I explained earlier, you are the manager of your family system, in the same way that companies, businesses and organizations have managers or supervisors. It is a manager's job to problem-solve, as well as to motivate and educate their charges, their employees. As a parent, you also have charges—your kids—and you are managing them just as a manager supervises his staff. Just as managers do, every parent has a certain way of relating to, and managing, their children. Every parent has an MO, an attitude of approach; every parent has certain behaviors and actions that they choose when dealing with their children. This way of managing, this parenting style, is particularly important for you to understand, because you can use your knowledge and insight to shape and determine how your children will respond to you.

There are three main styles, ways or levels of managing with which we deal with our children. Although there is invariably a dominant style that defines us in the eyes of our family, no style is necessarily permanent, and it can be altered to fit the family interaction. In other words, we may choose different styles in different situations and circumstances.

TAKING ACTION

Your first task is to discover and define your parenting style and your child's style, then figure out how to change and, if necessary, adapt in order to generate the best results. We are going to begin this process by identifying with a great degree of clarity your dominant parenting style—and the behaviors that define you as a parent. You have a predictable pattern of response, and as things happen from moment to moment, you make a statement to your children and your family that flows from that style and affects all your interactions. Very few parents ever stop to consider what their style is, yet it is a topic of utmost importance to family life. Why? Because as you continue to engage your family differently, then all of the responses and reactions you get from your family members change as well.

After we turn the floodlights on over your style, you are going to assess your child's style, with the same amount of bright-light clarity. Once you've completed this important work, we'll talk about where the real value of this knowledge lies: in how these styles fit together, how they mesh and how they clash. Knowing these relational dynamics, how to adapt your style to your child's style and applying that knowledge—will move you both toward what you want, need and deserve. You will discover how to adopt the attitudes, behaviors and characteristics that will generate what works best for you. You'll have your own unique formula for maximizing your family life. The edge this knowledge will create is an awesome advantage.

> **Survey Fact:**
> When describing the ideal parent, the three top qualities given were understanding, sensitivity and selflessness.

Please understand that there are many different kinds of parenting styles. I suspect your parenting is unique to your particular situation and influenced in part by your family legacy. Despite the variety of parenting styles and the labels that describe them, I chose this three-dimension assessment because it represents different points of reference on the parenting continuum: One is on the left part of this continuum, another on the right and another represents the middle ground.

These assessments are somewhat akin to an innovative model called the Response to Power Measure (RPM), developed by the renowned psychologist Art Sweney, Ph.D. RPM is a system that analyzes superior and subordinate roles in business and industry and how these roles interact in a managerial climate. There are similarities that exist between parents managing children, and managers supervising employees, but it is not exactly the same. Love, caring, bonding and history make a difference. Of that there can be no doubt. But there are lessons that apply, particularly regarding motivation. I think you will find what you are about to do here an enlightening exercise in self-discovery and the beginning of increasing your effectiveness as a parent.

I told you that this would not be one of those books that you just sit down and read, so get out your pen and paper or journal. You must play an active role from start to finish. Like any coach, I can go only as far as the sideline. You are the one who is on the playing field, and therefore you are the agent of change. Be totally honest with yourself, even if it is scary to admit certain things about yourself and how you interact with your family. With that in mind, let these audits be a place to start figuring yourself out and those you deal with. Remember: You cannot change what you do not acknowledge.

Step 1: Identify Your Parenting Style

Below you will find thirty direct statements describing various aspects of parenting behavior. Read them carefully and rate how well they describe how you parent. Some of these statements may sound negative or disapproving, but let me assure you, items may not be as they appear. No matter how negative a statement might sound, don't avoid the truth if you think a particular statement applies to you. In other words, don't mark the answer you consider to be the most socially desirable. You are the only person who will see your results, so it is to your advantage to be as honest as possible. The goal of this assessment is to identify your dominant parenting style, not to look for any downside or negative labeling regarding how you parent your children. In fact, you'll be able to draw nothing but positive conclusions with the insight you'll gain from this assessment. For each statement, choose: Agree (A), Mostly Agree (MA), Mostly Disagree (MD) or Disagree (D), by circling the number underneath the letter.

Section A

	A	MA	MD	D
1. I believe that I have clear expectations for how my children should behave, and I make sure they are rewarded or punished, according to that expectation.	4	3	2	1
2. I feel that it is my responsibility to set goals for my family and serve as their guide.	4	3	2	1
3. I believe that my values should be taught to my family and if my children have different values, they can choose those for themselves when they are old enough to make those choices.	4	3	2	1
4. I feel that one of my roles in the family is to determine the social image that our family displays to the public.	4	3	2	1
5. I think that I need to serve as a controlling force until my children can make their own decisions.	4	3	2	1
6. I may not be smarter or stronger than anyone else in the family, but I have the role of setting and enforcing values.	4	3	2	1
7. As long as my children live in my house or under my supervision, they will follow the rules.	4	3	2	1
8. This family is not run by democratic vote. I take full responsibility.	4	3	2	1
9. Most times I have to make decisions about the family behavior and discipline by myself.	4	3	2	1
10. I think that the most important attitude my family can have toward me is respect.	4	3	2	1

Section E	A	MA	MD	D
11. I believe that it is more important for my family to learn *how* to accomplish goals than to actually accomplish goals.	4	3	2	1
12. My philosophy is to develop a team spirit with my family in dealing with our problems.	4	3	2	1
13. Accomplishing a common goal is more important than the personal achievement of any one member of the family.	4	3	2	1
14. I feel that one of a parent's most important tasks is to teach a child how to set realistic goals for himself.	4	3	2	1
15. Learning how to trust one another in difficult times and relying on one another's abilities are very important skills for all family members.	4	3	2	1
16. It is important for the parent to listen to the child and respect what the child wants and needs.	4	3	2	1
17. Although the parent has the responsibility for the child, it is important to share the decision-making.	4	3	2	1
18. Children's behavior should always have consequences, good or bad.	4	3	2	1
19. A parent's rewards are in seeing the child achieve his goals.	4	3	2	1
20. The parent-child relationship is the most important lasting legacy in a family.	4	3	2	1

	A	MA	MD	D

Section P

21. I feel responsible for my family's success or failures and would probably do some of their work for them rather than let them fail.   4   3   2   1

22. I am too lenient with my child and allow him or her to get by when I should be more consistent.   4   3   2   1

23. It is probably partly my fault if my child gets into trouble, because I did not do my job as a parent as well as I should have.   4   3   2   1

24. My parents were too hard on me, so I try to give my children what I didn't have in terms of freedom to be their true selves.   4   3   2   1

25. My child sometimes blames me for a problem and part of me agrees because I feel guilty.   4   3   2   1

26. I try to motivate my family by making them feel guilty if they don't do the right thing.   4   3   2   1

27. I want my child to behave and be a good person because he wants me to be proud of him.   4   3   2   1

28. My child often expresses the thought that I owe him a good life because I am the parent.   4   3   2   1

29. I would like my family to remember how much I sacrificed for them.   4   3   2   1

30. I try not to put too much pressure on my child because it is not fair to him.   4   3   2   1

Scoring the Parenting Styles

Add up your totals for each section separately and write them here:

A:_____

E: _____

P: _____

Circle the meaning of your score in each of the three categories below:

Section A: Authoritarian

33–40   High identification with the Authoritarian style
25–32   Dominant behaviors for the Authoritarian style
18–24   Average or moderate behaviors for the Authoritarian style
10–17   Low behaviors for the Authoritarian style

Section E: Equalitarian

30–40   High identification with the Equalitarian style
23–29   Dominant behaviors for the Equalitarian style
15–22   Average or moderate behaviors for the Equalitarian style
10–14   Low behaviors for the Equalitarian style

Section P: Permissive

34–40   High identification with the Permissive style
27–33   Dominant behaviors for the Permissive style
18–26   Average or moderate behaviors for the Permissive style
10–17   Low behaviors for the Permissive style

RED ALERT: The labels of Authoritarian and Permissive may sound judgmental or negative to you. I want to emphasize that this interpretation is not accurate. An Authoritarian parent is not synonymous with dictator or controlling and should not be considered a negative or toxic style of parenting. This style is simply more directive and tends to problem-solve by taking primary control of a situation. In fact, using this style, you can achieve a high standard of compliance, as long as you approach your child in a loving, caring manner. The Authoritarian style of parenting is effective in another way too: It provides the important ingredient of structure, which is needed by many children.

A Permissive parent is not synonymous with passive, lazy, uninvolved, neglectful or wishy-washy. Nor is this style characterized by the type of parent who says to his kids, "Sure, go ahead and drink with your friends." In reality, the Permissive style actually requires more effort on the part of parents because they must instill a greater degree of self-determination in their children in order to get results. This approach is based on the familiar proverb, "If you give a man a fish, you feed him for a day. If you teach him to fish, you feed him for a lifetime." There's a lot of truth in those words, as they apply to the Permissive style of parenting. It is this style that does one of the most effective jobs of imparting skills, values and self-worth in children and ultimately empowers them to make responsible choices and decisions. For parents using this style, their interactions with their child often involve more trial and error, as well as more words spoken. But it is time and effort well invested in promoting the maturity and self-responsibility of their children.

Everything related to parenting styles depends on the type of child you're managing, which we will assess a bit later in this chapter. Sometimes, the Authoritarian style is best and is the only style that gets results with certain children and in certain situations. Sometimes, the Permissive style works the best of any style. So if your dominant style is either of these, please don't judge yourself; both styles can be acceptable and effective.

Authoritarian

If you scored in the dominant-to-high range in Section A, your dominant parenting style tends to be *Authoritarian*. This parent tells a child what to do and what not to do; the rules are clear and usually inflexible. It would not be surprising to find that an Authoritarian parent controls most of the decision-making processes in his or her family. Using the Authoritarian style, a parent sets family goals, gives the rewards and handles the punishment—and does so sensitively and usually not in an arbitrary fashion. There is absolutely no ambiguity in terms of what is expected, who does what in the family or how misbehavior will be disciplined. The Authoritarian style tends to be confrontational at times.

Equalitarian

Scoring in the dominant-to-high range in Section E indicates that you tend to use the *Equalitarian* style when parenting your children. You give your children a role in making choices; your family operates like a team, and decisions are made somewhat democratically up to a point. Your entire family is involved in goal-setting, decision-making and problem-solving, and there is usually an atmosphere in your family of effective communication and team spirit. The Equalitarian style of parenting is usually successful at negotiating compromises.

A parent using the Equalitarian style believes in giving children choices. Children in these families learn that their opinions and thoughts count. Rules in the household are simple, with reasonable consequences for breaking them, and children understand the reasons behind the rules. There is room for flexibility, however. If a child's bedtime is 8:30 P.M., it might be extended if there is a special show on television they want to watch. Generally, a parent using this style is responsive, attentive and sensitive to children's needs. Discipline is viewed as an opportunity for a teachable moment.

Permissive

If you scored in the dominant-to-high range of Section P, yours is a *Permissive* style of parenting. You generally take a more gentle approach, intervening only when your kids get off track or into trouble. You keep your children within broad boundaries, plus work to make everything seem as if it were your child's idea in order to give a lot of ownership.

Adopting this style, you act compassionately, empathetically, and encouragingly. You have the ability to tap your children's internal motivations, such as need for self-improvement, more personal goal attainment or even guilt. As a result, you know how to push the right buttons to motivate your child in the right direction. Many great inventors and sports figures had permissive mothers who maintained this primary pattern, including Lance Armstrong, Thomas Edison and Albert Einstein.

Permissive parents generally encourage freedom of expression so as to enhance their children's creativity and allow them to voice their opinions.

You may have scored in the high-to-dominant range of one of these parenting styles, meaning that there is a dominant theme of Authoritarian, Equalitarian or Permissive parenting running through your behavior. Or you may have scored high on each and every style dimension. That's a good thing, really; it means you have a well-developed range of styles. If you are high in one dimension and low in another, you need to recognize that you may need to make a conscious decision to step up and lead more effectively when it is called for, even if it means using the style with which you have the most difficulty.

What your score can also tell you is how people, including your children, may perceive you, based on your style of interacting with them. Given a dominant score in any of these styles, it is very likely that others perceive you as having certain traits, some may be reacted to negatively and some may be reacted to positively. These are listed in the table below. The aggregate of these traits is what defines your children's reactions to you, and therefore, your relationship with them. If you don't understand why your children react to you the way they do, it may be because they are simply responding to one or more of these traits. If that's the case, begin consciously, purposely and actively changing your style to improve your interactions with your family.

AUTHORITARIAN	EQUALITARIAN	PERMISSIVE
• Decisive	• Collaborative	• Accepting
• Requiring	• Team player	• Supportive
• Efficient	• Sharing responsibility	• Respectful
• Assertive	• Decision maker	• Open
• Task-oriented	• Not bossy	• Agreeable
• Controlling	• Ingratiating	• Assuring
• Strict	• Avoiding leadership	• Conforming
• Rigid	• Undisciplined	• Motivating from behind the scenes
• Inflexible	• Reactive	• Pushing the child on self-goals
• Domineering	• Manipulative	• Relying on internal structure
		• Too lenient
		• Too time-consuming

PARENTING STYLES: SCENARIOS

What I want to illustrate for you now is some specific language that typifies the various styles of parenting, Authoritarian, Equalitarian and Permissive. These phrases and terms and the attitudes they reflect will give you an idea of what you need to do if you determine it is best to shift into one of the styles that is not your most dominant or primary.

The scenario is the same for demonstrating each style: We have a child who missed school on Friday due to illness and has some makeup homework to do. The child is feeling better by the end of the day. From all accounts, it looks like this assignment will require about four hours' worth of work. The goal is to motivate this child to complete the homework quickly, with as little conflict as possible. The homework is due Monday.

The Authoritarian Style in Action

Parent: Okay, here's the deal. You've got to get this homework done, so I want you to start now. It's going to take just four hours.

Child: But I want to go to a movie sometime this weekend.

Parent: A movie is a lot less important to you than your homework. You will work from ten till twelve and three till five on Saturday in your room with no television blasting and no talking on the telephone. Then I will see how far you have gotten. When you finish, we'll talk about a movie.

Child: Can I go to a movie if I work for four hours?

Parent: If you get that homework done. Your priority is getting your homework done—and done right, so I'm going to check it. If you get it done in less than four hours, and it is right, you'll have time to go to the movies.

The Authoritarian parent is very direct and decisive, committed to structuring a specific time frame for accomplishing the task at hand. The rules are clear, and there is an emphasis on compliance.

Authoritarian parents use phrases such as:

- Right now, we're going to . . .
- Listen, you have to make better grades . . .

- The way we're going to do this is A, B and C . . .
- Your priority is to . . .
- You need to make a plan and stick with it . . .
- Let's follow the rules . . .

The Equalitarian Style in Action

Parent: Johnny, I noticed you have about four hours of homework to do before Monday. Do you agree that we need to make this a top priority?

Child: Yes, I guess that's at the top of my list or I'll get in big trouble and fall behind.

Parent: We can work this out. Okay. Let's make our plan. First, you map out the times you want to devote to it, and I will help you get it done.

Child: I guess my best time would be Saturday afternoon, but I don't work real well for a four-hour stretch.

Parent: Okay, let's break it down into two sessions. I'll wake you up early and make breakfast and we can focus on your work. How does that sound?

Child: Yeah, okay. That would work. I don't know if I can do it without some help.

Parent: I will help you. Let's roll up our sleeves to make it happen. I have faith that you have the abilities, and with a little teamwork we can get this done. Where are you going to do your studying?

Child: I guess in my room or in the living room.

Parent: How can I help you be in the right place?

Child: I need a place where no one is bothering me and I don't have to do something else in the middle of my work.

Parent: We can find that.

In this scenario, the Equalitarian parent approaches the situation with a spirit of teamwork and support. There is an implied sense of "we" in the interactions. Decisions were made jointly and goals were decided on jointly. Equalitarian parents use phrases such as:

- We can approach this problem and be successful . . .
- How can I help you be more efficient? (How can we work together as a team?)
- Let's roll up our sleeves to get it done.
- We can get this done. I know that you have the ability and we'll be a team . . .
- We have a common goal . . .

The Permissive Style in Action

Parent: Johnny, I noticed that you need to do four hours of homework before Monday. What's your plan?

Child: Well, I will get to it on Saturday.

Parent: I know you will. Don't you think it's important that you don't fall behind in school and that this is important to all of us?

Child: Yeah, yeah. I know it is important.

Parent: Then let's talk about making a plan. I know you want to go to a show and we are going to church Sunday night, so that does not leave much time. How are you going to make the time?

Child: I guess I'll do it after church.

Parent: I don't think that would work for you, do you? If we got home at 9:00, you wouldn't have time and you would be too tired. Besides, I don't think that this is consistent with what you told me about how important it was to you. It doesn't sound that way to me. Who are you fooling? Me or you?

Child: Okay, I will do it between ten and two on Saturday. That way I can get it out of the way.

Parent: That sounds more reasonable. Where are you going to do it?

Child: In the living room where I can watch shows at the same time.

Parent: Do you think that's a good idea? You know what will happen. Do you know yourself better?

Child: Yeah, it would take me forever. I will do it in my room so I can do it faster.

Parent: Are you going to do it haphazardly or are you going to do it so you'll be proud of yourself?

Child: I'll do it right. After all, I do need it for school, right?

Please notice that the Permissive parent does not just blow this priority off. Remember: Being Permissive is not synonymous with being weak or parenting irresponsibly. This parent gets to the same goal as the other parents, but in a way that makes it feel as though the plan was the child's idea. When a child has ownership in a plan, he or she is more motivated to see it through. The Permissive parent may spend more time getting to the end result but gets there nonetheless. This parent may work harder at achieving the desired result because this parent always asks questions and does a lot of probing. Most of the questions, however, are statements in disguise. Permissive parents generally use phrases such as:

- What is your plan for . . . ?
- Do you feel like that is the best course of action for . . . ?
- How do you take into account these other factors . . . ?
- If you did it that way, would that help you get to your goal?
- What is your ultimate goal and can you start there?
- Where are you going to do it?
- Is that working for you?

Let me underscore the point that each style arrives at the same destination: the successful completion of the homework that is due by Monday. However, each style takes a different road to reach that destination. Bottom line: All three styles describe effective, though very different, ways of getting the job of parenting done. As long as they work, the train is moving forward and family life has positive momentum. Managing your children is largely about style—how to get where you are going.

There is no bad or good, no right or wrong, no "best" style, because again, *it depends on the child you're managing.* Each of your children has tendencies, resistances and temperaments that are distinctively theirs. Because of this uniqueness, even children within the same family have a different style with which they engage you. Like Tammy in the opening case study, some children come across as *Rebellious*—a child who seems to resist authority, likes getting his or her own way or is very independent and self-directed. Other children are *Cooperative.* They like to share and help other people; they're "team players." Then there is the *Passive* child, like Bobby in the case study. They need direction, communicated in a clear, connect-the-dots fashion. They're not self-starters by any stretch of the imagination. Bottom line: When you know your children's styles, you'll be able to figure out what makes them tick. You have to know your kids to move them.

Step #2: Identify Your Child's Type

Is your child Rebellious, Cooperative or Passive? The next assessment is your chance to identify and profile your child's type. Here are thirty direct statements that describe various aspects of your child's behavior. As you did in the exercise above, read these statements carefully and rate how well they describe your child. Fill out this assessment for each of your children.

For each statement, choose Agree (A), Mostly Agree (MA), Mostly Disagree (MD) or Disagree (D), by circling the number underneath the letter.

	A	MA	MD	D
Section R				
1. My child can be described as a self-starter who likes to work independently.	4	3	2	1
2. My child is energetic.	4	3	2	1
3. My child enjoys getting his or her own way.	4	3	2	1
4. My child likes to be different.	4	3	2	1
5. Much of the time, my child acts uncooperatively.	4	3	2	1
6. When playing or interacting with other children, my child likes to lead and be in charge.	4	3	2	1
7. My child likes to express his or her own opinion, is outspoken at times and likes to argue.	4	3	2	1

	A	MA	MD	D
8. My child is a hard worker.	4	3	2	1
9. My child has a competitive streak and likes to win.	4	3	2	1
10. My child sometimes dresses differently and likes to be unique.	4	3	2	1

Section C

	A	MA	MD	D
11. My child is willing to go along with others.	4	3	2	1
12. My child can be described as collaborative and helpful.	4	3	2	1
13. My child is flexible in group decision-making.	4	3	2	1
14. My child enjoys participating, rather than leading.	4	3	2	1
15. My child enjoys teamwork.	4	3	2	1
16. My child understands the importance of sharing.	4	3	2	1
17. My child is generally agreeable.	4	3	2	1
18. My child generally asks permission before making decisions or interacting with others.	4	3	2	1
19. My child will fully give his efforts for his team.	4	3	2	1
20. My child will lead or follow, depending on the needs of the situation.	4	3	2	1

Section P

	A	MA	MD	D
21. My child needs to be instructed in what to do before taking action.	4	3	2	1

	A	MA	MD	D
22. My child is motivated when I give him or her direction.	4	3	2	1
23. I would not describe my child as a self-starter.	4	3	2	1
24. My child follows orders and rules well.	4	3	2	1
25. My child takes pride in following instructions and presenting a job well done.	4	3	2	1
26. My child gets confused without rules.	4	3	2	1
27. My child responds very well to praise and approval.	4	3	2	1
28. My child takes criticism very seriously.	4	3	2	1
29. When my child is given leadership for his own group, he takes it very seriously.	4	3	2	1
30. My child takes on the qualities of the person he recognizes as his authority.	4	3	2	1

Scoring the Child Types

Add up your totals for each section separately and write them here:

R:_____

C:_____

P: _____

Circle the meaning of your score in each of the three categories below:

Section R: Rebellious

33–40	High identification with the Rebellious style
25–32	Dominant behaviors for the Rebellious style
18–24	Average or moderate behaviors for the Rebellious style
10–17	Low behaviors for the Rebellious style

Section C: Cooperative

30–40   High identification with the Cooperative style
23–29   Dominant behaviors for the Cooperative style
15–22   Average or moderate behaviors for the Cooperative style
10–14   Low behaviors for the Cooperative style

Section P: Passive

34–40   High identification with the Passive style
27–33   Dominant behaviors for the Passive style
18–26   Average or moderate behaviors for the Passive style
10–17   Low behaviors for the Passive style

Your children may have scored in the high-to-dominant range of one of these styles, meaning that there is a dominant theme of Rebellious, Cooperative or Passive running through their behavior, or they may show behaviors in a number of style dimensions. The key is for you to recognize these behaviors, so that you know how to interact with your children when different situations and circumstances arise. The next section will help you become more adaptable in order to avoid clashes in style and become a better problem solver with your children.

Understanding styles is critical, but it is not enough. To solve problems effectively, you must be willing to adjust and adapt your parenting style to each child's needs, behavior and temperament. These parenting styles can be applied situationally and can shift from day to day, even from hour to hour, as the circumstances with your children change. The point is that you must be willing to move your position—that is, move out of your natural, more dominant style—and do some things differently. You have to be able to dance to whatever tune the band is playing, as we say in Texas.

Even so, it never ceases to amaze me that parents will continue to persist in an attitude or behavior that simply does not work. They continue the same rigid style or behavior, beating their head against the wall over and over again, seeming not to notice that they always come away with nothing but a headache. Being rigidly locked into one style will never shape a child's behavior in the right direction.

If you are used to approaching a situation in a certain manner or demeanor, but usually with disastrous results, you need to take specific note of that unsuccessful attitude or behavior and cross it off your list of options. You *must* be flexible. You cannot continue to live with certain behaviors, particularly rigidity.

Think of it like this: You wouldn't use a five-pound sledgehammer to drive a tiny nail into the wall to hang a small picture. Nor would you use a small hammer to break up concrete. You'd use your sledgehammer. Same deal with parenting. You use whatever you need, choosing from your range of traits, abilities and styles. You have to be fluid and do what works.

I am not suggesting that you become someone you are not. What I am suggesting, however, is that you become a chameleon. When a chameleon climbs on a green leaf, it turns green; when it crawls up on a brown rock, it becomes brown. Like a chameleon changing its colors to adapt to its environment, you must change your colors to manage the child you're dealing with. Everyone has a range of behaviors from which to choose. At times you may need to put on the color of "directive," at others, the color of "leniency," and even the color of "confrontational." Although you change and adjust your parenting style, this does not change who you are on the inside. A chameleon is a still a chameleon, despite the fact that it takes on the color that surrounds it. The same is true of you. All I want you to do is use the best of who you are to bring out the best of who your children are.

Relationships are mutually defined: You and your children contribute importantly to the definition of your relationship. You have taught them the rules and you have taught them the boundaries of the relationship. In turn, they have learned your response patterns and incorporated them into their actions. These patterns of relating are easy enough to spot. For example, if your son treats you disrespectfully, talking back, with little or no consequences for acting like that, then you have taught him to treat you that way. For years and years, you accepted and tolerated that behavior. You taught him that disrespect was okay, because you allowed it. Your attitude of approach dictates what you get back. He knows how to treat you to get his way. By letting each other get away with the problem behavior, you each have taught the other that his or her behavior was acceptable. Therefore, if you don't like the deal now, don't blame just your kids. You have ownership of the relationship just as much as they do.

Your kids will have to be retrained about what works and what doesn't. No matter how long you have let the unwanted behavior go on, even a pattern of relating can be redefined. It is in the give and take of relating, and of results, that relationships are successfully negotiated.

I strongly believe that it is beneficial to avoid head-to-head confrontations with your children whenever possible. What you are doing when you confront, deliver ultimatums or throw down the gauntlet does nothing more than breed more conflict, more power struggles and greater resentment. With confrontations, you are in danger of turning what should be a loving, supportive interaction into a fight for leverage and the upper hand. Worse, you're driving your children away. You create your own experience; stop these confrontations and you may see your children moving toward you rather than away from you. If you absolutely cannot avoid a confrontation, however, you must and cannot lose.

The work you do here will help you avert confrontations and keep your interactions on a more productive level of relating; however, it clearly calls for work on your part and willingness to undo and redo the ways you interact with your children and family. Learning the nuances of style—and how to change your colors—will dramatically transform your interactions with your family.

By the time we are finished with this chapter, you will know how to skillfully and effectively inspire in your children the kinds of responses that add to their lives. Your children will start responding to you in new ways because they know they will be treated fairly and with dignity. Encounters between you and your children will leave your kids feeling better about themselves for having had the interaction. The love in your heart will give you the energy to make this happen. Let's get started.

Step #3: Manage the Clash or Confluence of Styles

This is the step when you focus on what happens when those styles mesh and when they clash by acknowledging the interactive patterns that occur between parenting style and the child's type. Certain parenting styles link up and mesh well with certain children's response styles, as Figure 1 points out.

Styles do clash, however. When you see this happening in your own family life, it is worth your time to sit down and analyze why a particular relationship with a child is not working. Do you get certain feedback and responses in this relationship that say you're too rigid or strict or too

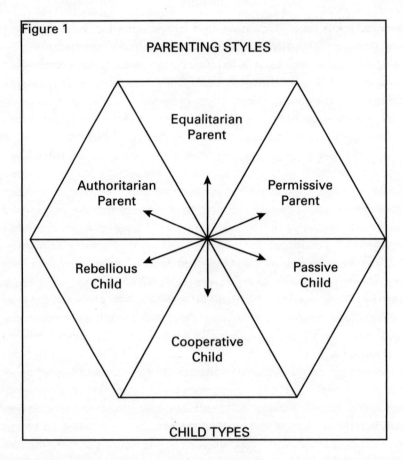

Figure 1

PARENTING STYLES

Equalitarian Parent

Authoritarian Parent

Permissive Parent

Rebellious Child

Passive Child

Cooperative Child

CHILD TYPES

This figure is adapted from principles set forth in Figure 10 from *Leadership: Management of Power and Obligation* by Art Sweeney, published by Test Systems, Inc., © 1981 Art Sweeney.

lenient or permissive? What is it about this child's attitude or yours that is causing the problem? Do you need to approach this relationship differently—investing more energy in it, for example? What style-related behaviors do you need to change in order to eliminate the confrontations, the conflict or the tug-of-wars that leave you drained and exhausted?

By questioning your style, even if it feels second nature to you, you are in a position to nurture or eradicate certain attitudes and behaviors. What follows from here is a look at the interactive patterns that predictably pay out in families. This information will help you identify negative dynamics that can keep you from forward motion. If you find yourself here, pay particular attention to the strategies that are listed. Let these strategies stimulate your own thoughts and actions for change.

I have also included two sample dialogues that illustrate how to problem-solve when a clash of styles exists. Applying this information, and using it as these sample scripts suggest, will give you a tremendous head start in the solution category.

Authoritarian/Rebellious

If your parenting style is mostly Authoritarian, and one of your children is Rebellious, you have a power struggle on your hands. It is an absolute fact that this dyad can be the most frustrating relationship to manage in a family. Most of the conflict erupts over the power in the relationship; both the Authoritarian parent and the Rebellious child crave power and control. Both try to dominate all of the interactions by being too controlling or too unreasonable.

Rebellious children seek power in different ways, including misbehavior, drama, catastrophizing (making mountains out of molehills) and attention-getting. These children feel important when they are in control and being noticed. They like to draw their parents into battle; doing so makes them feel powerful and influential over them. Rebellious children tend to be combative toward their parents and their authority (screaming, crying, spitting out food or otherwise asserting their will over yours). In addition, these children may be passive-aggressive, saying that everything is okay, when inside, they may be angry or frustrated about something. Too many rules generally frustrate these children, and they may disregard them.

I can assure you that with an Authoritarian parent and a Rebellious child, the struggles take on confrontational qualities. There is the potential for a lose-lose scenario because Authoritative parents and Rebellious kids don't problem-solve; they clash. You never get anything done because you are always butting heads. If you're arguing, you're not problem-solving. The more you push, the more your child will push back.

To keep you on task, moving forward and solving problems, you must:

- Avoid angry exchanges, raising your voice or issuing ultimatums.
- Take time to listen and make sure your child is heard; two-way communication is vital (see Chapter 8).

- Deal with misbehavior as calmly as possible.
- Move toward Equalitarian-style parenting, which will provide a team-spirit atmosphere in which your child can be channeled away from the power struggles and into more productive activities, such as play, projects, sports, homework or reading, among others. You will be so much more efficient at problem-solving.
- Give instructions with attention to timing and place. When my boys were younger and playing baseball, they would always fail to gather up their baseball equipment in time for us to get out of the house and to the ball field on time each Saturday. I had a hard time prying them from the television set on Saturday mornings. Then I discovered a simple solution: If after each game, I made it their job to put the equipment neatly back into the bag, and if they performed that task on the field as everyone was gathering up their things to go home, they carried out the job flawlessly. I further charged them with the responsibility of returning to the bag anything they removed, so the equipment was always ready to go on game day. I learned that kids can take responsibility for a task or a chore as long as they're in a situation where they can focus. Select the right framework of time and place, and you'll increase the odds of success.
- Learn how to compromise and move toward mutual respect, cooperation and shared decision-making.
- Stay patient and persistent.

Authoritarian/Cooperative

If you are using an Authoritarian style with a Cooperative child, expect some conflict, since these children like to share power and be involved in family decision-making and problem-solving. You may insist on the last word, for example, and this will frustrate your child. Cooperative children also like to be given responsibility, which Authoritarian parents are often reluctant to give.

Some important recommendations:

- Move toward the Equalitarian style of parenting and give your child more decision-making responsibility. For example, you might ask your child if he would like to take his bath before or after dinner. Giving a child a choice between two alternatives allows them some autonomy, but lets you maintain some degree of control.

- Increase your involvement in this child's life. Cooperative children respond well to high parental involvement in their lives. This can take many forms: attending their games, going to the movies together, checking their homework, doing projects together and being available to talk. The point is to find more ways to do things together, in a collaborative fashion.
- Listen to your children's opinions more often and let them have some say in problem-solving.
- Approach this relationship with a spirit of encouragement. Acknowledge your child's successes more often, give appropriate praise for accomplishments and interact in a way that is supportive. You will create a much more nurturing atmosphere, one in which your Cooperative child will flourish.

Authoritarian/Passive

As an Authoritarian parent with a Passive child, you have a good fit. This child needs a parent to tell him what to do; Authoritarian parents, with their take-charge attitude, like to tell their children what to do—a perfect mesh of styles. With a child who is Passive, you must be very instructive, because these children are not self-starters and they respond best to a direct approach. For example, you may have to sit down with the child and go over a checklist of what to do. Or you might say, "Son, you need to make a plan, and stick with it. Here's a plan of how to go about this . . ." Then outline for your child, point by point, what he needs to accomplish. When solving problems with a Passive child or giving instructions, the dots must be very close together.

Equalitarian/Rebellious

If you are using the Equalitarian style of parenting, expect to have some trouble communicating with your Rebellious child, who just does not seem to want to listen. Nor do Rebellious children want to share or give power away, but rather they want it all. This apparent selfishness on the part of your child can frustrate you. That frustration builds and builds, and you may become impatient with your child's behavior.

Some important strategies:

- Never overreact. Your child may be trying to get a rise out of you. Instead of lecturing, scolding or getting mad, explain your point of view and do it in a calm manner. This approach will keep hostilities from escalating in your relationship.
- Let your child disagree with you on a topic. Disagreement can be healthy, if it occurs within a spirit of mutual respect for differing opinions. Show your child this type of respect, and it will alter the nature of your interactions.
- Let your Rebellious child take a leadership role in appropriate family activities, such as organizing an Easter egg hunt, setting up family games or selecting family entertainment for the weekend.
- Include children in establishing clear rules about appropriate behavior and consequences. When this happens, clashes over rules and punishment generally end.

Equalitarian/Cooperative

Because the Equalitarian/Cooperative relationship is based both on teamwork and democratic principles, this is usually a good fit for success, and interactions are generally positive. The parent treats the child in such a way that protects and enhances his or her self-esteem, and the child in turn is confident and motivated in this relationship. There is a peaceful coexistence here because both parent and child relate well, and they accept and believe in themselves and in each other.

Equalitarian/Passive

Because Equalitarian parents generally expect children to enter eagerly into team activities—they encourage their kids to jump in and contribute—they may have a tendency to get frustrated because Passive children are often reluctant to get involved, due to shyness or timidity.

Some important recommendations:

- Encourage the Passive child to get involved in smaller-group activities made up of two or three children. This environment is less threatening and offers opportunities for Passive children to expand their skills.

- Voice your appreciation and give praise whenever a Passive child ventures into unknown territory and demonstrates greater flexibility and adaptability, since these children tend to withdraw if pushed into a new project or situation too quickly.
- Move toward a more Authoritarian style in order to provide the structure and predictable schedule this child needs to feel secure.
- Always give these children straightforward, step-by-step directions—how to do it, when to do it, and why it should be done—so that they can succeed.

Permissive/Rebellious

The Permissive/Rebellious dyad works well because both parent and child are sympathetic toward each other. They support each other and take an interest in what the other is doing. Dialogue such as the following works effectively with a Rebellious child: "Tell me what you think would be the best way to handle this . . ."

Generally, a parent using the Permissive style of parenting is strong on support, but may be weak on control. Because a Rebellious child does need some degree of control, a Permissive parent should learn how to place firm limits on any unacceptable behavior.

Permissive/Cooperative

This relationship may run into problems, with tensions emerging. A parent using the Permissive style may offer too much decision-making authority to this child, who is used to shared decision-making. Under these circumstances, the child may feel overwhelmed, disconnected and unsure of what to do. There may also be poor communication in this relationship.

Recommendations:

- Become more Cooperative in style in order to encourage two-way listening, participation in problem-solving and decision-making, goal-setting and overall better communication skills. Encourage children and allow children to speak for themselves and express their feelings.

• Work together on mutual projects, such as camping out, doing school projects or taking classes together.

Permissive/Passive

This combination plays into and amplifies the negative side of both people's characteristics. If you are a Permissive parent with a Passive child, you're vegetating; you're sitting around watching the drapes fade. You're not problem-solving. You're waiting for the child to initiate a project, while your child is awaiting instruction. A Passive child needs stimulation, initiated by you.

Recommendations:

• Encourage any interests or talents this child wants to pursue, such as art or music lessons, sports or dance instruction.
• Move to a more Authoritarian style of parenting for this child, who needs clear structure and boundaries in order to feel motivated.
• Require more of yourself in terms of providing challenges and stimulation in your child's environment. Learn how to give hands-on instruction for activities, play and assignments.

Sample Dialogue for Improving Grades

Using the following scenario, I coached a mother in how to make her Rebellious daughter improve her report card by having the daughter create her own strategy for improvement. When your child thinks something is her idea, she will own the idea, taking accountability for it, and see it through successfully. If you are facing a similar problem, let your child have ownership in decision-making, then embrace that decision.

Mom: I see your grades are not what you hoped for. I hate that for you. Won't that create real problems for you in terms of being eligible to try out for cheerleading?

Daughter: I know, I know . . .

Mom: What do you think you need to do about that? Can I help in some way? I want you to do well too; how can I help?

Daughter: Well, I don't know. I am just not doing it.

Mom: Well, what would help you do it? To do better?

Daughter: I know what to do . . . I need to spend more time doing it.

Mom: Would it help if we had dinner at a different time? Would it help if your friends weren't bugging you?

Daughter: I know I spend too much time on the phone.

Mom: Well, I don't know; maybe you do, maybe you don't. You probably spent ten hours last week talking to your friends on the phone. I wonder what would have happened if you had been studying instead.

Daughter: Well, I am sure I would have done better.

Mom: How would you feel if we just told your friends not to call during that time or we just turned the phone off during that time? What if we did something to make it easier to focus? You tell me; I want to help you here.

Daughter: Well, maybe I will unplug the phone from 8:00 to 10:00 so I can study.

Mom: Well, look, I'll help you do that. I'll answer the phone during that time and hold them off, and after that you're on your own. But I will help you between 8:00 and 10:00 P.M.

Sample Dialogue for Setting a Curfew

Try presenting facts when you problem-solve. This helps you stay on point and solve the problem.

Son: Dad, I want a later curfew—like 1:00 A.M. That's what my friends have, and they make fun of me because I have to come home before midnight.

Dad: Let's talk about this. The bars let out at 1:00 A.M. Most car accidents occur between the hours of 1:00 A.M. and 3:00 A.M. and as many as one in four drivers may be drunk. You're driving your car that you enjoy; we can't afford to replace it. I don't want you coming home at 9:00 P.M.

feeling like some nerd. I don't really have the answer; let's come up with one together.

Son: But Dad, all my friends are out having fun when I have to go home.

Dad: I'm willing to extend your curfew as long as I know you're not out on the road during those hours. What about if you bring your friends over here at midnight and they stay all night?

Son: Or I stay all night at someone else's house.

Dad: That would work, as long as you call us at midnight and let us know you're safe.

As a result of the work you've done so far, you have taken a giant step toward getting greater clarity on how you interact with your family and your children. Continue to massage this information, taking it to heart, because we will be referring to it throughout the rest of this book. Remember this: You are making a difference in your children's world, and one day they will go out into the world and make their difference. Stay the course. Do not be diverted from your resolve. You are on the right track.

6

Powering Up

Making the decision to have a child is momentous.
It is to decide forever to have your heart
go walking around outside your body.
—ELIZABETH STONE

As you begin to live the new ideas and plans you've been working on with regard to leading your family, you can expect your children to improve across all areas of their being, what is generally referred to as personhood. They can only benefit from a more purposefully defined family marked by healthy interactions and home environment.

There are also some more specifically targeted efforts you can make—what I call *powering up* your children. We will begin with what you can do to enhance their intelligence and cognitive efficiency, then progressing to other areas of their personhood, such as self-esteem and self-worth, social confidence, mental and emotional stability and spiritual maturity.

We've been talking about creating a phenomenal family, and phenomenal families are made up of phenomenal people. As discussed in Chapter 3, you want your children to be authentically who they are, and you want them to realize all of their potential and to rise to the challenge of being the best that they can be. If you stay focused on what you've learned so far, and now add to that knowledge and adopt these very specific action plans that target the five different areas listed above, you're about to see great progress in your children's lives. Be excited—this is one of the fun and rewarding parts of being a parent.

INTELLIGENCE AND COGNITIVE EFFICIENCY

Let's begin by focusing on your child's intellectual functioning, which many experts have long believed to be genetically determined and therefore unchangeable. Are they right or are there things you can do or stop doing that will increase your child's intelligence? I'm not talking about educating them more; I'm talking about actually increasing their mental ability. The answer may surprise you, although there are definitely differing opinions.

There's an older school of thought supported by a large, if somewhat dated body of scientific research (the references for which I have included at the end of the book) that says you cannot boost IQ because it's fixed at birth and based on genetic programming. However, as the sophistication of measurement devices has improved, this long-held position has recently been widely disputed. Intellectual ability is no doubt *primarily* a function of genetics; however, there are many experts who now believe that intelligence is changeable and that you can increase your child's intelligence, as measured by standardized, valid and reliable tests, by as much as ten to twenty points! Many experts believe that it's even possible to increase connections between brain cells, which in turn will lead to enhanced mental processing.

Understand too that your child's brain doesn't fully mature until the late teenage years or beyond, according to recent findings from the UCLA Medical School and the National Institutes of Health, so it makes sense that you still have time to enhance your child's brainpower. By the way, the part of the brain that fills in last is that which is involved in decision-making, impulse control and emotions—which may explain why teens are so prone to volatile and erratic behavior. In fact, the way the brain appears to optimize itself is by making mistakes, and then learning from those mistakes. So I guess there's a silver lining to some of our children's most frustrating behavior. They're at least "growing" their brains!

Neither side of the intelligence debate disputes that you can at least increase your child's intellectual *performance*. That fact is well established. But do you actually increase what was long held to be your child's "innate" intelligence, or are you simply optimizing it? Having reviewed both bodies of research, and having worked with fellow psychologists who deal exclusively with the neuropsychological population, I tend to take the position that you can actually increase your child's intelligence, and that's a very exciting prospect. However, I'm very much a results-oriented person, and I'm not sure I really care whether I'm increasing innate intelligence or just increasing intellectual efficiency. As long as there are things I can do to help my children function smarter and perform better, I'm going to do them. Bottom line: If there are things you can do to get your children to score better, reason better, function better and do better than they did before they had the benefit of those efforts, do you really care whether you've increased innate intelligence or simply tuned up and enhanced the intellectual power that was already under the hood?

Improvement in intellectual and cognitive functioning is important for many reasons, including the positive impact it has, particularly on mental and emotional stability and social confidence—which is why I'm beginning with it here. I strongly believe, and research bears this out, that when children accomplish something worthwhile, such as doing well on a test, earning good grades or achieving something they set out to do, that success builds a foundation of self-confidence, self-esteem and self-mastery. If children have a positive history—a successful track record—in intellectual and academic pursuits, they'll tend to be more calm, focused and efficient as they tackle intellectual challenges. It's a fact of human functioning that people in general like to do what they're good at. We develop vertically in the areas in which we enjoy success. Everyone likes to be a winner, and the expectations of success can energize performance. Positive experiences lift children up to help them see all kinds of possibilities for themselves. Having observed themselves succeeding, they're willing to reach for performance levels that they may not have had the confidence to strive for in the past. A sense of mastery is an amazingly empowering experience.

To help your children boost their intellectual abilities, I've supplied a list of activities below to bring about positive cognitive change. These activities work on two broad levels. First, they're intended to provide a program of training that may enhance some aspect of your child's intellectual skills and maximize his or her mental power. Second, a number of these activities, namely those that focus on increased mental stimulation ("brain workouts"), may help the brain form new connections between cells. As the number of connections increases, the brain becomes more adept at complex thinking.

Take care not to let your children be intimidated by these or other intellectual challenges. Make them fun—lots of fun. At the same time, avoid unrealistic expectancies about what your children can accomplish. Pushing your children into situations they can't handle will frustrate them.

In the event you feel like you don't have a clear view of where your child is currently functioning intellectually, I've provided on drphil.com an intelligence test that you can easily administer to your children. This test has been standardized and validated against some of the intelligence tests most commonly used by professional psychologists. No test, nor the score it generates, will fully and completely measure your child's cognitive skills and abilities, but it will give you at least some idea of your child's level of functioning. If you decide that using the test would be helpful, you can learn more about it, as well as the general concept of IQ, on drphil.com. If you're not interested in that type of evaluation, ignore it.

As we go forward, please understand that while gains in intellectual skills are possible and very worthwhile, no training program or change in any environmental condition can turn your child into a genius if they don't already have a fair amount of genetically programmed intelligence. You can very likely have a significant impact, but there are limits.

By the way, a lot of the information that follows has blown blizzard-like over parents for years, so you may have heard bits and pieces of it before. That's okay. I'm not trying to reinvent the wheel. What I want you to do here is organize this information into a usable form, develop a clear plan for implementation and be sure to put it on Project Status.

Create an Empowering Internal Dialogue

Even very young children have a running internal conversation with themselves. I introduced this concept of internal dialogue earlier in our discussion on overcoming your family legacy (Chapter 4). Internal dialogue can be made up of positive or negative messages, including judging, assessing, praise, criticisms, encouragement, disapproval, painting a rosy picture or sending messages of doom and gloom. Negative messages involving fears, doubts, worry, anxiety and pessimism are all too common.

If children, for example, choose thoughts that diminish their self-image, they choose the consequence of self-doubt. If children think they'll do poorly on a test, then they probably will. An internal dialogue that is negative promotes failure. It can drown out positive messages that promote success. Simply put, children can do and think themselves into poor intellectual outcomes.

There is also a strong mind-body connection. Every thought a child has engenders a corresponding change in their body. For example, immune cells are closely linked to nerve cells, and there's instant communication between the two. If a child thinks that a test will be too difficult, he or she will experience a negative physiological change. That change might take the form of a headache, stomachache, nausea, faintness, trembling, sweating, fluctuations in bodily temperature or other physical distress symptoms. These physical changes exact a high performance cost on their thinking ability. A child can blank out, have racing, out-of-control thoughts or simply forget what he's studied and have trouble concentrating or completing assignments. Bottom line: Depressed thoughts depress energy, action and the ability to think clearly. They shake your child's faith and create doubts about what he or she can really achieve.

I once worked with a family whose thirteen-year-old son Wayne experienced test anxiety on a chronic basis. Wayne was a very bright boy with an above-average IQ of 110 who did well on homework assignments, but when it was time to take tests, he'd panic, and his test-taking skills simply fell apart. He was a C student with the potential to be an A student. Even though Wayne studied thoroughly, his anxiety level during tests was off the charts. I deduced that his problem was not a lack of preparation, ability or motivation, but rather interfering and destructive self-talk. I asked him to recall and write down for me what his self-talk was during his last failed test. Here is what he wrote:

> *I'm starting to sweat and shake. What if I flunk another test? Everyone will make fun of me. But this test is too hard. I'm not smart enough to pass it. I should have studied harder. I'm such a wimp. My mom is going to be so disappointed. I wish I could leave. I hate school.*

It should be obvious that Wayne failed the test because of this negative self-talk. Combined with it, there was a physiological reaction—sweating and trembling. Even more significant, however, was the interfering nature of the self-talk. Wayne is a very smart boy who in this case began the test with 100 percent of his mental horsepower engaged. But the effect of his internal dialogue was to cut his horsepower in half. As he started the test, 50 percent of that horsepower was invested in the conversation he was having with himself, leaving only 50 percent focused on passing the test. Instead of maximizing his strong IQ of 110, he probably started the test with applied IQ of maybe about 55! Was it any wonder Wayne, when in a test-taking situation, usually failed? His problem was that he was trying to do two things at once: listen to himself rag on himself and at the same time take a test. Once the problem was diagnosed, and Wayne learned to manage his self-talk the same way I'm going to teach you to work with your children to manage theirs, his test anxiety was over and done with, and he went on to become the excellent and steady student he was always capable of being. Any time children divide their attention between their fear of failure, judgment and ridicule for a potentially poor performance, when they should be applying their full attention to the task at hand, then obviously intellectual performance will be decreased. It's like trying to run on one leg. You might be able to do it, but you are going to lose the race.

The flip side of what Wayne experienced is the kind of internal dialogue that is positive, realistic, empowering and above all controllable so it doesn't interfere during performance times. A positive internal dialogue can dramatically enhance intellectual performance. Later in this chapter, when we turn our focus to self-esteem, I'll give you a powerful exercise that will help your child eliminate self-talk that works to his or her disadvantage.

Practice Controlled Breathing Exercises with Your Child

One of the most efficient and effective methods for stimulating a child's mental processes and performance is controlled breathing. On its face this may seem like no big deal, but it is, in fact, a very big deal. Research shows that schoolchildren can increase their grades if they do breathing exercises prior to tests or assignments; these exercises also reduce test anxiety. Children competing in national spelling bees are encouraged to do this prior to competition to boost their powers of recall, and these kids are plenty smart to begin with. Controlled breathing increases oxygen flow to the brain, which in turn boosts memory, concentration and problem-solving abilities. The breathing technique I recommend is relatively easy to do, even for a child, and you can practice with him. The goal is to breathe out for the same amount of time as you breathe in, to prevent dizziness or hyperventilation.

When you try this, teach your child to count to five when breathing in, and then to five again when breathing out. Repeat this breathing cycle about six times; the entire routine will take only a minute. Instruct your child to use this breathing exercise before a test, exam or other assignment in which problem-solving or recall comes into play. Breathing patterns cannot be taught just once. They need to be practiced, so that they become a positive habit. Remember: Matching inhalation and exhalation time is the key.

Perform Mental Gymnastics

Playing games that stimulate the mind, particularly those that contain the element of strategy and that aren't mainly based on chance (e.g., a roll of the dice), will build verbal skills, plus improve powers of concentration, perception and reasoning. Here are some recommendations for brain-building games you can do as a family:

- Chess
- Checkers
- Crossword puzzles
- Cryptograms
- Word jumbles
- Scrabble
- Solving mathematical puzzles

Increase Opportunities for Verbal Interactions as a Family

Engaging your children in conversation helps develop their language and vocabulary skills, particularly between the ages of sixteen and twenty-six months when a child's language is developing very rapidly. Studies suggest that the more talkative parents are, the larger their children's vocabularies will be. No matter what your children's ages you should discuss with them topics such as school, friends, their interests and activities, projects they create, trips you've taken together or current events. Make these conversations a regular part of life. What emerges from these interactions will be children who feel valued and are smarter, better adjusted and more intelligent.

With my own sons, one of my favorite word-building activities when they were younger involved having them make up and tell a story about some topic. We made it a game. And my kids' goal was to either make me laugh, scare me or surprise me. The story had to incorporate each member of the family, including two dogs, a cat, a gerbil and a lizard! And it all had to be included in a meaningful way. We always approached this in a fun, even silly way. For example, if Robin was involved, sometimes my sons would try to gross her out. If they could make her cringe, squeal or grab her stomach, victory was at hand. The boys absolutely loved it.

Disguised in this fun activity were a number of mental gymnastics. Jay and Jordan had to rely on their short- and long-term memories; they had to deal with intertwining concepts and relationships; and they had to use their imagination and verbal skills. Often, the events had to be framed against a timeline (temporal reasoning), and they had to present their narrative with feeling and emotion to get the desired result of laughter or whatever the objective was.

Another activity I devised to nurture my sons' creativity required them to do some creative selling. They had to sell me a certain item based on two factors: its designed use and a fictional or a novel use. In this game, I'd pick some random item in the room and hand it to them, and one minute later, they had to begin selling it to me until I was motivated to buy it. For example, if I handed them a pencil, they had to passionately describe what a great and wonderful writing tool it was, telling me the many different ways I could use it during the day. Next, they had to come up with a nontraditional use of the pencil, which was often silly, but fun. For example, they'd promote the pencil as a way to prop up a box as part of a trap for catching a woolly booger, or as a great back scratcher. To make the game more fun, I sometimes "bought" the item, paying up with another fun activity.

> **Survey Fact:** Twenty-eight percent of parents said that their children had or have academic problems in school.

Again, they were using imagination, verbal skills, persuasive skills, short- and long-term memory, conceptualization and presentation abilities. They were also having a great time, and so was I. These particular activities really prepared them well for such academic pursuits as English class, literature and speech and debate. I have no doubt that my boys are smarter today for having participated in these games. Games taught them how to think and reason. The key is repetition. Make all of these activities part of your child's role.

Encourage Repetitive Reading

It's no big news flash that reading to your children helps nurture a love of language and promotes bonding—both of which optimize a child's intellectual potential. The latest word on reading, however, is that repeated exposure to a beloved book helps a toddler enhance his or her memory, improve attention span and build vocabulary.

I once tested a nine-year-old girl named Amy whose parents wanted assistance in improving her academic skills. The problem, as her mother said, was that Amy did not like to read, because she thought it was boring. After the initial testing (she scored in the average range), I recommended several of the exercises mentioned in this chapter, but I emphasized that she should read aloud to her mother at least thirty minutes a day. Did she roll her eyes and resist the activity in the beginning? Absolutely, but she did it and it helped. After one month of following this read-aloud program, Amy's verbal skills tested in the *above average range*, impressive for such a short amount of time. Bottom line: Reading to your children, as well as encouraging your children to read, leads to optimal language development. Read with and to your children as often as possible.

If you have trouble getting your kids to read, try something that worked exceptionally well for a father I know. As a condition for purchasing a video game, he negotiated an agreement with his children that they could use it only on Sunday mornings, provided that each child fulfilled reading requirements throughout the week. This agreement proved to be a reliable motivator and even stimulated the kids to read more than they were required to.

Create a Stimulating Environment

As a young child's brain develops, trillions of connections are formed between brain cells and developed through such stimuli as light, color, smell and sound. These connections are vital to learning: The more connections a child has, the faster he or she can process information. Many experts believe that by stimulating an infant's senses through an enriched environment, you can quite possibly increase his or her IQ. Since I don't see any downside, I'd encourage you to provide toys such as mobiles that can be moved and touched, or colorful pictures and other objects that may help develop an infant's brain. Many other ways to create an enriching, stimulating environment for your children are listed in the box on pages 122–23.

FIFTEEN WAYS TO CREATE A MENTALLY STIMULATING ENVIRONMENT FOR YOUR CHILDREN

1. Hold your baby frequently. In a recent research study, the findings showed that the more a baby was touched by the parent, the less likely that infant would develop attention deficit problems later in childhood.

2. Use expressive facial gestures. Infants respond to parents whose facial expressions are more animated. In one experiment, babies turned away from mothers with dull facial expressions, but turned toward those whose faces were more expressive.

3. Do wordplay games in the form of rhymes or songs that you make up with your child. This activity encourages the development of language skills.

4. Cut the captions off cartoons; create new captions with your child in order to boost thinking skills and creativity.

5. Have your child read age-appropriate stories out loud from newspapers or magazines.

6. At least once a week, take your children to the library, where they can read on their own or attend storytelling groups. Have your children get their own library cards so they can learn responsibility for taking care of books and returning them on time.

7. Take your children to appropriate cultural events throughout the year, such as plays and concerts.

8. Limit your children's computer time, unless they are doing schoolwork that requires the use of the computer.

9. Travel to new places, including local museums. While on vacation, take them on tours of interesting sights even if they don't expect to like going.

10. Use dinnertime for mental stimulation. Encourage your children to talk about their day and express their viewpoints.

11. Sing lullabies to your infant; these stimulate the development of brain connections, particularly during the first three years of life.

12. Use complex, multi-clause sentences when talking to your children, such as "I'm going to the grocery store because we need cereal for breakfast," as opposed to simple, single-clause sentences such as "Drink your milk." Children who are

exposed to more complex grammatical structure show a higher degree of language development.

13. Enroll your children in dance classes (if they show an interest), since dancing requires the memorization of specific movements—a mental activity that helps build brain connections.

14. Provide stimulating age-appropriate toys that invite interaction and thought. For infants, look for toys that engage as many of the five senses as possible (color, texture, sound, sight and smell). Toddlers benefit from balls, blocks, cars, pull toys, simple puzzles, musical instruments and stuffed animals and dolls. From ages three to five, children begin to use their imaginations, so encourage them with construction sets, washable crayons or markers, and modeling clay. From ages six to nine, building self-esteem is important. Hobby sets, sports toys, computer software, construction toys and books with uplifting messages all make good playthings. So do educational toys that promote problem-solving skills, such as counting, math games and more challenging board games. From ages ten to twelve, children need to develop independence, responsibility and self-expression. Your best bets are complex construction sets, age-appropriate board games, science kits and artwork kits.

15. Limit television-viewing time to ninety minutes a day for preschoolers and two hours a day for older children, since kids who watch a lot of TV suffer academically. However, make allowances for television content that is positive and educational, such as the programming found on the Learning Channel, the Discovery Channel and similar networks.

Introduce Music and Rhythm into Your Child's Life

Children should be given opportunities for the constructive pursuit of things they show an interest in. If music is one of these, encourage it. Not only will you help your child's gift blossom, you'll simultaneously help promote his memory and language development. The younger the better too. Research with preschoolers shows that enrolling them in keyboard and group-singing instruction (choir) enhances their spatial-temporal reasoning—a skill that helps with puzzles, geometry, fractions and ratios. Instruction in musical skills also helps children develop in other intellectual areas, such as math and complex reasoning.

Even if your children aren't musically oriented in terms of singing or playing an instrument, introducing music and rhythm into their world may enhance many aspects of their academic performance. For example, many children find the rhythmic stimulation of drumbeats makes it easier to focus on doing homework (some kids will find this distracting, however).

There has been a lot of controversy surrounding something known as the Mozart effect, in which listening to the music of Mozart may enhance how we think and reason. Whether this effect is valid is uncertain; however, we do know that music provides mental gymnastics through the learning of its symbol system, plus it increases creativity. Anything you can do to enhance the creativity of your children is certainly worth doing.

Nourish Young Minds

The importance of nutritional balance, with foods that provide a high yield of vitamins and minerals, cannot be overstated when it comes to supporting your child's mental capabilities. Deficiencies of iron, iodine, vitamins A and B and other vital nutrients are prevalent in schoolchildren today and can affect their mental development and learning ability. Better-nourished children simply function more effectively on a cognitive level, and studies carried out in other parts of the world clearly show that improved nutrition leads to an improvement in IQ scores.

When you fail to feed your kids wholesome foods, instead serving overly processed foods high in sugar and fat, it can negatively impact their mental processing abilities—and potentially affect IQ. In a well-publicized study of one million schoolchildren enrolled in the New York City school system, IQ scores improved by 14 percent after additives, dyes, artificial flavorings and colors were removed from their lunches!

Nutritionists tell us that because the human brain is an extremely active metabolic organ, it depends on a steady supply of circulating glucose (blood sugar) from carbohydrates to support cognitive functioning. Natural, unrefined whole grains, fruits and vegetables are the best choices to drive mental activities, since they are also high in vitamins and brain-protective antioxidants. You can guard against nutritionally sabotaging your children by serving foods that can enhance their brainpower and mental energy. A number of these foods are listed in the table on page 125 of this section, along with their mental fitness benefits.

Researchers have also found that when kids eat breakfasts rich in natural carbohydrates such as whole-grain cereals, along with a lean protein such as eggs, this can help maintain their mental performance over the morning. By contrast, sugary cereals, donuts or pancakes with syrup are too high in processed carbohydrates and sugar, which will accelerate the production of a brain chemical called serotonin. High levels of this brain chemical can induce sleep and mental grogginess—exactly what a child does not need for alert, effective performance in school or prior to taking a test.

BRAIN FOODS FOR BRAINPOWER

Foods	Benefit and Function
Citrus fruits	Foods such as oranges and grapefruits are high in vitamin C, which improves memory and performance.
Eggs	Eggs are high in a memory-building vitamin called choline.
Fish (at least two fish meals a week)	Fish contains important brain-building fats.
Green, orange, yellow, and purple fruits and vegetables	These foods are rich in antioxidants that can protect brain cells against damage, as well as potassium, which helps prevent mental fatigue.
Lean meats (beef and poultry)	These foods are high in iron; deficiencies in iron impair learning and memory.
Whole-grain and iron-fortified cereals	These foods are excellent sources of carbohydrates, which are required for sharp mental performance.

Active Body, Active Mind

Physical activity, including playing sports, boosts blood flow to all parts of the body, including the brain. When the brain is supplied with freshly oxygenated blood, concentration, thinking speed and complex reasoning are all enhanced. Children who are physically active as a matter of habit perform better in school—a finding that has been confirmed by more than fifty years of research. Physical activity in children:

- Promotes clear thinking
- Boosts creativity
- Stimulates the brain and learning
- Increases energy and mental concentration
- Produces positive changes in the body that enhance self-esteem (which in turn supports better cognitive learning)
- Helps develop motor skills and coordination
- Helps manage stress and anxiety
- Reduces depression by increasing levels of important brain chemicals that are often depleted in depression

There are many activities kids can do for exercise, most involving an element of fun (exercise doesn't have to be something a child dreads doing); for example, team sports, martial arts, biking, Rollerblading, swimming, dancing to rhythmic music, hiking or working out with a friend. These exercises increase respiration rates and heartbeat, enriching and strengthening both the body and mind. Of course, exercise should be appropriate to a child's age and stage of physical and emotional development (see the accompanying chart on page 127 for guidelines).

How much exercise is enough for children? The American Heart Association recommends that all children age two or older should engage in fun physical activity at least thirty minutes every day, plus thirty minutes of more vigorous exercise at least three to four days a week to build and maintain healthy heart and lung fitness. Encourage your children to relax after exercising too, since relaxation is essential to restoring physical and mental energy.

One of the most effective ways to motivate your children to become more physically active is to be active yourself. Activities such as hiking, biking, in-line skating, and certain outdoor sports can be easily enjoyed as a family. Be someone who sets the right example and inspire your children to rise to a better, more active level. Children rely on the role models in their lives—and that's you. Through your action and your lifestyle, you can direct your children toward where you want them to go and all that you want them to be.

AGE-APPROPRIATE EXERCISE FOR CHILDREN

Age 6 and Under	Gymnastics (tumbling), hopscotch, jumping rope, swimming, karate, playing tag, outdoor play, dance, unstructured play
Ages 7 and Up	Soccer, field hockey, basketball, lacrosse, swimming, in-line skating, biking, other organized sports, dance
Adolescence	Organized sports, competitive running, weight training and exercise classes

---

OTHER DIMENSIONS OF YOUR CHILD'S PERSONHOOD

I've set the stage for enhancing your child's functioning using intelligence as the working example. Now let's look at what you can do in some other important areas of your child's personhood.

Self-Esteem and Self-Worth

Positive self-esteem is achieved through properly interpreting yourself through accurate, positive and healthy internal dialogue. Let me be absolutely clear on what I mean. For many kids, self-esteem is measured as a function of what they accomplish or accumulate externally, from the world, in the form of grades, trophies, recognition or material stuff. But this form of esteem can be elusive, fickle and completely vulnerable to the whims of the external world. When kids keep trying to meet internal needs from the outside that can only truly be met from the inside, they'll never hit the spot. True self-esteem is *internally* defined; it comes from the inside out. It means that you love, believe in and accept yourself because you accept and appreciate that you are a unique, quality and authentic person. These are all big words that children seldom understand. As a result, your emphasis must be on the result, not on the language to describe it.

In children, true self-esteem, along with confidence, hope and optimism, is generated by internal dialogue that tells children they are okay, loved, appreciated and special. Positive and realistic self-talk also creates children who live up to their own expectancies (in contrast to those imposed by other people). Clarity of focus and cognitive efficiency are enhanced as well. Having high self-esteem and high self-confidence will ensure that those self-expectancies are high yet realistic, and carry your children to their highest possible level of achievement and performance.

Important: Trying to boost a child's self-esteem with random, overblown, false or insincere praise independent of actual achievement is not a good idea. Unconditional love is one thing; giving a child a trophy for coming in last in a race is another. Children who are led to believe they can do something, when indeed they cannot, will suffer greater disappointment later. There's a delicate balance here, and at the tipping point one finds realistic encouragement and confidence about the task at hand.

If you suspect your child may be sabotaging himself with disruptive self-talk, you should work together to create a new, more accurate internal dialogue. As your child begins to think differently and behave more authentically, he'll begin to experience a new, more positive history that will predict a new future of successful life endeavors in a variety of pursuits. The exercises you're about to do with your child are designed to help you do just that—make changes internally to ensure he's accepting himself and therefore living with inner peace and confidence. Let's turn now to the specifics.

First, help your child recognize some of these negative self-talk traps by asking him or her to write down, or if they can't yet write well, tell you, the "bad things that I say to myself"; for example, "I'm not good in math . . . I worry about getting bad grades . . . I won't do well on my test." Be careful to remain age appropriate in discussing this with your child or you will just be talking with yourself. Children hear what they understand.

Next, you can use a technique with your child called fact-finding to see if there is any validity to the negative self-talk. Ask: "Why do you think your thoughts are true or not true?" Your child might respond by saying: "I got As and Bs on my report card last time, so I do get good grades . . . I got a B on my test last time . . . my teacher says I'm a hard worker in math." The point is to help your child identify whether these thoughts are correct or incorrect.

As you work through this exercise with your child, you may discover that a thought is true, such as "I'm a bad speller." Look upon this opportunity as a teachable moment, asking your child: "What could you do differently now to change that?" Have your child come up with his or her own plan for improvement, such as studying a little longer or spending more time checking over assignments for spelling errors. When your child is involved in devising the solution, he has ownership in the plan and is better motivated to carry it through.

As a way to eliminate any negative self-talk and build self-confidence, teach your child how to substitute, and practice, positive responses. For example:

> I'll do the best I can, and that will be the best I can do.
> I studied hard for the test, so I should do well.
> I worked hard on my homework.
> I know my stuff.
> I'll be okay; I can do this.

Finally, as you perform this exercise with your child, encourage him or her to express his/her new thoughts out loud. Research shows that working out solutions aloud helps in solving problems, such as mathematics or understanding words.

Another key to developing your children's self-esteem is acknowledging their self-worth. Self-worth refers to things we have come to believe about our importance and value. If children don't have feelings of self-worth, they're less resilient in facing adversity, and they have trouble solving problems out in the world. Effectively helping your children develop their self-worth demands that you help them maximize all their distinctive gifts and qualities—and let them know that they do matter in their family and in society.

The following exercise is one you can do with your children. It is designed to help your children acknowledge their gifts and their importance in your family. Have each of your children fill out the following form and display it in their rooms. That way, they can see the positive and affirming foundations of who they have become. By taking your children through this kind of exercise, it forces them to objectify themselves in such a way that they consciously acknowledge their worth and value.

My best talents and skills are:

My best school subjects are:

My best physical qualities are:

My best accomplishments are:

My best relationship skill (e.g., making friends) is:

My best problem-solving occurs when:

I look the best when I wear:

My best friends like my:

My friends think I:

My family thinks my talents are:

I excel in:

People can depend on me to:

I've made the following positive contributions to the family:

I've made a positive impression on my teachers by:

The following family members have expressed their love for me:

Other members of my community (e.g., religious group, teachers, uncles and aunts, etc.) have told me how much they appreciate me, including:

The following people have told me they respect me:

I feel worthy of love and respect because:

Social Confidence

As I said in Chapter 1, one of the greatest mistakes children make is to compare their private reality with the "reality" others exhibit, and as a result, they come away feeling socially and comparatively inferior. As you increase your family's connectedness and peace and decrease conflict by better managing the parenting-style and child-type combinations, expect to see greater confidence on the part of your child in the social world. When children learn how to get along socially, particularly with other children, their self-confidence is increased, and they learn about values such as loyalty, supportiveness, compassion and empathy—all very powerful strengths. Here are other ways you can help enhance your children's social confidence:

- Teach your child about socially acceptable values and actions, such as being patient while other kids receive attention, taking turns and sharing toys. Children who snatch toys or don't know how to share often have trouble making friends.
- Make sure your child has a plan for social situations. Discuss and role-play what to do in a new situation: for example, how to get involved in a game or conversation, how to participate in a project or how to start a conversation. Make sure your child has a preset plan to strike up a conversation, which can be an effective tool for success in social interactions.
- Have your child use mental rehearsal as a way to prepare for social challenges. Mental rehearsal builds self-confidence and self-assurance. I would suggest mental rehearsals such as the following:

Situation: Dealing with a Bully

- Have your child imagine in his or her mind's eye his or her worst experience with a bully. Then ask your child to describe that experience to you.
- Have a creative discussion about what options he/she may have in coping with the situation. You may even role-play each circumstance.

- Have your child imagine the same situation and the outcome, using one of the options both of you considered. Next, repeat this imagery exercise with another optional response and get your child to talk about how he/she feels in terms of self-confidence. Repeat this process until your child has at least three optional responses that provide a sense of mastery.

Mental rehearsal and imagery can be used for any number of social challenges, such as coping with an unfair event against your child, handling an embarrassing situation with the opposite sex, communicating with an older person who misunderstands him/her, interacting with an authority figure or dealing with a negotiation.

- Get your children involved in age-appropriate team sports or other group activities so they can share their interests with other kids and learn how to function in a team environment.
- Allow your kids to invite other children to your home so that they can learn positive social interactions and manners under your supervision.
- Encourage play opportunities with other children, since these experiences help children become more socially confident. They'll also develop leadership and cooperation skills.
- Teach and model for your child what healthy friendships and relationships should look and act like.

Mental and Emotional Stability

Raising an emotionally healthy child is a worthy goal, since children with mental and emotional strength do better at coping with whatever life hurls in their path. Emotionally healthy children tend to be more resilient and more able to bounce back from setbacks and disappointments. They're also more effective guardians of their authenticity. As a parent, you can help your children embrace the full continuum of emotions they will experience, from the positive to the negative, and this will help shape their outlook on life for the better. Helping your children acknowledge and deal appropriately with emotions is simply another crucial step toward developing the authenticity we talked about in Chapter 3. With that in mind, here are some steps you can take to help your children enhance their emotional well-being:

- Let your children know they are entitled to their emotions, that it's normal to feel angry, sad or frustrated and that it's okay to share these feelings. Give them the opportunity to express themselves without fear of judgment or retribution; this enhances mental and emotional stability because they have appropriate outlets. Emotional expression is healthy.
- Talk to your children about the fact that they own their feelings. Their sadness or anger is not caused by someone else. They are not mad because someone else made them mad. They're angry or sad because of how they choose to respond. Emotional responses are triggered by our interpretation—the meaning we assign to a situation—and our corresponding reaction to that interpretation. In other words, our emotions flow from the meaning we attach to situations. By helping your children understand this connection, you can help your kids become more accountable for how they react to stressful situations and problems in their lives. Whatever the situation, they can choose their reactions.
- Respect your children's need to grieve, be sad or joyful or to cry in privacy.
- As in almost every aspect of purposeful parenting, you must model good emotional and mental stability. All eyes are on you, particularly in times of stress or crisis. Be a role model your children will remember—how strong you were, how resilient you were, how you held things together when life seemed like it was breaking apart.
- Encourage your children to articulate the different emotions that they have experienced, and teach them coping skills for managing different emotions. You might try the following exercise with them:

Which of the following emotions have you felt over the last six months?

Anger	Happiness	Fear	Contentment	Joy
Dread	Excitement	Frustration	Concern	Panic
Contentment	Satisfaction	Pleasure	Irritation	Pressure
Sorrow	Intimidation	Worry	Sadness	Terror

In what situations have you experienced these emotions?

_____

_____

_____

How have you handled them and how do you feel about the ways you have managed yourself?

Relaxation strategies?

Distraction?

Reading books?

Negotiation?

Humor?

Taking a break?

Playing games?

Playing/listening to music?

Talking it out?

• Help your child explore aggressive emotional reactions, such as the desire to harm another person or an animal. Show your child how it would be helpful to channel those feelings into positive actions. For example:

Instead of harming another . . .	Find a minimal effective response that would suffice for the same feeling, such as writing a letter.
Instead of revenge . . .	Find pleasure in self-approval.
Instead of feeling victimized . . .	Take control of his or her own feelings.

Spiritual Growth

You'll discover that as you establish a harmonious rhythm in your family and reduce the conflict in your home, your child will be quieter on the inside and better able to rise above the noise of the world. As this happens and your child matures, consider more spiritual topics. Spiritual growth or maturity is a complex and sophisticated journey, one that can go on for the entire span of our lives. Even so, here are some things you can do to help your children begin to develop a deeper spiritual focus, whether your definition of "spiritual" is a relationship with God or other concept of higher power, or simply transcending day-to-day existence:

- Create within your home the symbolism and ethics of your spirituality or religion. For example, use religious symbols as a part of your decor as well as in your practice of parenting.
- Practice your religion as a model for your child; go to your church, your temple, mosque or natural place of spiritual inspiration. Participating in spiritual traditions and rituals gives your children a sense of being a part of something greater and more meaningful than themselves.
- Study the principles of your faith so your child can understand your role in it and choose to follow your values accordingly. Show your children that spirituality can be a powerful source of peace and strength.
- Pray or meditate with your child. Teaching children how to be still and listen to their hearts or to the depths of God will strengthen their sense of peace and integrity.

THE UNDERLYING FAMILY CONNECTION

There is one more piece to all of this that cannot be measured, scored or counted, yet it must be taken very, very seriously: the love and nurturing you bring to everything I've offered here. Children who grow up in a secure and loving relationship with their parents tend to be smarter and more resilient; of that there's no doubt. You can play all the word games you want with your kids, spend money on music lessons, and work on emotionality with them, but none of it means much unless it happens with the right spirit, the spirit that says you love and value your children and believe in them. When children feel this from you, they flourish.

Part Two

7 TOOLS FOR PURPOSEFUL PARENTING

7

Tool 1:
Parenting with Purpose

Define Success

Children are one third of our population and all of our future.
—SELECT PANEL FOR THE PROMOTION OF CHILD HEALTH, 1981

One of the most important and exciting decisions you can make as a parent is to define success goals for your child. Success goals are tools that serve as guidance systems for parents and their children. Once you decide on the goals that will serve as the measure of your child's success, those goals will help you make decisions throughout the child's trip to adulthood.

Much like the navigational system in a car that keeps you on track to your favorite vacation spot, success goals help you get where you want to go and make the trip a whole lot more fun. Raising children isn't just a job, it's an adventure. The objectives for this chapter are:

1. To give you some steps for identifying your and your child's specific goals.
2. To begin a plan to successfully accomplish those goals.
3. To take responsibility to be accountable for those goals as a responsible parent.

Choosing, communicating and pursuing clear and age-appropriate goals for your child will give them a sense of purpose that brings them the experience of mastering their world as they achieve the designated benchmarks in their life. It will also bond you and your child, bringing you together and energizing you both. Everyone loves success! A goal is different from starry-eyed dreaming of greatness and fame. A goal is realistic. It is measurable. And it can be clearly monitored day in and day out. It is a point of clarity in what are sometimes messy, noisy and crazy lives. Goals, clear objectives and the plans for attaining them can contribute mightily to the rhythm I talked about in Chapter 3. As the leader of the pack, you must make sure you are parenting with a purpose. Your hands are on the steering wheel of the old "Wally wagon." Your decisions must be guided by the plan and made as a parent who wants the best for your child. The only way you can evaluate the choices that confront you every day is if you know exactly what you want for your child.

As the driver, you have to know your goal so well that you can automatically envision the final destination as if it were a bright red X on a crystal clear map. Your first turn out of the driveway and onto the road of your child's life sets you off in the direction of that big red X because that's where you want to take your child, and it is where the child has been passionately inspired to go. That should be an easy sell, by the way, if you have properly set the goals by making sure they are based on your child's unique skills, abilities and interests and not just your own.

For the rest of the trip, every turn you make can be evaluated and designed to move you and your child closer to your agreed-upon destination. If your destination is due south, you don't get on the east-west tollway. You stay on course. The same holds true as you lead your child toward your shared vision of success. As the responsible adults in the driver's seat, you as a parent stay focused on that clear objective, mentally and spiritually. You do all that you can to keep your child moving toward it in a world full of distractions and temptations.

Every decision, every turn you take on this trip must be made with the ultimate destination—your shared vision of success—in mind. Parents can't go to sleep at the wheel or they'll put everyone else in danger. You've got to stay alert for obstacles. You've got to keep those you love on course.

TAKE A MOMENT

Sometimes it can help to step back and just think about the big picture and your own success. One of the ultimate measures of your success in life will be how good a job you do in raising your children. That's not a burden or some cross to bear. It is one of the great blessings and joys that life has to offer. There is nothing in this world like seeing your children successfully take their first steps, discover their talents and thrive at something that fulfills them.

That's why it is so important to start out with specific and detailed visions of what a successful child means to you and your loved ones. That clarity will keep you from wasting time and energy. And most important, you want your children to one day sit before you and say, "Mom, Dad, thank you for guiding me through the maze. Thanks for not believing my lies when I was fourteen and foolish. Thank you for making me do right and realize my potential. Thanks for modeling passion and commitment and a loving and caring spirit."

If you don't have a plan, I can promise you with equal assurance that things can and will get ugly in a hurry. But you won't make wrong turns if you always have that clear vision in raising children.

Help Your Child Achieve Personal Goals

If you were headed somewhere important like, for example, a hospital when your child was gravely ill, you wouldn't just get into the car and start randomly driving around in hopes that you would run into a doctor or a hospital before the worst happened. What kind of parent—or person—would take a chance like that? That is the same situation you are in now as you are confronted with the responsibility of raising your children.

You've got to have a plan that will help guide you through all of the distractions and temptations and general messiness of life. One of my goals as a parent was to help my children achieve their own goals while pursuing their own passions. I don't want my boys to just be another me, and Robin doesn't want them to be carbon copies of her either. They are two terrific young men, and we are getting great kicks out of discovering them and watching them grow and develop as individuals.

In certain areas, I am so different from my two sons it's hard for me to believe that we share any DNA at all. I am a softy when it comes to critters of all kinds. I'm an "all creatures great and small" kind of guy. But I also realize that there are legitimate and purposeful reasons for things like deer hunting, which helps control the herd population and prevents the weaker animals from suffering and starving. Still, I have no interest in shooting a deer. I'm no outdoorsman. My idea of roughing it is watching a big-screen TV inside a fully equipped RV. Nonetheless, I felt like I

should expose my sons to hunting, fishing and camping so they could decide for themselves if it appealed to them.

For ten years, I regularly went hunting with the boys. I intentionally
never shot to hit anything other than a can or a rock. But we had a lot of
fun and, as it turned out, my older son Jay absolutely loved it. He became
an amazing marksman and hunter, and he competes in a major bass tour-
nament every year. Jordan, Jay's younger brother, turned out to be pretty
much like me. He has no more interest in hunting or fishing than I do.
That's okay. My goal was to expose them to things that might stimulate
them, whether I was interested in those activities or not.

A successful parent helps children find their unique gifts and talents.
This may mean that you'll have to sit through recitals and soccer
matches, and muster enthusiasm for stamp collections and the complete
recordings of the Insane Maniacs of Rock. But I guarantee that along the
way you will laugh and experience closeness to your child that will last a
lifetime. And, believe me, there is no greater gift you can give your children than introducing them to their life's passions. Jordan recently had a
career-day field trip at his high school. He absolutely loves music and was
fortunate to get to go to a recording studio here in Los Angeles. Because
the man who runs the music company is a father and a softy, Jordan left
there with a pile of CDs, not one of which was by anybody I had ever
heard of. He was so excited to get all of that new music that he was wired
for hours that night. He wanted me to listen to first one band and then
another. He played his favorite songs for me from each CD. I'm sorry, and
I *don't* want to sound like my dad, but I would just as soon have been listening to three idiots banging garbage can lids together. But, you know
what, there wasn't another place in this world I would rather have been
than in his room listening to that "music" for several hours. We laughed,
we talked, we each rolled our eyes and made fun of the other's music. In
short, I got to share in his passion and be a part of his excitement on that
day. It was a privilege, and it was an honor. I hope to do it again and
again and again. I wasn't there for the music; I was there for my son. (I
have to confess, I did hear a few that were just pretty darn good. God
help me, but I do love that Kid Rock!)

Benjamin West was a great American painter of historical scenes and
portraits and was one of the leading artists in the nineteenth century.
When he was a very young boy, West decided to paint a picture of his sister while his mother was out of the house. He got out bottles of ink and

started, but soon, no surprise, ink was everywhere. His mother came home to the mess and was not pleased. But before she could scold her son, she saw the portrait he'd made. The mess was instantly forgotten in light of the beauty created. The mother picked up the portrait and declared to her son, "What a beautiful picture of your sister!" Then she kissed him.

Later in life Benjamin West wrote: "With that kiss I became a painter." Maybe with that night Jordan and I spent together, he became a musician. That frankly wouldn't be my first choice, but if it's his first passion, I am totally all over it. Remember, goals; your definition of success for your child must reflect your child's interest, skills and abilities, not just yours.

Putting Plans into Action

West's mother knew instinctively the importance of that moment. But we can't all rely on instinct. More and more it's obvious to me that today's busy parents need to set specific definitions for success with their children. I was amazed at the results of the survey we conducted with the parents we polled from across the nation. Many parents confessed that they had no clue about what goals they should set for their children. They claimed to be too busy to bother with plans. They were caught up in their jobs and the whirlwind pace of modern life. Some said their children set their own goals. One after another, the parents we interviewed offered a multitude of excuses for not doing the most important job they'll ever be given. It told me something too when I saw that 25 percent admitted their primary goal was to create a teenager who would just stay out of trouble. Five percent said they had goals, but only in the vaguest terms, such as "I want my children to be happy."

> **Survey Fact:**
> **The two top challenges for parents are making punishment work and improving school performance.**

Reading the results of that survey made me want to drive door-to-door across America, shake every one of those parents by the shoulders and shout: "Wake up!" Obviously, we need greater dialogue about the incredible importance of setting well-defined parental goals for children and specific steps for achieving those goals. My college football coach drilled that same sort of message through our helmets and into our thick heads every day before we left the locker room: "It's one thing to talk a good game, it's another thing to do it."

Mythical Goals: Beware

Before I get to some truly specific goals, let's define what I mean by vague goals. Take "happiness," for example, as in "I just want my children to be happy." I hear this all the time from parents and it makes me crazy.

Happiness is an *emotional* state. It's not a goal. Emotional states change with the weather, with your hormones, your bank balance or the last episode of *Friends*. If you base your goals on an emotional state, I advise you to strap yourself in and keep your arms and elbows inside the roller-coaster car because you are in for one scary ride. And so is your child. How do you define "happiness" anyway? Is it a warm and fuzzy feeling? A belly laugh? A hearty chuckle? A satisfying feeling of a job well done? These are all good experiences to have, but they are not specific enough to define success in your child's life.

Happiness can be a by-product of some achievement in your life, or it may come in the aftermath of some struggle or sadness. You can't use something so ambiguous as a goal for your child. I'd rather see you tap frustration as a goal than happiness. At least frustration is an emotion that drives you to take action and move ahead. In fact, irritation is the major source of motivation among all species.

Another mythical goal that drives me up the wall: the jaw-dropping concept of the "convenient child." Time and again, parents tell me: "I just don't want any more problems with her." Having a convenient child who always does everything right and never causes problems is the *last* thing you should set as a parental goal, unless you are a Stepford wife. There is no such thing as a flesh-and-blood convenient child. When parents tell me that their child never causes any problems two images come to mind:

- The Robot
- The Quiet Beast

The Robot child makes no decisions for itself. Robo-Kid only follows the rules while trying to hide from the world. What sane parent wants such a child? A child who never crosses the line will never experience an authentic life. Soldiers march. Children scamper. Sometimes motivating your children will be as frustrating as trying to herd chickens. They'll be off in one direction and then another. There may be times when your goal is one of simple containment. That's okay; a child without curiosity, a child without energy may be convenient, but that's not what you want. You want a child who is curious and energetic, a child who colors outside the lines as well as inside the lines. You want a child who is a unique being pursuing unique interests.

The Quiet Beast is the kid who pulls the fire alarm when the teacher leaves the room. It's Eddie Haskell from *Leave It to Beaver*. Or Beavis and Butt-head masquerading as the Olsen Twins. Every generation and every group of teens has Quiet Beasts. In mine, it was the PK—the preacher's kid. The minister's daughter grew up bowing to her father's strict rules of conduct. She was required to be a convenient child to preserve his standing in the religious community. But when her teenage hormones started to rage, the Quiet Beast was unleashed. She broke every rule in the Good Book. Another myth that clueless parents have about goals for their children is that "Nature will take its course." This myth sometimes is translated also as "God will decide what is best for my child." I've got my own translation. This myth is really about the parents refusing to take responsibility. Yes, there is always the possibility that a child will find his or her own path to an authentic and fulfilling life. But it is the parents' responsibility to serve as each child's guide and protector on this good earth. Alexander Hamilton and Abraham Lincoln grew up without much parental involvement. But the same was true of Saddam Hussein and Adolf Hitler.

Loving parents choose to take responsibility for their child's direction in life. You must determine both the path and the destination for the adult you are raising, or prepare yourself to deal with potentially disastrous consequences down the road. As you learn more about your child, as your child learns more about himself or herself, you become partners in defining success in life—and in designing the plans for pursuing it. Until then it is your job and you need to do it.

Parenting by Design

Now I'm going to equip you with at least the basics of a guidance system for parenting. It is based on the concept of an operational definition of goals. Big words, simple idea. Parents need to discipline themselves before they can discipline their children. One of the most important parental self-disciplines is forcing yourself to move from the general to the specific. Rather than saying, "I just want little Susie to be happy," you need to define clearly what sort of happiness you are talking about. Happy as in giddy with laughter? Or happy as in living an authentic and fulfilling life? Does happiness mean that little Susie has good friends, close family or an outstanding academic record? Maybe it's all of the above. Whatever the heck it is, the parents need to define it so they can cut a path to it and know it when Susie's got it. Get it? Dr. Stephen Covey coined a good name for this concept. He called it "beginning with the end in mind." That's exactly what you have to do. First you decide what your destination will be, and then you look for the best route to get there.

The second step in this process is to be able to articulate that destination and measure your progress toward it. It never fails when I try to teach this concept that some goofy parents will decide they aren't going anywhere. "We just want to stay put with little Sammy." Their goal is apparently maintaining the status quo. They've given up on any higher aspirations for Sammy. They've decided he'll never be a National Honor Society member or a McDonald's All-Star or a Juilliard candidate. So they've adopted the turtle's tactics. They are pulling all exposed limbs into the shell and just hoping that Sammy reaches the age of eighteen without hurting himself or others. In other words, their goal is containment.

This is also known as a "not" goal. And it's *not* a good idea. Any goal that contains a "not" doesn't work over the long term. Negativity is rarely a positive. There is no such thing as not doing something. The brain doesn't process negative instruction as a goal. Here's an example: Try *not* thinking of a blue elephant. Amazed, aren't you?

When you set a goal of not doing something, it has no meaning because there is no way to measure that which is not present. Not being a drunk, not being a drug addict and not being a prostitute are *not* goals. So it makes sense to state your parenting goals in positive, declarative statements that can be objectively measured.

There's another advantage to doing this. Clear guidelines make it much easier for your children to make their own decisions and, in the process, develop their problem-solving skills while using your criteria. If you were walking across the desert and you wanted to make certain that you were following the straightest path to the oasis and not going miles out of your way, you would instinctively pick out some palm tree or boulder to serve as a reference point, right? So will your children, as long as they are given a clear destination. And that is what parenting with purpose is all about.

Parenting with purpose is a long and challenging trek, it's not a frantic, mad dash. It's not about where your child's developmental progress stands this afternoon or tomorrow. It's about the type of adult your offspring becomes ten or fifteen years down the path. Getting to adulthood as a self-contained, authentic and fulfilled individual with sound morals and values requires making thoughtful decisions step-by-step, hour-by-hour while never losing sight of the guidelines or the long-term objective.

One more thing. This process that you and your children are going through? It's called *life*. As difficult as it may be and as rough as the ride may get, I encourage you to savor every moment, laugh together at every opportunity and always express your love for one another whenever you can.

Taking Measure

Most adults have a basic grasp of goal-setting, but sometimes they need ways to measure and monitor their child's progress. I have designed a short audit to stimulate your thinking about the goals you want to set for your child. Take a minute for this short questionnaire to see where you are and where you need to be.

Circle one of the two descriptions from each row:

Your goal is trying to deal with each crisis as it happens.	You are achieving at least one step toward a goal every day.
You feel that you are happy if the kids don't create a crisis today.	You feel some accomplishment if you can see some steps toward a goal today, even if there is a crisis, because there are times when crisis serves as a step.
You think a goal is to keep your child from causing a disruption in your plans.	You feel that if your child doesn't create a challenge that you are not fulfilling a goal of expression and authenticity.

You want your child just to be quiet and accept your rules with no question.

You encourage your child to ask questions, even if they challenge your ideas.

Your motto is "Children should be seen but not heard."

Your motto is "Children grow into life by being respected and acknowledged."

You had the idea that your child would be a source of glue for the family.

You had the idea that your child should receive your attention for his or her individual abilities and interests.

You are committed to controlling, directing and maintaining an environment that is described as excellent by your ideals or some other authority, like your own parents, social group or community.

You are committed to the protection, socialization and authentic development of your child, regardless of the external sources that might define these for you.

You have not defined what your goals for your child are, other than to get them through their teens without drugs, pregnancy or flunking out of school.

You have definite goals for your child, such as learning empathy, finding resources and personal goals or working toward discovering skills for success.

Your usual goal for the day is to have the child complete his or her assigned tasks and stay out of your way.

Your usual goal for the day is to see some learning in your child about himself or herself that promotes better understanding of abilities or insight in the world.

Scoring: If you circled ANY of the items on the left, I want you to decide immediately to develop a plan with specific goals. For each item you circled on the left, add 10 percent to the probability that you will have major problems with your child by the time of seventeen.

If you notice, the items on the left are descriptive of those behaviors that do not immediately and deliberately lead to goals of success for your children. Those on the right confirm that you are on course toward your goals. It might be helpful for you to retake this little exercise every week or so to monitor your progress.

Finding Appropriate Goals

Goal selection is a personal process in which the parents must collaborate and agree. I won't decree a one-life-fits-all master plan for every parent and child in the land. Each blessed young person has unique needs, talents and visions, and we should be grateful for that diversity of passions. Rather than setting out a master plan, I'm only going to offer two possible goals as examples, with the recommendation that you consider them for your top ten guidelines because they are so important. They are:

- *Socialization*
- *Authenticity*

Socialization

Socialization involves finding your place in the flow of life. It's not about going along to get along, it's about learning to swim with both the sharks and the dolphins, and the occasional piranha—all the fish up and down the food chain. It's about learning to be successful in this mad, mad, mad and wonderful world. As I have said in *Life Strategies*, people either get it or they don't. But as a parent, you have the responsibility to teach your child *what* to get. There is a learning curve. Socialization is not mastered in an hour at the dinner table. There are objective, measurable steps— smaller goals as stepping-stones—that need to be mastered along the way. Let's take a look at them.

Learning to be a responsible citizen. For a small child, this process begins with the understanding that, as sad and shocking as it may be, the universe does not revolve around him or her. Each of us, at some point, has to deal with the humbling fact that we are part of something bigger. The goal for a small child would be to understand the needs of the larger group. Later, the parent's goal should be to teach the child to take responsibility for contributing to the welfare of the whole group, providing leadership and expertise when needed. Some recommended activities that teach citizen skills are:

- Volunteer work. Regardless of how old your child is, there are always volunteer jobs for cleaning up the environment, taking care of animals, going on errands for the sick and a thousand valuable tasks through your church, civic center or Scouts.
- Work for a political campaign. It doesn't make any difference which candidate or party, as long as the child gets some understanding of the responsibilities in our political system.
- Talk to the people who are trying to make a difference in the world, the heads of organizations who have a missionary focus, such as the Peace Corps, Special Olympics, ecology groups, animal rights or anyone who needs help.

Learning how to work in harmony with other people. Sooner or later, we all have to learn to play well with others. We've got to share toys and take turns. Parents begin this process of socialization by guiding their children to scoot over on the play rug and not eat all the cookies. Having your child serve the greater good by providing the cookies at some point is a helpful goal too. Later steps would include participation in team activities and democratic processes and creating game plans in cooperation with others to achieve objectives—as long as it doesn't involve soaping the windows of the principal's house. I am concerned about children being overscheduled by their parents simply to keep them busy and out of the parents' hair, so these recommendations come with the caveat that parents should be involved too, and the child should still have plenty of free time to practice that truly important art of just being a kid. Some recommendations for activities for your child might be:

- Forming an informal club or group of children to play together, going to the zoo or on field trips and going to cultural events. These activities would bring your child into contact with sharing and cooperation.
- Have a neighborhood project like a lemonade stand, a talent show, an original play performance or a clean-up-the-block project organized and conducted solely by young people.

- Create a band. This activity may sound strange, but it is surprising what will happen if you get some old rhythm instruments, like drums and cans, and get them to make some noise. Who knows? But it is amazing what they learn.

Developing intimate and trusting relationships. Hopefully, your child learns very early on to trust family members and extended family members, but it is also important to show how there are many levels of intimacy and trust in the wider circles of friends, acquaintances and strangers on the street. Parents can begin this process by showing a child how even board games are based on trusting that the other players will follow the same rules. Later, children need to become comfortable with sharing their inner emotions at appropriate times, and they need to be taught to respect the feelings of others.

These activities might be helpful in your initial planning for this arena:

- Go on a campout, especially if it is an organized plan. In the unprotected environment away from the city, kids begin to understand trust on a survival basis.
- Create simple contracts with your kids. This will start an understanding of trust and commitment.
- Talk, talk, talk. The more dialogue in a family, the more the child begins to understand others' motives and plans. Don't underestimate the value of listening to discussions and opinions. Children may not understand all the complexities, but they begin to understand attitudes.

Learning to pay attention. Watching and learning from others is a critical goal for your child's socialization. By paying attention to another child's efforts to properly hold a pencil or solve a puzzle, your child learns to advance her or his own learning curve through observation. The parent can help develop this socialization skill by simply pointing out the successes and the mistakes of others as lessons to be noted. I have found the following activities to be helpful in this dimension:

- Introduce your child to some heroes in real time. Professional sports figures and media stars love the attention, especially by children and teen fans. Kids get a close-up of real achievers who know something.

- Talk about, read and listen to biographical sketches of successful people. These might include ancestors, like grandparents or great-grandparents who achieved success in some endeavor. Have them check out the website for the Horatio Alger Association, www.horatioalger.org, which is full of great rags-to-riches stories about real people, some of whom they may know.

- Take them to workplaces and let them observe. My favorite suggestion is a used car dealership, but drugstores and post offices are fun as well. Teach them to people-watch and to converse with all types of people. I had a boyhood friend who we often teased because he could talk to adults at a level that none of the rest of us could match. We didn't see it as a gift at the time, more of an oddity. But that friend turned out to be a huge success because he had the ability to talk to people from all walks of life and all ages. Encourage this in your children by exposing them to a wide variety of people and model it for them by engaging with all sort of folks yourself.

Authenticity

Authenticity is fostered when you set goals suited to the youngster's interests, abilities and talents. While Jay took to hunting like a bird dog to water, Jordan couldn't care less about outdoor sports. But as I said, early on we saw that he was drawn to music. Where that interest came from is a mystery to me. I'm not just tone-deaf, I'm musically impaired. Church deacons invite everyone in the congregation to sing, "except Phil, of course." I'd never held a guitar until we bought one for Jordan. When he took it in hand that first time, I swear, fireworks went off and angels that looked like Willie Nelson strummed on harps. The kid absolutely lit up. Now he has a band. The flicker has become a flame. It's all about the goal of helping our children discover and pursue their individual passions. Every parent has to be sensitive to their child's individual needs and sense of self in doing that, but here are basic and objective steps that can be followed. They'll serve as measures of progress.

Teach them who they are. In order for you to understand your child's talents and abilities, you have to open many doors for them. Be willing to expose your child to varied types of music, sporting events, art, science, business, books, cars and cooking. Get your child out of the house and away from the television, home computer and video games. You don't accomplish this goal in a couple weekends. It can be exciting for both of you, because at some point a light will go off and together you will begin to discover your child's unique gifts and interests. Prepare to be surprised.

As an animal-hugging, tin-eared father with one son who is an outdoorsman and another who is a rock 'n' roller, I've certainly had my share of surprises. To raise an authentic adult, you have to encourage your child to discover and embrace those unique talents and interests.

Teach your child that life ultimately rewards the pursuit of authenticity. One of the great responsibilities you have as a parent—and one of the greatest gifts you can give your children—is to teach them to develop their gifts fully and to build their lives around whatever it is that fulfills them. You may not have any desire to go anywhere near an opera performance, but if your little girl has an inner diva, you'd darn well better check out *Madame Butterfly*. Teach your child that the world has a place for all sorts of interests, talents, knowledge and experience. It's important that we show our young people all the possible ways of creating fulfillment in their unique lives. Getting paid to do what you love to do is just one way of succeeding, but there are other currencies. Self-acceptance, approval by others whom you respect and making a difference in people's lives all generate emotional reward that are like money in the bank, maybe better. A child needs to learn that personal passions may or may not be rewarded or accepted as initially valid by the external world, but being true to yourself will ultimately pay off.

Allow your child to set personal goals within the framework of the goals you set for them. You don't want your child to grow up and become an unguided missile. It's important that your adult in progress learns to set their own goals. Whether it is mastering a new song on the guitar or bicycling a little faster down a track, allow your child to set personal goals to cultivate both authenticity and confidence and to develop internal frames of reference too.

Clear a path that encourages self-discovery. While your ultimate parenting goal is to give your child the opportunity to explore and develop his or her own unique gifts fully, it's also your job to equip your child with filters for the barrage of outside stimuli. There is a lot of noise out there, folks. Consumer product companies spend trillions of dollars trying to convince your child that life has no meaning without Nintendo or MTV or computers. You have to help them stave off the retail roar from advertisements, television, radio shows, music lyrics and movies. Teach your children that this Bud definitely isn't for them. Help them analyze media messages so that they learn to distinguish hype from reality. Teach them to guard their own interests. Sharks come in many forms. From rent-to-own companies and paycheck advance outfits that charge exorbitant rates to car dealers that slip hidden fees into the final bill, they are out there in the water.

The Goals Revisited

There is no doubt that all parents want their children to be loving, caring, motivated and honest. Every thoughtful parent wants his or her children to grow up with integrity, a good work ethic, a caring heart and the desire to make a difference in some way. But as I've tried to make clear, it is your responsibility as a parent to set much more specific goals and develop a plan for your child. I've put together a worksheet to help you get started. On it, write down a maximum of three goals that both parents understand and agree upon. Work backward from destination to starting point by first determining the ultimate result or vision you seek for your child. Then look at what smaller, more specific goals will move your child toward that ultimate goal. Next, break these more specific goals down to behaviors that can be observed. The last step for this chapter will be to write down some steps you can take today, in a week and in a month to achieve these goals.

1. Ultimate results or vision for your child: _____

Goals to achieve result or vision:_____

Steps toward that goal: 1. _____

2. _____

3. _____

2. Ultimate result or vision for your child: _____

Goals to achieve result or vision: _____

Steps toward that goal: 1. _____

2. _____

3. _____

3. Ultimate result or vision for your child: _____

Goals to achieve result or vision _____

Steps toward that goal: 1. _____

2. _____

3. _____

Checklist

Goal-setting requires more than wishful thinking. It is a daily monitoring process in which both you and your child participate. There will be times of absolute hair-pulling frustration as you miss some targets, and there will be times of jump-up-and-down celebration in which you delight in your child's achievements and growth. And you'll be surprised at how much you grow as well by being an active goal-setting parent fully engaged in your plan for a successful child. Their success is your success.

8

Tool 2:
Parenting with Clarity

Talk, Listen and Learn

If you don't talk to your kid about the little stuff,
they won't talk to you about the big stuff.
— JAY MCGRAW

Most of us got our first lesson on the importance of communication from our parents as we were growing up: "The good Lord gave you two ears and just one mouth." The not-so-subtle message of that old saw is that listening is twice as important as talking. Once again, an age-old parental catchphrase proves out, both practically and scientifically, and suggests a tool that must be employed if you're to achieve your goal of creating a phenomenal family. I'm talking about communication, including but not limited to the instructive kind that can be used for teaching, problem-solving and raising your children in such a way that they'll become successful adults. This tool is based on the principle that communication between parents and their children is essential for building and maintaining a loving and productive relationship.

I've really fretted here over how best to communicate about communication. It's a challenge because "communication" is probably the most overused and poorly understood concept in all of human functioning. It's become what I call a wastebasket catchphrase. No matter what the problem is between two people, it always gets described as a "breakdown in communication." I'm not even sure what breakdown in communication means, but I'm absolutely certain you don't want your family to suffer it. As I've said, one of your jobs as a parent is to successfully socialize your child. If you can't talk to him in a way that he'll hear—and hear him in the way he talks—you won't succeed in that socialization process. My objective here is to equip you with a working knowledge of how to connect with your child. To do that you must know where the pitfalls are, and I'm going to show you precisely how to make this all-important connection through specific action-oriented communication skills. But first, before anything else happens, you have to get your mind right and approach this with a really good, open attitude or we'll just be wasting our time by embracing hollow behaviors. Having an open attitude begins with committing to being a good listener. Whether your child is three years old, seventeen years old or anyplace in between, you have to be willing to react to her point of view in a way that makes her feel good about having opened up to you.

You can have just that effect by learning to really tune in and receive the messages sent. There are a few secrets to convincing your child you're tuned in. Think about it this way: Talking, seeking to convey a message and communicating in any fashion is a behavior, and all behavior is motivated. Whenever a child says or does something that is communicative, he's doing it for a reason. Rather than just listen to the words being spoken, you have to "listen" for the need driving the communication. Your child will only communicate with you if that behavior is rewarded by your reacting in a way that the child perceives as meeting her need. You don't necessarily have to agree with what's being expressed, because your agreement or compliance is very likely not the kid's primary goal in engaging you. In fact, as strange as it may seem, children of all ages tell us that often they don't expect or even want you to agree, concede, fix the problem or give permission. Sometimes, they just want to vent, to feel like they've made their case or just have you to talk to about things that are of interest to them. Whatever the content, they want to know that you think they're important enough to be listened to in a serious way. By the way, this is true for children of all ages.

An example: One night during my junior year in high school, my friend John came by at about six o'clock to pick me up for an out-of-town high school basketball game. It was the dead of winter. There'd been a pretty bad ice storm that had moved in. The distance to the neighboring community was only thirty miles, but he felt like we needed to start early because the roads were so treacherous. John's parents had told him to be careful. When we went downstairs to announce our plans to my parents, my dad threw up a huge stop sign. "Just hold on there," he said. "You aren't going anywhere on these icy roads. There's no way I'm letting you get on the highway under these conditions. Ain't happening, you aren't going anywhere, end of story." I actually thought he had a pretty good point, but since my friend was already there and ready to go, I argued my case vigorously. I was glad my dad didn't relent. When we went back upstairs and took off our coats, I could see that John was really upset. I told him that I was sorry to ruin our plans and that I understood if he wanted to go on without me. He looked at me through tear-filled eyes (an amazingly rare occurrence for a tough guy like John) and said, "I wish my parents cared enough about me to tell me I couldn't go. They wouldn't care if I drove straight off a cliff." It struck me that though John had asked his parents for permission to go to the game, what he had really needed was for them to provide some boundaries and leadership. I had a need to make my case, but I was relieved when my parents refused to buy into it.

Children need to feel that they have certain power and influence within the framework of the boundaries you've created in your family. They really don't want to run things; they just want to feel like they have input and hopefully sometimes get their way. The primary way to promote that feeling is to give them your full, undistracted attention and weigh very carefully what they're seeking to convey. Again, listening, really listening, is the key.

Making sure that your children see that *they* are being heard is extremely important in ensuring *you* too will be heard. Bottom line: You have to listen to be heard. Children don't tune into the messages of their parents unless they believe that their parents truly hear and understand their concerns and needs. Think about it: If your children believe you really understand their positions because you have listened to them, whatever response you then give becomes highly relevant because it's tied directly to their message. Alternatively, if they believe you haven't really heard their position, whatever you have to say becomes irrelevant. Let me put it another way: Kids don't want to hear a bunch of random preaching that you were spring-loaded to give before they ever opened their mouth. What they do want to hear and are willing to hear is your response to *their* position and message. The *consequence* of not responding to what they're saying, or more accurately, the need they're expressing, will be frustration, anger and relationships marked by resentment and disconnection. Shouting and slammed doors or silence are pretty good clues that that is where you are. The good news is that the basic human need to be heard is so strong that a relationship can be renewed with improved communication. If you and your child are disconnected, it's not too late. Listening and really hearing and responding to your child is the key. Don't just go through the motions here. Resolve to genuinely listen and treat your child and his or her point of view with dignity and respect. Turning off the television, stopping other activities and giving your child your unhurried and undivided attention speaks volumes to your child about how important he or she really is. Children know the difference between real and fake.

It is up to you to define—or as the case may be, redefine—your relationship as nurturing and open. You can't wait for your child to turn the corner. Sure, your efforts may be met with suspicion at first, but you have to be patient and persistent as you seek to redefine this part of your relationship. It's not enough that you just resolve to have a new, open-minded position; you have to declare it and then show it once you get into an exchange. Children often feel that their parents don't recognize or give them credit for the fact that they're maturing and growing mentally and emotionally. They also feel that if they have violated a parent's trust in the past, they're doomed to serve a life sentence. If you expect them to really plug in to you, you must assure them it's a new day. Let them know that they do have a chance to redefine themselves in your eyes in the here and now. Getting that chip off their shoulder won't be easy, but children are both resilient and hungry for your acceptance, so you *can* get there.

So far, I've recommended that you:

- Adopt a genuinely open attitude and treat kids' communications as legitimate.
- Give your children your undivided and unhurried attention when they reach out.
- Truly listen to what they're saying so that your responses are relevant and therefore of interest.
- Listen for the underlying *need* that is motivating your child's communication.

Here are some additional tips that have proven useful in getting children to communicate:

- Embed your conversation in some activity that helps your child not to feel conspicuous or on the spot. Talk while the two of you are playing catch, playing with dolls, taking a walk or driving. But remember, your focus is on them and not the "lubricating" activity.

- Whenever possible, do a little homework so you can be up-to-date. If your child wants to talk about a certain cartoon or a particular band, take the time to actually watch or listen so you have something to offer.
- If you're having a disagreement, have the courage to state their position back to them in a fair and balanced way. You might say, "So your position is that so-and-so is correct and you feel it's only fair that you have the right to do what you want to do." Be sure not to do this sarcastically, but instead in a fairly stated fashion. This doesn't mean you do or will agree but they will know they've been heard.
- Be quick to admit any mistakes or flaws on your part.
- In every situation, find something positive to acknowledge about your child. For example, "I can see you have really thought about this carefully, which is good."
- Ask for your child's help in resolving a given situation. Make them your partner; they'll be much more likely to buy into the process.

All of these tips will help you connect with your child because they communicate that you understand and appreciate his or her feelings and that you have empathy, a quality you either have or can develop to make you more approachable and to help you relate to your child. Empathy is a personality trait that reflects maturity, caring and unselfishness. It is not the same thing as being sympathetic and it sure doesn't mean that you agree with your child's position or point of view. Sympathy is an emotion expressed when one hears about a problem and offers pity or condolence. Empathy is taking the time to really understand how the other person is feeling by putting oneself in that person's position. The willingness to walk a mile in your child's shoes can be a great gift of the heart, particularly if he or she feels alone, frustrated and misunderstood. It can help the child feel safer, more secure.

True empathy goes far beyond saying "I understand" or "I know just how you feel." To really have and communicate empathy, you must connect with your child's point of view and effectively explain to her what you believe she is feeling. This is what famous psychologist Carl Rogers referred to as a reflection of feelings. The following types of statements can help:

- You must be feeling really sad (scared, happy, excited, left out, worried etc.).
- That must have really hurt your feelings and upset you.
- You must have felt really alone.
- You must be so excited, you can hardly sit still.
- You must be really scared about what's going to happen.

These types of statements can then be followed up with similar confirming and validating observations to make the child feel like someone understands. This isn't about fixing things. It's not about going back over the facts; it's not about agreeing with or challenging and arguing the merits of the situation or coming up with a solution to fix the problem if one exists. Empathy is about truly making the effort to understand and going to the trouble of showing that you understand.

It's all about focusing on the other person's *experience* of the situation at hand. It's a way of validating another's feelings, which they have the right to. This can be very important to your child, because an empathetic acknowledgment from you can convey to them that they matter and that you've taken the time to get in touch with what they're experiencing. That kind of connection can really encourage your child to communicate without fear of judgment.

There is also a selfish motivation for putting yourself in your child's shoes. If you can understand his emotional position, you can gain powerful insights into his needs. If you can then go on to meet those needs, your child's relationship experience with you is going to be very positive—and that will lead to a stronger relationship in the future. Empathy is the opposite of emotional knee-jerking. It calls for thoughtfulness and self-control. It does not call for agreeing with the child's behavior or validating his choice. There will be time to disagree and even punish the behavior after your child knows you understand the reason for his actions.

Consider the following dialogue, which demonstrates how empathy and reflection of feeling, or their absence, works when a daughter has run away from home and ends up in police custody.

Daughter (crying): I am so sorry, Mom, I just want to come home and start over. This has been such a bad night. I'm confused, and you hurt my feelings about the report card. I just thought I would run away from it all.

Mother's Nonempathetic Response: You should be ashamed of yourself. Do you know how worried I've been about you . . . ?

Mother's Empathetic Response: You must have been really mad at me, or even mad at yourself [hugs her]. If I'd run away like that, I probably would feel like there was nothing I could say and I'd just want to escape. Is that the way you feel? Tell me this: What could you have done that might have been more useful than running away? I understand you were emotional, but don't you agree that you could have done something that might have been more constructive?

If you can show your child that you get it, she is going to be more open to accepting any help and intervention you may offer later. You'll also be demonstrating by your actions an important quality for your children to develop as they mature.

RULES OF ENGAGEMENT

Effective communication isn't just a free-for-all and it certainly isn't a no-holds-barred argument where disrespect from your children is tolerated in an effort to show you're an enlightened and modern parent. It's important to set rules, guidelines or boundaries for these interactions with your kids. My father's cornerstone rule was that I could talk until I was blue in the face as long as I didn't get disrespectful. I could argue a point for hours to try to persuade him to change his mind or do things differently. He'd let me go on until I went hoarse, but if my words, tone or attitude became less than respectful, he turned me off quickly. If that happened, I had no right to appeal. I learned quickly to make my case like a lawyer in front of a no-nonsense judge. I think he even caved in a couple of times just to reward me for making my case in a respectful way, even if he wasn't fully persuaded.

Just as my father policed my tone and attitude, you have to police your tone and attitude. You won't always get the response you want while trying to communicate with your children, but you must discipline yourself to keep trying to get your message through in the right way. Older kids are often self-conscious around adults, so they may appear to be inattentive or disinterested. Don't be intimidated or angered by eye rolling and heavy sighs. If the child sits there and refuses to engage, that doesn't mean her ears aren't working. You'd be surprised how your words will be played back in her mind later.

Often, teens just don't want to admit that their parents might be making sense. But they still listen. Sometimes you have to take what you can get. Just getting a teenager to stay in one place long enough to receive a message can pay dividends down the road. Here are some guidelines that can be particularly helpful when you're trying to get through to a child. These suggestions, when followed, have proven to be very effective in drawing children of all ages out of their shells and into an exchange:

- Approach all communications in a way that protects or enhances your child's self-esteem, even when you're in discipline mode. For example, it would be wrong to handle unacceptable academic performance by saying something like "You're lazy and irresponsible, and I'm so sick of your not doing what you're supposed to do." A better approach might be "You and I know you're capable of doing so much better. As your parent, I'd be cheating you if I allowed you not to use your wonderful mind and intelligence. Let's find a way that *you* can perform at a level that you can be proud of."

- Narrow the focus of your task-oriented communications as much as possible. Decide in advance what your objective is and don't allow yourself or your child to jump around to a number of different topics. Hopping around will just create confusion and make it difficult for you to reach a resolution. If you find yourself drifting, simply say something like "That's a discussion for another time, but right now I want us to stay sharply focused on what we came here to discuss."

- Use your communications to generate solutions rather than to relive problems. No one can change what's already happened. Problem-solving communication should be focused on moving beyond what's happened toward what you want to happen in the future. Be very specific about the behavioral changes or outcomes you expect. An admonishment to do better is not very helpful. Questions that can help you stay solution-oriented include "How can we avoid this occurring in the future?"; "What have we learned, so that we can specifically do something different next time?"; "What would have been a better approach or solution to the situation?"

- Focus on the issue at hand, and avoid personal attacks and character assassination. Stay focused on the behaviors and the consequences of the behaviors, rather than on the child and character traits such as honesty and integrity. Those traits may in fact be extremely important, but it's better to talk about how behaviors reflect on those traits, rather than questioning whether the child exhibits them. Avoid comments like "You're a liar and not trustworthy." Instead, say things like "That kind of behavior or choice reflects poorly on your honesty and integrity. If you choose differently, then others will be able to see your good qualities. I really want you to make some different choices in the future. Let's talk about what those choices might be."
- Stay in the here and now. Throwing old behaviors and circumstances in your child's face is nonproductive and will cause him or her to feel helpless. Focus on the current situation only. If you solve problems in the present, the past will seem increasingly remote and irrelevant.
- Keep your problem-solving communications and exchanges private. Don't ever take your child to task in the presence of peers, relatives or siblings, unless they're directly involved in the situation. Dressing the child down in front of others will cause humiliation, embarrassment and resentment. Even though you may feel that's not what you're doing, it might be seen very differently by the child. Take it private and keep it private.
- Conclude on a positive note. It's important for your child to feel there's an opportunity for rehabilitation and that he or she has some formula for success going forward.

Younger children can be even more difficult to communicate with because they have a smaller vocabulary and less impulse control. It's also true that they may not yet be very well socialized and usually have very little interest in any point of view other than their own. Communicating with a young child having a tantrum, for example, can be very difficult, but it is possible. Again, people in general and children in particular want to be heard. That's a universal truth even with children as young as a few years old. If a child is crying, yelling and screaming—presumably because you won't do what they want you to do or they can't have the toy they want—the quickest way to ease their pain and stop the tantrum is to let them know you understand what's upsetting them, even if you don't give in. Tantrums often start for one reason but persist for another. A tantrum may begin because the child's desires are frustrated, but it usually isn't long before the original frustration is forgotten. The child then becomes upset about being upset. If you plug in to the child at that level, and they see that you appreciate their hurt feelings and frustrations, they quickly realize they no longer need to cry, scream and yell to get you to understand. Sometimes you simply need to say, "Doggone it, that hurt your feelings, didn't it? You're really mad because you couldn't get that toy." Repeating that kind of reflective language several times can defuse a tantrum in a hurry because the child's real need was to be heard. I'm betting that you don't even almost believe me on this. But, the next time you're trying to tame a tantrum, give that approach a try. I think you'll be surprised.

TIMING IS EVERYTHING

Too often, the only communication that takes place between you and your child is when a crisis has erupted. It's important to talk about critical issues outside of stress-packed situations. The time to discuss curfew, for example, is not when the child comes home thirty minutes late. The rules should be established before the kid goes out at night. If he breaks curfew, save the discussion of consequences until the calm of the next morning when you both have clear heads. Yelling and screaming in the heat of the moment is the poorest form of communication you can practice. Sometimes when it comes to communication, timing is everything.

Also, don't restrict your communication efforts just to problem-solving. As I've said, if problems are all you ever talk about in a relationship, you'll likely have a problem relationship. Talking about things that *don't matter* can be just as important, because it serves as practice, and creates a trusting foundation, for those times when you need to talk about serious stuff. Kids are much more open to talking about things that have no downside for them, like movies, sports or what cousin Billy did last weekend. If your child is used to talking to you on a really regular basis he won't feel nearly as conspicuous when it comes time to broach the really important subjects. He'll know you better if he talks to you frequently, and that familiarity can be very comforting. If the child has come to appreciate many different aspects of your personality, such as humor, compassion, commitment and vulnerability, he'll be much more at home in knowing how to start a meaningful conversation and in predicting how it's likely to turn out.

You Get What You Give

It's important that you recognize the rule of reciprocity. If you are respectful, genuine, open and candid with your child, he or she will be much more likely to treat you in the same fashion. You get what you give. I know that can be really hard to carry off sometimes. Sometimes our children say things or take positions that are so outrageous we go ballistic. Don't take the bait. Doing so only shuts down communication and makes the neighbors call 911. I'm always astounded when I see parents yelling, screaming, cussing and even throwing things around during a disagreement with their children. I'm even more astounded when that same parent looks at me with a straight face and says, "My child is so disrespectful, he yells, screams, cusses and throws things." Well, *duh!* What do you expect? You get what you give.

Remember, your goal is to communicate, not dominate. Getting the point through to them is more important than asserting control over them. Think about it this way: If you dominate and dictate, you can have full and perfect control of your child, as long as you're standing right there next to him or her. But what about the next day, when your six-year-old is on the playground and you're at home or at work? Or how about the next night or the next weekend, when your teenagers are out by themselves and you aren't standing there in all of your overbearing, dominant and dictatorial splendor? Aren't you going to have a lot better chance of influencing your children long-term if you can *persuade* them to see things your way rather than just getting them to acquiesce in the moment so you'll finally shut up? The truth is, if they don't get persuaded and internalize your values and beliefs, your parenting and control is limited to those times when you have them on a really short leash. You may not like the idea of having to talk them into your point of view, but like it or not, that's your only real chance to truly impact their behavior when you're not around. And in case you haven't noticed, the older they get, the less time you get to be around them and the more important their decisions become.

That point was driven home recently when a teen went out drinking after a series of big-time clashes with his mother, who'd freaked out at early warning signs he and his friends were buying booze. There was no persuasion on the part of this mother, only rigid edicts about how she'd turn his life into pure hell if she ever found out he was even thinking about drinking. Unfortunately, he did go drinking—I'm sure at least in part because he'd been given no logical rationale for not doing it. His mother never told him why it was a bad choice; she never reviewed with him the potential downside of drinking, just warned his life would be pure hell if he did. Once he'd made the choice and gotten quite inebriated, he was terrified to call home and ask for a ride because his mother had been so vehement in her demand that he never let a drop pass his lips and been so explicit about the wrath he'd endure. Instead, he tried to drive himself home to hide the transgression and escape accountability. Driving drunk, he caused a terrible accident. Tragically, he was killed and a woman and her ten-month-old baby were severely burned. Only after that horrible outcome did the mother consider that if she'd been less rigid and controlling and had instead sought to persuade her son to buy into her position, he might have been less likely to drink and drive. He might have been more willing to communicate to her his need for help. Was she to blame? Absolutely not. Her son made the choice and created the terrible outcome. But could she have avoided the problem and become part of the solution? Would less dictatorial and more collaborative and persuasive communications have generated a different result? I guess we'll never know, but I can tell you that I will improve my family's odds

> **Survey Fact:** Parents said their two greatest mistakes were being too lenient and taking out their stress on the kids.

by trying to persuade my children in a way that they can internalize rather than dictating a course of action I cannot enforce.

Having unbridled and largely unmonitored authority over your children is a huge responsibility, and how you wield that power and communicate your positions is critical. What *sometimes* happens, even with well-intentioned parents, is that by the time most children are old enough to walk, they've heard an awful lot of negative reinforcement in the form of "You're a bad boy! No, no, no! Don't throw your toys at your sister!" There's far less comment about their positive behaviors. Children will seldom fill in that gap by deducing what the positive alternative behavior might be. Worse, far too many parents still spank and even slap their children, even though research has shown that corporal punishment provides very little in the way of constructive, long-term learning. Instead, it stirs feelings of shame, resentment, bitterness and confused disconnection. Think about it from a child's perspective. Children believe you're supposed to love and protect them and be their safe harbors in what can otherwise be a hugely intimidating world. Then all of a sudden, you're attacking them and inflicting physical pain. They don't understand that, and frankly neither do I. Will inflicting that pain suppress an unwanted behavior? In the short term. But there's little if any message worthy of internalization. What you need to communicate if your child is behaving in an unacceptable manner is a lot more complex than a spanking could ever convey.

An awful lot of parents who believe in spanking tell me they never do it without also providing an explanation as to why the child is being punished. Sorry, that just doesn't do it for me. Ask yourself just how open to input you'd be from someone who'd just yanked you up by the arm and hit you several times. Corporal punishment is neither necessary nor the most efficient way to modify your child's conduct. Even if you think it's okay to spank and that it works, you cannot deny that there are more efficient ways to get the same result, without the side effects.

Spanking is like digging a large hole with a soupspoon. You can do it, but a good, sturdy, sharp-edged and long-handled shovel will get that job done a whole lot faster and better because it's a far superior tool for the job at hand. The same is true with the behavioral-change tools I have included in this book; they're a whole lot better than spanking and communicate a totally different message. (By the way, there are millions of parents and a large body of child-rearing experts who passionately disagree with me. In the back of the book, I've listed a number of articles with those dissenting opinions. I think they're wrong, but I wanted you to be able to read their arguments as well, so you can make up your own minds.)

I'm troubled and surprised at the number of parents who still use physical methods to keep their children in line, but you could have knocked me over with a feather when I saw the data from my National Parenting Survey indicating that 44 percent of the respondents admitted their only means for motivating their children is to yell at them.

We don't have to guess that the yelling was not at a pep rally in which they cheered their children's successes. There are just too many parents who really have no blessed idea of how to communicate with their children in a way that will nurture their talents, self-confidence and dignity. I've often had parents, even those who don't actually yell and scream, do some self-checking, using a sheet of paper to record how many positive versus negative comments they communicate to their child during the course of the day. Sometimes, for objectivity's sake, I have a family member do the recording. I have the parent or family member simply mark a plus sign (+) each time a positive communication occurs, and a negative sign (−) each time a negative or critical communication occurs. Even with a loving and caring parent, the imbalance between negative and positive communications is often staggering. It's not unusual for a parent with a child four years or older to record zero positive communications, and over a hundred negatives per day! I've counted over two hundred negatives for one parent in a two-hour grocery trip—and that was on a day when the parent was in a *good* mood. Your goal should be to have twice as many positive as negative exchanges with your child each day. Double your pleasurable comments and you'll maximize the chance that your child will grow up to be a secure, confident and successful adult. If you're like most parents, you probably think there's no way you're that negative. If so, I suggest you try this positive/negative recording exercise, and without altering your typical behavior, you allow one of your older children or your spouse to do the recording and scoring. Sometimes it's hard to catch your child doing something good so you can reward them with a positive communication, but those positive behaviors are there if you'll just look for them.

Demystify Communication

We've been talking about the mind-set you should employ in communicating with your children. Now I want to be very specific about some of the skills and objectives you should embrace as you develop yourself into an effective communicator. It's time to break down communication into some simple elements. First, I believe there are five different categories of communication:

1. *Information Exchange:* These are the communication scenarios in which you're simply trying to impart or gather information. These exchanges are very matter-of-fact and straightforward. They can range all the way from a casual exchange to pointed interrogation.
2. *Persuasive Communication:* These are the communication scenarios in which you're trying to convince someone to change his mind or move her position. This category contrasts markedly with the matter-of-fact, information-sharing category. It's marked by passion, emotion and, oftentimes, persistence.
3. *Motivational Communication:* These are the communication scenarios in which you're trying to motivate someone to get involved or work harder or simply care more. These are different from persuasive communications in that you're not necessarily trying to get the person to change his mind or position, but to embrace it more passionately. Like persuasive communications, inspirational interactions are usually marked by emotion and animation. They can vary from casual interest to pointed interrogation.
4. *Problem-Solving Communication:* These are communication scenarios in which you're faced with a problem or crisis and there may be time pressure. For you and your child, managing scenarios well means approaching them as a team, shoulder-to-shoulder, even if the problem is the child's or brought on by the child.
5. *Connection Communication:* These are communication scenarios in which you're simply trying to connect to or relate to someone in a meaningful way. These interactions are

marked by emotional commitment. As the old saying goes, If you want a good friend, be a good friend.

Be mindful at all times of the communication scenarios you enter into with your child so that you can have an objective in mind. Know where you are and what you're about when communicating with your child in important moments. Having a goal will help keep you on point.

In addition to these five categories, I believe there are also two broad models of communication: one-way communication and two-way communication. One-way communication is, in my opinion, all too common and highly dangerous. The most frustrating example was when Robin and I would buy our boys bicycles, a swing set or a jungle gym that came in a condominium-size box with a couple hundred pages of "easy-to-assemble" instructions. These were seldom decipherable by a nonmechanical engineer and there was no phone number that any human being would answer when you needed clarification at 2:00 A.M. on Christmas morning. One-way communication is just what it implies; there's an outgoing message and that's it. There are no responses, feedback, questions or clarifications.

The other model, two-way communication, is exactly what I'm hoping you will learn, embrace and practice in your family situation. Unlike one-way communication, the two-way model is dependent on a communication loop in which senders and receivers exchange and adjust a message to ensure accuracy and clarity. The two-way communication model incorporates four steps:

1. *Initial Communication:* The sender formulates the message in his mind, evaluates, edits and then sends. A thoughtful communicator does not adhere to the "ready, fire, aim" plan.
2. *Feedback Loop:* The receiver communicates what's being heard back to the sender. The feedback can be elicited by the sender by simply asking, "Tell me what you hear me saying." Or it can be offered by the receiver: "What I hear you saying is . . ." This allows both sender and receiver—in your case, parent and child—to verify whether accuracy and clarity of the message are being accomplished. Obviously, if your intention is to send Message A and your child is receiving Message B,

you have a problem that can lead to very negative consequences and mischaracterizations. Verification of messages sent and received is critical. If you're in a situation where you simply cannot risk miscommunication, this feedback loop is the answer.

3. *Restatement and Clarification:* In this step, the original sender refines the message for a greater degree of accuracy in response to the feedback and/or questions obtained from the receiver.

4. *Confirmation Loop:* In this step, the feedback and restatement and clarification process is repeated until sender and receiver agree and concur on what's been sent and received. This doesn't imply that the receiver will act on the message as the sender wishes, only that both parties agree on what the message is.

The following is a brief but highly representative dialogue that took place between a forty-one-year-old mother, Rebecca, and her seventeen-year-old daughter, Sloan, about whether or not Sloan could go to an after-prom party at a house on a nearby lake. The conversation took place after I'd spent considerable time with Rebecca, discussing the elements of two-way communication.

Rebecca (initial message): I've decided that I just cannot allow you to attend the party because there'll be no adult supervision. I don't want you to take this wrong, so tell me what you hear me say.

Sloan (feedback): You just don't trust me; you think I'm going to go drink and have sex and be completely stupid.

Rebecca (restatement and clarification): Sloan, that's not it at all. I do trust you, and I don't think you'd go out there with the plan to drink or have sex, but I'm smart enough to know that those things are very likely to be going on. There could be problems and trouble, and I don't want you to get painted with that brush. If you get there, and a lot of drinking is going on and someone gets hurt or drowns in the lake or the house gets torn up, you're going to wish you weren't there. It's my job to see around corners, and I'm not going to put you in a situation that I don't think is going to have a good outcome. Now tell me what you hear me saying.

Sloan (confirmation loop): Mother, okay, I get that you think the situation is the problem and not me. But I'm smart enough to leave if things get out of hand. I think it's going to be okay and that you should let me go.

The conversation proceeded from there. Sloan was not allowed to go to the party. But you can see that in just one pass through the two-way communication process, a serious misperception—in which the child wanted to play the victim—was clarified by Rebecca, who provided additional information. Had Rebecca handled this in a one-way fashion by just saying, "You're not going because I'm your mother, and that's the end of it," she would have had no idea what Sloan was thinking or of what thoughts she was assigning to her. By adhering to the two-way model and listening to each other, the two were able to agree to disagree. Sloan didn't get what she wanted, but neither was she left with the false impression that her mother viewed her as an irresponsible kid.

Be Thoughtful and Be Strong Inside and Out

To communicate effectively, you can't be giving yourself one message—such as "This can never be worked out"—while at the same time offering your child a message of hope and forgiveness. Solid external communications must be congruent with internal communications. You can't ride to the rescue if you sabotage yourself along the way. This isn't the time for self-doubt, self-incrimination or self-criticism. Sure, even adults have self-doubts and insecurities. We moms and dads can psych ourselves out too, so you need to be conscious and careful about your inner thoughts during a time of crisis. Banish the following messages from your brain because they'll only get in the way of your rescue attempts:

- This is all my fault.
- There's no way we're ever going to come out of this one okay.
- I always knew things would end up like this.
- I can't deal with this.
- I can't face this.
- I can't get through this.

When those phrases pop up, bite your inner tongue. Counter self-defeating thoughts with more positive messages that will move you through the crisis, instill confidence and energize you. Say things like:

- We can work this out.
- We'll get through this.
- I'm going to do the best I can and it will be enough.
- I know I can handle this.

There's plenty of research to support the theory that positive inner thoughts are much more effective than negative messages in times of crisis. If you tell yourself you can do something, you're much more likely to actually do it than if you spend all your energy thinking about how badly you're going to screw it up. Don't get down on yourself in the midst of a crisis. You don't need to add to the negativity and pressure. Instead, work the problem; don't become part of it by contributing to the stress.

And be careful not to drive your child's internal dialogue in a negative direction. For example, you must be extremely careful about hanging labels on your child, even if you think those labels are accurate. Labels can be especially dangerous because young people tend to internalize them. Often they then act according to the expectation. The father who introduces one son as "my athlete" and the other son as "my bookworm" may be unconsciously locking both boys into boxes that could limit them down the road.

Even a label that you think is positive can be very hurtful. For example, I often encounter parents who label their child a genius. They think this is a very positive characterization, but often when the child hears that, she becomes condescending about school, feels that day-to-day work is beneath her and begins to experience problems in her schoolwork and her relationships with teachers and other children. The labeling of a child as ADD or slow or clumsy can even more obviously implant messages and self-images that will restrict or disable. Such labels will likely dampen a child's interest in acting on opportunities and could also cripple the all-important ability to get beyond failure or disappointment.

While we're looking at the power of language in communication and how it can affect your child's success as an adult, let's take a look at a truly *catastrophic* problem—catastrophic language. This is the exaggeration of situations and circumstances through the use of hyperbole and overstatement.

Last night was the worst night of my entire life!

You made an unbelievable, fatal mistake that I will never, ever be able to forgive!

You are a parent's worst nightmare and you've broken my heart!

This sort of language is easy to use, but it's very hard to mend the damage it can cause. Catastrophic language is intended to jolt the listener's emotions and it can have powerful physiological effects on those who take it seriously. Blood pressures shoot up. The heart pumps harder. Muscles tense. And one bad word can lead to all sorts of bad repercussions. Parents, don't play that game. Don't exaggerate your child's mistakes or misadventures. Be the adult and the caring guide that parents are supposed to be. If you're going to exaggerate anything, go nuts in describing the good things your child does or the admirable qualities he exhibits. Be a cheerleader, not a doomsayer.

Use Communication to Prepare and Rehearse for the Future

Communicate with your children to anticipate the temptations and challenges they're likely to face. Get them to rehearse through role-playing. Have them play out scenarios in their minds to determine how they might handle difficult situations. Obviously, parents don't want a sixteen-year-old girl to be in the backseat of a car alone with a boy at midnight on Saturday night. But if she finds herself there, we want her to be prepared to handle that situation. If the boy is trying to talk her into doing things she doesn't want to do by trotting out lines like "If you really loved me you would . . . ," it would help her to have responses ready and to recognize that these are age-old, boy-to-girl manipulations. If prepared, the girl might well see that the boy is full of it and respond: "That's just dumb and manipulative. If you loved me, you wouldn't try to manipulate me."

The Boy Scout motto has it right: Be prepared. Parents, take that to heart in communicating with your children. Look ahead and prepare them for the typical scenarios that may play out. Lawyers never go into a trial without anticipating what the other side will pull in the way of surprise evidence or testimony.

Learn from Successes as Well as Failures

As a parent, you need to be there to help your children acknowledge and reinforce their successes, their good decisions and wise choices. How powerful and empowering it is for a child to hear a father say, "I think you should be proud of the way you handled yourself this season. The coach didn't give you much of a chance, but you hung in there and improved your game, and when you got the opportunity, you showed you've got talent."

Help your children learn from their successes. At every opportunity, review for them what they did right. Tell them why you think they were successful; point out their positive attributes. Every time you feel the need to criticize, soften it with something positive. It's critical for children to learn to build on their strengths instead of always trying to compensate for their weaknesses. Help them understand what their strengths are so they can go to them and develop their talents. When children learn to build on their strengths, they are more likely to respond to challenges with determination rather than fear.

Humor Helps

"Jeez," you're probably thinking, "not only has this guy lost his hair, but he's lost his mind. Besides being the disciplinarian and the facilitator of all my family's big decisions, I'm supposed to be funny too?"

Let's back up the truck. I'm not saying you need to be the family's class clown. I am suggesting, though, that if you want to raise children who have the ability to laugh at life's insanity, you've got to help them see life's funny side. How much fun are you to live with? Are you always cracking the whip? Well, cracking jokes works too. Being a parent means making tough decisions and being serious when the situation demands it, but that doesn't mean you should never lighten up, laugh or make fun of yourself.

Laughter is an important part of being human and if you laugh with your child, you strengthen the connection with him or her. Laughter is also a terrific way to reduce stress and your child needs to know that it has healing power. In the first weeks after her move to a new school in a new town, a friend's fourteen-year-old daughter had to stand up in front of a bunch of strangers in her junior high chorus class and sing a song about herself. She was so nervous her whole body trembled, making her voice sound like it was stuck on vibrato. She came home that night and cried in humiliation and embarrassment. But when her father went in to talk to her, she was sitting in her room laughing to herself.

"What's going on? I thought you were sad because of what happened today," he said.

"Oh, I was just thinking that tomorrow kids from my chorus class will probably come up to me and say, 'Hey, guess what's shaking—YOU!' "

Her father later told her that from that point on, he knew she was going to be a success in life because she had the gift of seeing the humor in difficult situations. Laughter is a great medicine. The more you laugh, the less stressed you're going to feel. The daughter was able to heal her hurt feelings and embarrassment by stepping back and seeing the humor in her situation. Hey, life really is a sitcom, only it's a reality show too. So laugh whenever possible; it makes you less crazy and it makes you more approachable than if you're scowling and being grumpy old Dad or Mom. Even when things go horribly wrong—the dog poops on the floor, the dinner burns and your child spills milk on the carpet—instead of getting upset, try laughing at the ridiculousness of it all. Clean it up and get on with life, but first, have a good laugh at how really unbelievably awful everything is.

There is a difference, of course, between self-effacing humor and having a laugh at your child's expense. The daughter mentioned above was able to laugh at her predicament and her reaction, but her parents needed to laugh along with her, not at her. Help your child find the humor, but don't make her the butt of your jokes. When people have the ability to find humor in their situations, they're much less likely to be defensive or stressed-out.

One of the marks of a successful family is that it has plenty of inside family jokes to share. It's a healthy sign when you and your children can cite story after story about the time Dad dressed the baby backwards, Mom thought a new band was a brand of dog food and the kids made purple egg omelets for breakfast. Keep crazy family moments alive by repeating them and having a good laugh at them. This provides a shared connection and reminds everyone that you're all just nutty people who make crazy mistakes, but you love and respect one another. Sharing laughter is an expression of humanity and community. Laugh with your children and the world will smile on you.

Audit

Let's do an evaluation in which you create communication opportunities. For each of the following statements, choose either Consistently (C), Often (O), Inconsistently (I) or Never (N).

	C	O	I	N
1. I acknowledge when my child does something that is positive and I give him full credit for that event.	4	3	2	1
2. I acknowledge when my child does something that is negative and I try to understand her feelings.	4	3	2	1
3. When my child achieves something, I like to review without criticism his thinking, intentions and the behavior that brought about the results.	4	3	2	1
4. When my child achieves something negative, I like to review the thinking, intentions and behavior that brought about the negative results.	4	3	2	1
5. Can your child name five good qualities of himself or herself to you? Can you affirm them?	4	3	2	1
6. Can you describe your child's feelings?	4	3	2	1
7. Can you and your child reach an understanding of your intentions and behaviors?	4	3	2	1
8. Do you and your child talk on a daily basis?	4	3	2	1

	C	O	I	N
9. Do you and your child recognize each other's feelings and purposes or someone he or she can envision as examples of success?	4	3	2	1
10. Do you recognize your child's definition of success?	4	3	2	1

Scoring: If for any item you chose 3, that behavior should go to the head of your to-do list. And if you chose less than 3, it becomes a must-do.

We've covered a lot of ground in this chapter and I hope you'll give all of this information on communication time to sink in. Contemplate the importance of talking to your children and, more important, listening to what they say to understand who they are. If you do that, you'll have a much better chance of influencing who they become as adults. Oh, and one more thing—don't forget to laugh with your children, even if YOU are the occasional butt of their jokes. Humor heals!

9

Tool 3:
Parenting by Negotiation

Partner with Your Child

*You know your children are growing up when they stop
asking you where they came from and refuse to tell you
where they are going.*
—P. J. O'ROURKE

*L*et's Make a Deal: Whether you're aware of it or not, you're involved
in countless negotiations every day. I truly believe that life is one
long series of give-and-take interactions, and it begins pretty much from
birth. When you cried for attention as a baby and then stopped when
your mother picked you up, your first successful negotiation was completed. Later, in kindergarten, you negotiated for your space on the playground. You negotiated to win the attention of that first crush in school.
Getting your first high school date or steady boyfriend or girlfriend probably required a little more sophisticated give and take. Then you moved
into the marketplace and negotiated things like your hourly babysitting
rates or lawn-mowing fees with the neighbors. Your first car, your first job
and salary and your first house were all acquired through negotiations.

You may not have thought of yourself as a negotiator and you may
not have used the word "negotiation" to describe the process, but that's
what you were doing. As parents, we need to be aware of the importance
of thoughtful negotiations in our family relationships. The objective in
relationship negotiations is, as the carnival barkers like to say, "Everyone
walks away a winner!" You want both sides to feel satisfied and fulfilled so
that the relationship can continue successfully. In a relationship, making
a deal that totally favors you and ignores the needs of your partner or
children may seem like a good idea at the time, but it will never last.

All relationships are mutually defined, and the definitions you reach are a product of the negotiations you conduct with each other. You may say, "I didn't negotiate this relationship, I just inherited it." That's not true. You teach people how to treat you, and this includes the way you relate to your children. If you don't like your relationship with a child, you need to *re*negotiate it.

Whatever definition your family relationship has, whether your kids are in control, Dad's in control, Mom's in control or you all share control, everyone has negotiated their role in the family—even Sparky the dog, whose tail-wagging and barking are persuasive negotiation tools. Consciously or unconsciously, we put negotiations into play in every relationship and in every family. The process goes on constantly. You negotiate the rules, the power distribution, the standards, the goals, the patterns, the practice and the rhythms of your family.

Herb Cohen, an international negotiation expert, teaches that any time you attempt to influence, persuade, manipulate or direct a person or group of people, you're negotiating. You're involved in a negotiations process when you attempt to reconcile differences, manage conflict, resolve disputes and create change in your relationship. Let's be clear on this: Negotiations are the absolute lifeblood of relationships. Negotiation skills figure prominently in how successful and effective you become. Hence, it's astounding that most people have absolutely no training in negotiation. Society doesn't teach you this invaluable and important tool, so I'm going to, right now.

Negotiation Tactics

As I made clear in Chapter 5, as a mother or father, you can negotiate with many different styles. The first step is to assess the kind of personalities and types you're dealing with. That will tell you what type of negotiation approach to take. If you've got a highly rebellious kid, you don't necessarily want to approach the negotiations in a heavy-handed, badge-heavy, "I'm the boss" manner. That will only spark resistance. You want to be more of a consensus builder. You want your child to buy in and feel ownership, like it's his or her idea. It's also important for your child to understand the basics of negotiation, because it's such an important life skill.

From the time our oldest son Jay was ten years old, I had him sit in on many of my daily negotiations—especially when I was buying a car or lawnmower, or trying to resolve a conflict with a neighbor about where to put a fence or park a car. Sometimes I even let Jay do the negotiating so he'd gain confidence in his ability. One day on the spur of the moment we decided to go to a Dallas Mavericks basketball game, even though we didn't have tickets. When we got to the arena, people were selling tickets on the sidewalk. I sent Jay off to negotiate the deal with the ticket hawkers, but first I negotiated my deal with him. "We want to be in section three so we can see the game. Here's two hundred dollars, enough money to buy two tickets. I want you to get the best price you can, so here's our deal: If you negotiate a ticket price of two hundred dollars, that's fine. But if you can get him to take less than that, YOU get to keep the difference. So if you negotiate the price down to one-fifty, you get to keep fifty dollars."

Jay did all right that day. And the ticket seller walked away a happy man too. My goal had been to teach Jay to be comfortable in negotiations and to not get taken advantage of. People sometimes think "negotiate" is a dirty word and they get anxious about it. They don't like doing it because it can often be tense, high-pressure and confrontational. But it doesn't have to be. It can be amicable and solution-oriented. Think of it as a process of working together to find a solution.

> **Survey Fact:**
> Forty-six percent of parents said that their children's biggest emotional issues were coping with stress and dealing with depression.

In relationship negotiations in particular, you want to foster mutual respect by treating each other as reasonable and intelligent human beings. I think my kids are really great people, and I want them to know that's how I feel about them when we negotiate. When there's dysfunction in a household, it's easy for parents and children under stress to perceive one another as enemies. Doors slam. Angry words fly. Emotions remain on the surface where they can easily be ignited. In the explosive environment it's lost that parents and children love and need one another. When you negotiate with your children, you don't want to browbeat or bully or intimidate them because your deal with them is a long-term deal.

In family negotiations you're not looking for a quick give and take. You're in it for the long haul. You have to be sensitive to family members' feelings, so it's a little different from negotiating with the guy selling tickets on the street corner (even though I think it's important to conduct

yourself with dignity and respect there as well). You should always negotiate from the high-road position, but most especially with your children
so that they come away with their self-respect intact.

In a successful negotiation with your child, both of you will buy into
the solution because both of you will feel a sense of ownership toward
that solution. When the deal is done, hopefully both of you should be
able to look at it and see that your most important points are in it. When
you negotiate properly with your child, each of you should come away
with the attitude, "I can support what you want because this isn't your
deal, it's *our* deal."

Start negotiating with the right mind-set. To be effective, do your
homework and understand your children's objectives before you begin
negotiations with them. Make certain that what you're trying to negotiate is in the best interest of everyone in the family and not just a matter
of convenience for you. Be a good and benevolent steward of your power
and control. It's easy to get one-sided when you hold all of the chips.
Recognize that when you negotiate with children, they may not have a
full understanding of what's in their best interest. Try to get your child to
see your rationale, which is about protecting the family, but don't feel
guilty if they don't. Once you've performed that little checkup, don't feel
guilty about pursuing what you want out of the deal.

Don't Hesitate to Negotiate

Many parents and children refuse to sit down at the negotiation table because of the demons already in the room due to past failed attempts. If
previous efforts have been conducted in a ham-fisted, head-butting manner, it's likely there will be reluctance to return to the table.

When Frances and her sixteen-year-old son Sean came to me, they
were at a stalemate over his use of the family car—a very common point
of conflict between parents and teenagers. Frances had been a single
mom for seven years. Sean had harbored resentment over his lack of a father and they'd had other conflicts, but this two-driver, one-car family
situation had put them on a collision course, especially since Sean had
started dating.

Frances came to these negotiations with some baggage of her own,
which is something every parent should be aware of. The family legacy
we discussed in Chapter 4 can show up in so many areas of your relationship with your children. How that legacy can affect your attitude about

negotiating with your kids is just one of many examples. If your childhood negotiations with your parents were confrontational experiences,
don't do a flashback and avoid the situation; rather, resolve to do better
with your child. Don't give up on the process. Change it for the better. Frances's father was a tyrant and physically abusive. From childhood, Frances had learned to avoid any kind of one-on-one with him
at all costs. She certainly would never seek to persuade him to do
anything he didn't want to do. Her son had his father's looks but his
mother's temperament. Sean didn't know much of his mom's history, but
from his limited experience, the negotiation process was more about
manipulation and arguing than reaching a consensus through reasoned
dialogue.

To get these two on track, I presented a new definition of negotiation
for Frances and Sean, which you will read more about later in this chapter. Because conflict avoidance had been the rule in their household,
both the mother and the son had become frustrated over unresolved issues. My negotiation format offered a safer environment for them to work
things out. Both had a stake in resolving their car conflict. That's no
small thing. A shared desire for resolution is the most important factor in
the negotiation process. If one or both sides don't really care if the matter
is ever resolved, it's going to be a tough row to hoe.

Frances and Sean were able to work things out once both felt safe in
negotiating. They put together a schedule that reserved the car for each
of them when they most wanted to have wheels. Frances, as the person
paying the bills, claimed the right to know where Sean was going and
what he was doing when he had the car. For Sean, there were also consequences and chores that accompanied car privileges. Both were fairly
happy with the resolution, although Frances reserved the right to fret and
Sean made it clear that he'd just as soon have permanent use of a car. You
can't negotiate away human nature or a teenage boy's road lust. In short,
both walked away feeling just okay but not feeling they had gotten 100
percent of what they wanted. There was some give and take. That feeling
is a pretty good standard for knowing that you made a fair deal.

Kid Power

Over the years one of the most common complaints I've heard from children is that they feel powerless in negotiations with their parents. Many

also perceive their parents to be arbitrary in their discipline and decisions. Nobody likes being treated that way, child or adult. We all want
our voices to be heard and our feelings to be considered, even if we don't
own the car keys, control the money or make the rules of the house.
Children thrive in situations that are orderly, have boundaries and are
predictable. But at the same time, they like to have a sense of self-
determination within that framework. They want to know that they can
earn certain rights and privileges if they do what is expected of them.
They want to have a perception of some power, some ability to create
what they value. If they feel your position is locked in, and that no matter what they say or do they have no ability to influence you in any way, I
can guarantee you they'll unplug from you and figure some other way to
get what they want, whether by hook or by crook. Sometimes children
who are made to feel inept and powerless in their family situations decide
it's easier to ask for forgiveness than permission. If they believe you've
long since made up your mind that they're not ever going to get what
they want and that you're holding them as a powerless prisoner, they're
likely to figure they have nothing to lose by ignoring your rules and taking what they want. They figure, "Hey, I'm already shut down, so what's
the difference?" Children often tell me that they believe their parents
hold fixed beliefs about how they're going to behave, and there's no hope
of ever changing their minds. They believe that if they've made mistakes
in the past, been irresponsible or gotten caught lying or misrepresenting a
situation, their punishment is a life sentence with no hope of pardon or
parole. They feel destined to live under suspicion and without trust. It's
important that children perceive you're coming to the negotiation table
with an open mind and a willingness to look ahead, instead of at the past.
It's important that they perceive themselves as having a degree of power,
persuasion and influence in an open-minded family situation. When kids
feel that their parents listen and take their concerns into account, it
boosts their self-confidence and self-esteem. Your job as a parent is to set
the boundaries, direct the important choices and instill the values and
morals you deem important for your child. At the same time, when involved in any negotiations, you should always strive to listen to your children's concerns so win, lose or draw, they at least know they've been
heard. Children who feel they have a voice, feel they have power. Children who feel they have power, feel safe and secure.

Clarity of Purpose

We've all done it. When passing a decision on to a child, every parent, you and me included, has failed at some point—and probably at many points—to provide a "why" (whether it's *why* the child can't have a Super Size milkshake or a Corvette as their first car). It's also true that children will demand a "why" in an effort to wear down parental resistance. I advise you to give it to them. Providing your child with an understanding of your underlying reasons helps them learn how to make their own judgments. Your rules will make more sense and carry more weight if you provide a foundation for them. Conversely, they'll have very little lasting power if you simply follow a command model of parenting.

Take, for example, the age-old "eat your vegetables or you can't have dessert" parental directive. Sure, most kids will do it as long as you hover over them like the Un-Jolly Green Giant. But the next time you're *not* there, what's going to compel them to eat the greens before they go for the goodies? Without any internal motivation or perspective, they'll sure as shooting gulp down the cobbler and leave the collards. Talk to your children and provide them not only directives but an understanding of the purpose for them.

My clinical research has shown that the more parents talk with their kids every day and help them understand why you want them to follow your directions, the more you explain things to them, the fewer conflicts arise. Talking confers a fringe benefit in terms of your child's ability to deal with other authority figures such as teachers, employers, even the police. You could say that parent-child conversation saves lives, or at least a whole lot of angst. The father who tells his sixteen-year-old son he can't drive his company car to a friend's party is only inviting conflict when his answer to the inevitable "Why not?" is "Because I'm your father, by God, and I said no!"

The kid who hears that answer on a regular basis is destined to resist authority throughout his life. Consider a more appropriate alternative response: "Let me tell you why. You're not covered by the insurance. It's a company car, which means only I am supposed to drive it. If you wreck that car or if some drunk runs into you, not only can't I get to work, I'll be in trouble with my bosses. And if I lose my job, we lose the car."

The typical kid may not be thrilled at that answer, but he can't deny the logic behind it. And once he has that logic, he has a foundation for making his own decisions when you aren't around. Let's say you've flown out of town on a business trip, leaving your company car in the driveway and the keys hanging in the house. Your son might be sorely tempted to defy your authority and take the car for a joyride if all he's ever heard from you is "Because I said so!" But once you've shared your logic with him, he has the basis for making his own decision. "If something went wrong and I wrecked that car, I'd put myself and my dad in a very bad situation."

Parents should note that providing a basis for a decision doesn't necessarily open the floor for debate, although debating is a great mental exercise for children. The appropriate close to a "why" conversation that threatens to mushroom into a debate that you don't think is best or timely is to simply say, "I've made my decision based on what I told you. That's final."

Rehearsal

Although it's true that your child knows you better than you know yourself, you have the advantage of experience. Most of the time you'll know what is coming in terms of requests or demands, allowing you to be prepared. Remember that it is better in any negotiation to persuade rather than coerce. It is better to partner in a decision than to dictate a decision. To have your responses ready, I'd suggest you practice mentally by rehearsing what you'll say the next time your child wants something you don't want him or her to have. Once they buy in to your point of view or a compromise position, you will find that you are not having to repeat the discussion over and over. Here's a simple exercise to get you thinking. Make a list of likely requests. In the next column write down the response and clarifications you might want to have at your disposal; require yourself to move to a higher level of interaction and resist the power play:

Probable Unreasonable Request	Clarity Response
1. Can I have the car to take my friends out?	
2. Can I watch television until 9:00 P.M. tonight?	

3. Can I go to a slumber party
   with the rest of the girls in my
   fourth-grade class?

4. Can I skip school? No one
   is going tomorrow.

5. Can I go to the midnight
   movie?

6.

7.

8.

9.

10.

Consequences and Choices

Tennis professional Andre Agassi has an array of tools and weapons for
the sport he's mastered. He's got a forehand, a backhand, a volley, an
overhead, a power serve and a variety of finesse serves and returns. With
his mastery of those tools and weapons, Agassi can play opponents with a
number of different styles and yet still compete at the highest level.

I'm an amateur but avid tennis player with my own, monumentally
more limited set of tools. I know what those tools will allow me to do and
what they won't. I show up with what I've got and give it my best shot. I
don't try to reinvent the wheel with every opponent. The same holds
true with negotiation. You are only as good as the tools you've got. The
same holds true for your child. That's why you should master the art of
negotiation and then pass this critically important tool on to your child.
By properly negotiating for what you want in your relationship with your
child a good result will be attained and additionally the child will see
how it's done, a double-bonus good deal.

One of the first steps in teaching your child negotiation basics is
to make sure he or she can predict the consequence of their actions so
they have a sense of responsibility for the outcomes generated. If as your
daughter leaves for school on a Friday morning she tells you to drop dead,

then she'd darn well better be able to confidently predict that she'll be spending the weekend cleaning her room and folding laundry instead of hanging out at the beach with young Mr. Wonderful.

It needs to be made clear: When you choose behavior, you choose the consequences. You'll know they've absorbed that fundamental principle when you hear them say things such as "I blew it, didn't I?" or "My mom didn't ground me, I grounded myself" or "If I'd just kept my big mouth shut, I'd be at the beach with you guys right now." If both sides of a negotiation don't have requirements to meet in a relationship, there can be no negotiation because there is no buy in.

Once you've made clear both your expectations and the consequences of failing to meet them, your child will get the picture. That sets the foundation from which the rest of the negotiation can begin. Your child needs to know that there are some absolute deal breakers. They need to know that violating any of these deal breakers means the negotiation is over and they lose. Your child will learn that and respect it in order to keep a dialogue going. It may take a few trial runs, but believe me, most kids catch on pretty quickly.

This choose-the-behavior-choose-the-consequences standard for how they behave in the negotiation process teaches accountability, which is important in getting them to own the outcomes in their own lives. Therefore, parents should consistently emphasize the rules of engagement, such as:

"I hope you choose to have a good time on spring break by getting your grades up this winter."

"You know the law, you know our rules too. I hope you choose to keep your driver's license by keeping your car's speed under the limit. It's your decision; the law is the law."

Consistency Invites Ownership

Again, for the choose-the-behavior-choose-the-consequences aspect of negotiaton to be effective, it must be wielded with consistency. Once you've negotiated the ground rules you can't level consequences willy-nilly. You must respect your child's right. If they choose inappropriate behavior, you must be prepared to deliver the consequences you have committed to. Just because you've had a bad day and are on edge, you don't have license to ground your daughter for no reason. Arbitrary punishments will foul not only existing negotiations but all future attempts at negotiation. Your children have to be able to predict what you will do in order to feel that all important sense of power to create their own lives. If your child lives up to her part of the bargain, you've got to live up to yours.

Cut Them In and They Will Buy In

The negotiation process is designed to give your child a greater sense of self-determination, security and belonging. When carried out correctly, your child will feel more like a partner than a pawn. It can be extremely helpful also to engage children in making decisions about rules, guidelines and family behavior patterns. Any time you can get someone under your supervision to buy into your management plan, you'll achieve several desirable effects:

- If someone has pride of ownership in a plan, they're much less likely to rebel against it.
- People who have ownership in a plan are much less likely to thwart it, because that would amount to an admission of failure on their part.
- Children, especially, will gain a sense of security if they feel a sense of power. They absolutely love it when theirs is a plan they can control or at least have input into.

It's great for children to know up front that cleaning their rooms, doing their homework and completing chores while being respectful to their parents earns them the right to a reward they've sought, such as a Friday night sleepover with friends. Once you've instilled in your child this sense of life being a series of quid pro quos, if she doesn't fulfill her obligations and the sleepover is canceled, you probably won't get a lot of grief about it. Instead of "I hate my mother, she is so mean," you'll more likely hear "I guess I blew that one."

Most kids don't want to rule the roost, but they do like ruling the section beneath their feet. They know they're small and are aware of their inadequacies, so they don't really want the responsibility of being totally in charge. They want just as much control as they can handle and just enough power to make decisions that directly impact them. That is the natural order of things and it is a big part of the rhythm of life that you can absolutely soothe the savage beast if you take the time to put it together right. In this case "right" means that you maintain authority, but you make sure that your child feels that he has the opportunity for input and influence. You and your children need to work together and in stages when it comes to sharing the privilege of power. We don't hand them driver's licenses without making them practice and pass written and driving tests; it's wise to be as careful when giving them the license to make their own life decisions.

The Negotiator Skills

Bottom line: Negotiation is a form of currency exchange, but in the best sense of the word. The definition of currency exchange has two criteria. First, the process must be overt, not insidious. Second, the methods must be motivated by a desire to further the child's best interests, whether the child agrees or not.

The following are key steps, techniques or principles for successful negotiation.

Five Critical Steps to Successful Negotiation

1. Narrow the area of dispute. It can be very helpful to first identify everything the two sides agree on. Oftentimes, we make the mistake of thinking we're totally at cross purposes with the other side, when, in fact, the areas of dispute are rather isolated. By identifying what you can agree on, positive energy is injected into the situation and some bonding occurs. For example, let's assume your child wants a one o'clock curfew instead of a twelve o'clock curfew. You can simply say, "No, because I'm your parent, and I say no." Or you can discuss it openly, identifying some things you both agree on. I suspect your child would agree that safety is a priority. Perhaps you can begin by saying, "Can we agree that the number one priority here is for you to be safe, and not placed unreasonably in harm's way?" Once that's agreed on, you have a starting point for your negotiation and it then boils down to whether one of you can persuade the other whether or not it's safe to be out on the road after the bars close and drunks are making their way home. If you've done your homework, I'm betting this is a logic battle you can't lose.

2. Find out what it is they really want. Notice I didn't say, "Find out what it is they want to do or not do." This is about what the other side *wants*. Your child may say, "I want to stay out until one o'clock," but there is a *need* or *desire* behind the request. What does your child hope to accomplish by staying out until one o'clock? It may be that all the cool kids are able to stay out until one o'clock and she doesn't want to lose "cool" status. Whatever the itch is, you need to determine whether there's a safer and more mutually agreeable method for satisfying it. In the example I've just given, you might be able to find many different ways to help your child feel "with it" without her driving at such a dangerous hour. There is more than one way to skin a cat, and if you're creative, you can come up with an alternative way to get your child what she or he is really motivated to have.

A family I worked with had just this sort of dispute in which the mother and daughter reached a compromise. It was agreed that the daughter could stay out until 1:00 A.M. if she was at the home of a friend in the neighborhood and she could get home without driving on any busy streets. Or she could have friends come over to her house from midnight until 1:00 A.M. Mom, in an amazingly unselfish effort to bring about a resolution, even agreed that they could blast the stereo during that hour with no protest from the parents. It worked for the mom, and it worked for the daughter. Negotiation completed. Some people tend to be selfish and overreaching in negotiations. They think that if they get everything they want and yield nothing, then they've made a really good deal. As I've noted many times, parenting is a marathon, it is not a sprint. As a result, it's really important that you conduct yourself in a gracious and generous fashion. Any time I go into a negotiation, I devote myself to this step so much that I end up working as hard for the other side as for my own. But I've found that if the other side is getting what they want or feel they need, they're much more likely to give me what I want or need. You should try to figure out as many different ways as possible to get your children what they want without violating what you hold dear.

In dealing with my TV production team I've established what I think is a really good rule, that is, we "love" every idea for fifteen minutes. If someone comes up with an idea, even if I or others don't think it will work, instead of being negative, we spend fifteen minutes trying to figure out how to make it work. My goal is to try to come up with a way that the idea can be part of the body of work we generate during that season. That means the producer who brainstormed the idea gets more of what he or she wants, which is to make good television that impacts people's lives and to feel like he or she has made a meaningful contribution. By not just dismissing an idea out of hand, what I get in turn is some really good "outside the box" thinking that has generated some amazingly interesting shows.

3. Work hard to find a middle ground in which both sides give a little and get a little. Maybe there are some limited risks you're willing to take, and maybe there are some concessions your child is willing to make. The potential problem with negotiations is that they can degenerate into ultimatums and hardheadedness. You get nowhere, forging only resentment and rebellion. So look for that middle ground, such as in the curfew example cited previously. One A.M. socializing becomes a lot more palatable if it occurs at someone's nearby home.

4. Be specific in your agreement and the outcome of the negotiations. If there are behaviors you feel are important for the child to exhibit, describe them in great detail so it's easy to measure whether there's been compliance. Don't simply tell your teenager, "I want you to be more respectful to me." State specific examples such as "When I ask you to take out the garbage, don't say 'Later' or 'After I download this song from iTune,' say 'Okay,' and do it immediately."

5. Make negotiated agreements, shorter term in the beginning and longer term after a period of adjustment. You might negotiate a new curfew for two weeks, and agree that it will be revisited at the end of that period to see how things are going. After this has worked through a few cycles, you might agree to revisit the policy in thirty days, and then six months. That way, you and your child establish a successful pattern. Probably the most effective approach in negotiating with your children is to appeal to their greed. Children typically don't take the long view of things. Remember, they want what they want when they want it, and they want it right now. If you want to motivate them for change, then appeal to that hedonistic impulse. Their greed doesn't make them evil. They're just not yet socialized to the point of putting others' interests ahead of their own. So use that to your advantage in negotiations by catering to their short-term vision and building long-term behavior patterns.

Self-correction

The five steps I've just presented give you a step-by-step map for negotiations, but mastering the skills takes practice. It's like learning to ride a unicycle: You shouldn't plan on going very far the first day. The process can break down quickly unless you self-correct as you go. In the negotiation process, this means checking to be certain that at each point you fully understand the other side's position. You may think you know what your child is requesting because you were young once yourself and remember how you behaved and even how much you lied. In reality, though, there's only about a 25 percent chance you really know what's going through your child's head.

Here are a few methods for self-correcting during negotiations.

Self-correct your understanding of your child's position. To do this you can use the cybernetic approach to communication, which means checking out what you're hearing before assuming you understand. I often have those involved in a negotiation process write down what they're trying to achieve. The next step is to have the opposing side read the other side's description, and vice versa. Then they try to translate each other's desires in their own words. The person writing the request can correct the perceptions if incorrect. By taking turns, there's the assurance that all parties are talking about the same issue.

In my example of Frances and Sean, they started out with very different perceptions of what the other was saying. When Frances described Sean's note, she said that what he wanted was a new car and she couldn't afford one, nor could she just give him hers. Sean corrected her by explaining that this wasn't his need. What he wanted was the use of the car at certain times until he could afford to buy one himself.

When they did the "translation" exercise, Sean described his mother's note as meaning she didn't trust him, despite his good grades and clean driving record. He wanted to prove that he was responsible but could not. Frances corrected this perception by explaining that she was at a loss to work out a solution, but she did trust him.

During parent-child negotiation practices, I often leave a tablet of the forms listed below for family members to keep on hand when they begin the process. I invite you to copy them and use them both as a beginning for negotiations and as a means for making self-corrections.

Person 1   Description of what he/she wants from the negotiations

Person 2   Perceptions of the description of number one

Person 1   Corrections

Person 2   Descriptions of what he/she wants from the negotiations

Person 1   Perceptions of the description of number two

Person 2   Corrections

Keep the eye on the donut, not on the hole. Stay focused on the final result, not on the intervening distractions. During negotiations, discussions can wander far from the primary topic unless you maintain a tracking system. In fact, there's a natural tendency to go off track as emotions build. Sometimes one of the individuals will break off the discussion prematurely out of fear of hurting the other's feelings or because of some personal baggage. The purpose of negotiation is not to hurt the other person or to gain power. The number one requirement for successful negotiation is safety, and the best way to establish safety is to form a partnership dedicated to finding mutually satisfying solutions. Repeating the ultimate goal, even writing it down and taping it to your forehead, will create clarity and help achieve success. To have faith in the process, it remains critical to keep the end goals in mind.

Create closure. Reduce the end product to a contract so you and your child feel a sense of accomplishment and mutual understanding. It can be as simple a statement as "You do this, I do that." Write the essence down as an agreement so when you disagree later, you can go back and see what was agreed on. It might not be what you meant, but what you said. This will help identify any misunderstandings or misconceptions and serve as another correction. Keep in mind that individuals interpret certain words differently. "Argue" is a good example, arguably. For some people, it carries only a faintly negative connotation. They see it as meaning to debate in playful or provocative ways. Others view the word as a synonym for fighting. Even if both people are using the English language, perceptions differ. What is required is patience and a commitment to gain a common language. Ultimately a contract merely serves a corrective function, and it shouldn't be used as a basis for a lawsuit.

• • •

As I said in the beginning, these negotiation tools are a gift that just keeps on giving, and they can be used in a wide variety of circumstances. Keep in mind, parents, that the goal of true negotiation is to come up with a deal that benefits both sides. You aren't trying to put one over on your children; you're trying to get them to buy into your vision of success for them and for the entire family. When that happens, it's the deal of a lifetime.

10

Tool 4:
Parenting with Currency
Performance and Payoffs

*No matter how calmly you try to referee, parenting will
eventually produce bizarre behavior, and I'm not talking
about the kids.*

—BILL COSBY

I cannot count the number of frustrated parents who have come to me,
certain that something is terribly wrong with their children. They say
their kids are messed up because they do not respond to standard parenting techniques. These children cannot be motivated. Typical punishments don't work. Time-outs or grounding has no effect. Threats to take
things away don't work, the parents say, because these kids don't care
about anything. Their children don't respond to lecturing or even spanking like other kids.

Believe me, these parents need help as much as, if not more than,
their kids. But when I try to guide them they invariably respond: "Sorry,
tried that, doesn't work."

Well, there is an old saying: "A poor workman quarrels with his tools."

If your child's behavior needs to change, this chapter is where the
rubber meets the road. Shaping behavior is a science. There are very specific and precise principles and techniques for doing it. You can learn
them and become a powerful change agent within your family. Simply
put, these principles work. If you follow my instructions, you can—and
you will—modify your child's behavior in a productive way.

In the pages that follow, you will learn how to get your children to do
those things you want them to do, and to stop doing things you don't
want them to do.

The truth is that most parents know just enough psychology to be dangerous, extremely dangerous. You may be thinking, "Hey, I took Behavioral Psych 101. I know about rewarding good behavior and punishing bad behavior. It's not that tough."

Well, you're sort of right, because it is easy when you know how. But chances are you don't—yet. My approach is not new if you have spent your adult life studying human behavior, but if you haven't, there is a whole lot more to it than what you learned watching mice in a maze. Still, it is easy when you are given the proper tool. I am going to share with you the how-to nuts and bolts for repairing and fine-tuning your child's behavior patterns. You will learn how to get rid of the behaviors that have you tossing and turning at night, and how to inspire those that will help your child become an authentic and fulfilled adult.

Principles used in this tool come from the established fields of behavioral modification, cognitive behavioral psychology, social psychology and other scientifically based approaches to human nature. I've pulled out the best of the best from each of these disciplines to teach you so that you can create a solid strategy for making lasting behavioral changes that will help you effectively and lovingly parent your child.

I must caution you that if you misuse this tool—if you play at this instead of making a serious commitment to learn and apply the principles—you might create more problems than you solve.

But properly used, the principles you are about to acquire are proven to be effective for eliminating undesirable behaviors and creating desirable ones. Understand that I am not talking about applying them to those complex issues that may be at the root of your child's unacceptable behavior. If in your opinion those underlying causes need to be addressed, then you should seek professional help to get that done. In most cases I do not believe that such an intervention is required, but that's your call and you will have to make it. I believe behavioral change is a valid primary goal in a high percentage of most cases, so I am going to tell you precisely what you have to do to change your child's problem behavior.

There is legitimate room for both approaches to dealing with maladaptive behavior. Sometimes it is important to get to the root cause as part of your solution, but there are other times when it is appropriately or even critically important to stop the maladaptive behavior within a more immediate time frame. For example, I have worked with children who persistently banged their heads into tables, walls or other unmovable objects when they came under stress. Was it important to figure out the root cause of that disorder? Absolutely. But in the meantime, to protect the child's health and life, it was critical to modify the behavior right then, whether the root cause was known or not.

The directions for using these tools are deceptively simple, but the nuances are critically important. The principles are based on decades of scientific research, and the applications are universal. I say that with such conviction because in addition to a large body of research, the tools are based on laws of human behavior that are as unwavering as the laws of physics. Primary among them is that all humans—and especially children—tend to seek pleasure and avoid pain. I'm not talking about modifying behavior with physical pain, mind you. But I am talking about knowing your child's currencies and controlling them to create the behavioral patterns you desire.

If you're wondering whether you have the right to shape your child's behavior so powerfully, trust me, you not only have the right, you have the responsibility. The truth is that the forces that shape your child's behavior are already active. They are being shaped and programmed this very minute. My belief is that process should not be random. There is no one better than you to help your child because no one else in this world wants the best for your child as passionately as you do. But this is an awesome responsibility and one for which you must be a good steward. You must remain focused on discovering your child's authentic self. You must be determined to help your child become the best, unique person he or she can become. You must be careful to avoid pursuing unrealistically high expectations or pushing your own agenda as to likes and dislikes, skills and abilities, onto your child. Shape them, but shape them within the frame of who they are authentically meant to be.

I am eager to get started in imparting this information to you because, although I know you are well intentioned, you are very likely violating some of the laws of behavioral shaping at this very moment because you don't fully understand them or their effects. If you are facing stubborn problems with your child, take heart because it is not too late—if you are willing to learn how to use these techniques (and more important, how to use them correctly), I predict that you are going to be pleased to discover that there isn't something terribly wrong with your child after all. Happily, you are going to find that they do in fact respond to guidance.

I know you may have doubts, but you must have faith. Your child is not an exception, because there are no exceptions. Whatever your child's problem behavior is, bed-wetting, baby-talking, back-talking or lying, you can bring about change. Tantrums, rebellion, underachieving at school, drinking or drugs, fighting, whining, overdependency or worse, all behaviors can be changed. You must believe in your child and in your own ability to master what you need to know to be an effective parent. Barring some genuine medical or developmental anomaly that affects your child's ability to learn, you will discover that you have the power to shape your child's behavior in a highly efficient manner.

Four-year-old Susan was one of the first children I helped with the methods I'm about to teach you. Susan wouldn't talk to her mother. The mom came to me beside herself, thinking that there was something terribly wrong because Susan would only grunt at her. This child was the youngest of three daughters and she basked in their attention as the baby. But she refused to speak. "I feed her cookies, I plead with her, I spank her, I tease her, I do everything, but all I get are grunts," her mother told me. "I am embarrassed to take her out to see my friends. I feel like I have a little ape with me."

There were several cues in the mother's remarks as to her own issues. And in just observing her daughter as she spoke, I could see that this obviously intelligent child had found a way to manipulate her mother to get her attention. I could see her eyes light up when her mother talked about her frustrations with Susan, compared to her successes with the first two daughters. The mother was so wrapped up in her own emotions that the initial session was over before I had a chance to interact at all with the child. Still, I was impressed with how passively little Susan sat on the oversize chair during the whole session. Obviously, there was nothing seriously wrong with this child.

Before the next session I picked up a box of Cheerios and a little child's purse on the way to the clinic. I asked Susan's mother to remain in the waiting room while I talked with Susan in my office. The little girl walked into the office, climbed into a big chair and made herself at home without a word. She got very interested when I brought out the Cheerios, grunting to indicate that she wanted a handful. I took my cue to begin the behavior modification process. "This is the deal. I want to have a good conversation with you about anything you want to talk about, but I know that you want to be paid for your efforts. I will pay you in Cheerio money," I offered. "You can eat them or save them in this little purse I bought. Deal?"

I could tell that Susan comprehended exactly what I said. But she did not say anything. It was a game to her. I asked her the first yes/no question, "Are you comfortable in that chair?"

She nodded, and grunted for a Cheerio.

I told her I needed to hear a verbal yes or no.

A bell-clear little-girl voice rang out: "Yes."

Cheerio time! I rewarded her with exactly one, and she quickly gobbled it down. The next series of questions required only yes/no responses. Susan had no problem with them. Then I began asking for responses in complete sentences. Again, the child spoke clearly and with obvious intelligence, which was also reflected in the fact that she began building up a Cheerios savings account. She stacked them like chips at a poker table. By the end of the session Susan was chattering like a typical four-year-old and I detected similarities to her mother's speech patterns. The child also had her purse packed with Cheerios, which she'd been using to create pictures to illustrate the stories she told me.

As we left the room and rejoined her mother, Susan proudly displayed her bulging purse, but she reverted to grunting instead of speaking. I observed as Susan quickly regressed to that undesirable behavior in front of her mother. The mom found it hard to believe when I assured her that Susan and I had been conversing for the last hour. I promised her that the child was very verbal and well adjusted.

We had two more sessions that followed the same pattern. Susan chatted me up for Cheerios, but only grunted for her mother. Her mother did get to see and hear her daughter's verbal exchanges with me by observing behind a two-way mirror, yet she reported no change later in behavior at home. I gained a deeper understanding of that problem when I asked the mother if she tried the Cheerios at home to elicit speech from her daughter. She responded that she didn't have time for those games.

In a professional perspective, this was a successful case in which I got the desired behavior from the child. But from a family perspective, it was a failure because Susan was not speaking at home. Her mother's failure to follow through should serve as a good bad example to other parents. You need to understand and embrace the principles of behavior change if you hope to be successful with your child. You can carry the poor kid off to a therapist every year until he or she is eighteen, but until you bring the principles to bear at home, your child probably will not respond with the desired change in behavior.

The remainder of this chapter is divided into two sections. In the first, you will learn about identifying, specifying and creating behaviors that are desirable. In the second, I'll offer guidance in identifying, specifying and eliminating those behaviors that are not desirable. As you read through this material, it's likely that you may realize mistakes you've made in the past with older children. Don't fret, please. You'll be able to correct those errors with the same processes.

PART I:
BASIC STEPS IN IDENTIFYING AND CREATING DESIRABLE BEHAVIORS

If you want your child to behave appropriately, you have to first set the standards for the behaviors you want. You need to specify exactly how you want your child to behave, but it must be behavior appropriate for the child's age. You can't expect a five-year-old to have the table manners of a thirty-year-old. And you must present a unified front. It is important for the parents to sit down with each other and be very clear in terms of how they want their children to behave. Then they need to develop strategies to achieve those behaviors. I'm going to give you plenty of help there because I want you to focus on the positive.

Too often, parents look only at undesirable behaviors, and consequently their parenting styles dissolve into complaining and reacting and, well, the old crash-and-burn pileup in the family room. This is like trying to drive a car by looking through the rearview mirror. You see only what is being done instead of what lies ahead. The list of proper behaviors isn't all that long or complicated. Kids should be expected to follow directions, respect adults, stick to schedules, and act like they have good sense in public, at least. If you focus on developing the positive behaviors in your child, then the negative behaviors won't be so overwhelming and you can feel good about your parenting and your children.

Step 1: Identify Specific Target Behaviors

Focusing on the positive is always the best way to deal with a child, so we'll first target those behaviors that you want your child to begin performing. This category may also include behaviors that your child may occasionally perform but you want to increase their frequency, intensity or duration. You may, for example, value a behavior such as reading, but your child rarely sits down with a book, so you want to encourage more of that. As a reminder, be sure to target behaviors that are developmentally appropriate. Reading might be a great goal for a five- or six-year-old, but not a two-year-old. Also, don't make the mistake of targeting an emotion rather than a behavior. A father once said to me, "I wanted my son to eat spinach, and he finally did. Now I want him to like it and *feel* excited about it!" Hold on there, Dad! You can influence behavior in hopes that it catches on, but you cannot legislate emotion.

That father was confusing emotions with behaviors. To help you keep the two straight, here is a list of characteristics. For a behavior to be an appropriate target, it must be:

1. Within the scope of the child's abilities. Avoid overreaching and make sure that what you are asking the child to do fits the specific circumstances in which it is to occur. They have to be old enough to do it and have ample opportunity. For example, it would be unfair to expect a ten-year-old to read quietly and comprehend *War and Peace*, especially if you stick the kid in the kitchen, which is a zoo of activity, with TVs blaring, phones ringing and other kids running in and out.

2. Narrow in scope. An appropriate target behavior should address a specific action rather than a broad array of issues. If a child is resistant to performing personal hygiene, you would want to address only one or two behaviors at a time. A sensible target behavior might be one of the following:
   - Brushing teeth for two minutes without prompting.
   - Taking a shower after playing outside and before sitting down for dinner or study.
   - Brushing or combing hair in the morning before starting the day.

3. Unambiguously defined. It should be clear not only to the child but to the whole family what the target behavior is. This might be helpful if a sibling can offer support when you are not there. Make this a family affair. Do not expect the child to guess at what you

want. Use your two-way communication model to ensure that your child knows and can articulate exactly what is desired. "Be good!" just isn't enough instruction. You have to break down what you want into what we call operational definitions. That is, you must break the desired end product down into the operations that define it. What do you mean by "be good"? Does that mean sitting quietly, watching TV, doing chores, playing a board game? What exactly do you mean? Be precise.

4. Measurable. Whenever possible, the target behavior should be quantifiable. If it is a target behavior you can count or measure in some objective way, it is much easier to keep track of progress; it is also easier for your child to recognize their own progress, which can create momentum in sustaining the positive behavior.

The following are some example target behaviors that are quantifiable and can be used as measures of improvement:

- Number of times showing a happy face (tough for teens)
- Number of words spelled correctly on tests
- Amount of time studying (be careful to define studying)
- Number of times room was cleaned per week

A positive target behavior is a well-defined action that you wish to introduce or increase in your child's pattern of conduct. It can be confusing just to ask a child *not* to behave in a certain way in order to receive reinforcement. Doing so would be to violate what we call the dead person's rule. You don't ever want to assign your child something a dead person could do! A dead person can*not* run through the house or *not* be rude or *not* talk back. Since you are dealing with a living, breathing child, you'll want to focus on guiding *active*, positive behavior. This may sound silly, but parents do it all the time. Think about it: If you tell Billy to stop hitting his sister, you may not have made any real progress, even if he complies. He can immediately start kicking her, pinching her or pushing her down. You didn't tell him not to do that, and kids will split hairs with you every time. Instead, tell him to do something a dead man can't do, such as "Billy, tell your sister you are sorry for hitting her and help her put her toys away." You have now given him a very precise *behavioral prescription* that calls for affirmative action of appropriate and desired behavior.

Simply telling a child what not to do is not an effective management approach.

You don't ever want to judge the success or failure of your parenting based on the absence of negatives with your child. As I have said, the convenient child is not necessarily a successful child. What you want is a child who actively engages the world with positive, productive and results-generating behaviors. In order to have that, you need to ask. You, the parent, need to positively reinforce and reward those behaviors to encourage them. So, bottom line: Don't waste your time just telling your child what *not* to do. Spend your efforts and energy guiding your child in what *to do*.

Step 2: Determining Currency

Based on human nature, there must be a reward or payoff for your child to actively adopt more desirable behaviors. That's not an indictment of your child as being unduly selfish. It is human nature. Everyone approaches a given situation thinking "What's in this for me?" to some degree. Children are certainly that way, because they have not yet been socialized to spend much time considering the thoughts or feelings or needs of others.

Children can be both selfish and power-seeking. I'm not saying they are *Children of the Corn*–style evil beings. They are just kids looking to survive and looking to get their needs and wants met. I'm pointing out their nature because if you want to be successful in dealing with people you have to understand what makes them tick. You have to meet them where they are, and if children are greedy, then appeal to the greed. *Children want what they want when they want it and they want it now*. So figure out a way for them to get as much of what they want through appropriate behavior.

All of us work for payoffs at some level. That's just human nature. What constitutes a payoff varies from one person to another. As the old saying goes, "One man's trash is another man's treasure." It is for that reason that you must *empirically* define whether a given consequence is truly positive for your child. That means that you just can't decide that some consequence is a reward just because *you* think it is or ought to be. You must determine a positive currency for your child based on what she likes or dislikes and what she is willing to work to get. One of the most powerful currencies for a child is the parents' acceptance and approval. If your child *isn't* influenced when you say "great job" or "you are disappointing me," then they don't care what you think. And that's a sad commentary on your relationship. You will need to do some major repair work because you have been written off. In most cases, children write off a parent if they think the parent doesn't truly care about them. They shun you and your influence to strike back. That way, if you hurt them, they can say, "I don't care."

As I said earlier, I have had so many parents of "problem" children tell me that their children value nothing, respond to nothing and are willing to work for nothing. Those parents are wrong. They just haven't found the currency yet or they have arbitrarily decided what works as a reward for their child. All children have currency, levers and hot buttons. If you want to have influence over your children, you must *empirically identify* and then control their favorite currency.

> **Survey Fact:**
> **Twenty-nine**
> **percent of parents**
> **allow their kids to**
> **sleep with them,**
> **but don't know how**
> **to stop it.**

In my clinical practice, I once worked with a young mother, Teresa, a third-year psychology major who was attempting to potty-train her three-year-old son, Javier. Teresa was one of those parents who knew just enough psychology to be dangerous. She knew that if you wanted to increase the likelihood of the behavior reoccurring, you should reinforce that behavior by introducing a positive reward whenever the behavior or some approximation of it occurs. Her choice of reward was the Hershey's Kiss, the popular chocolate treat. But Teresa was totally confounded. Although she was quick to reward him any time Javier even moved toward the potty-chair, he simply did not—to put it delicately—make any progress. Well, it turns out that poor Javier was allergic to chocolate! For him, those Hershey's Kisses were the kiss of death! Think about it from his point of view: Every time he went near that potty-chair, his mother shoved a toxic substance into his mouth that triggered a stuffy nose and itchy eyes. Any intelligent person would avoid the potty under those conditions!

Teresa did a lot of things right, but she failed to properly identify what was a genuine reward for her son. She was like a lot of parents who struggle to identify a positive currency for their children. Sometimes that difficulty is due to the fact that the parent has already given the child everything she could possibly want. So the kids—being kids—take everything for granted. It may be that they need to dial their children's world back down to the basics and require them to learn that television, Nintendo, stereos, DVDs and an army of stuffed animals are privileges to be earned in exchange for good and proper behavior.

Children need to recognize a direct connection between their levels of performance and their quality of life. There are a number of different currencies that can vary with your child's age. One currency for adults is monetary. At least in theory, if adults do an excellent job, they get an excellent paycheck. With your child, one form of currency, for example, would be grades earned in school. I believe it's important to teach children how the world works, so I believe that if grades are designated as an important currency and a child has an A level of performance, they should enjoy an A *level lifestyle*. If the child has a B level of performance, they should have a B *level lifestyle*. If the child makes Cs in school, they should have a C *level lifestyle*. This teaches them how the world works. It also gives them that sense of kid power and mastery and control of their existence that is so critical to the development of a child's sense of self. They also learn that valuable lesson: *When you choose the behavior you choose the consequences*. This is critical for learning responsibility.

So it's important to determine what currency works for your child and for you too. Do you know your child's currency? Do you have a plan for using it to shape behavior? Or do you just hand out candy indiscriminately, because they are entitled? Here's a definition of exactly what I mean by currency. Currency is anything that when presented *during* or *immediately after* a target behavior will increase the likelihood of that behavior occurring again. In other words, it is something the kid will work to get.

Note the emphasis on "during" and "immediately after." You must be very careful about your timing or you can inadvertently reinforce the very behavior that you're trying to eliminate. Here's a common example: Many parents complain that their children will not stay in their own beds. They come into the parents' bedroom late at night and beg or cry to sleep with them. I've had parents say they respond by getting up, giving the children hugs or even bribing them with cookies to go back to their own beds.

In doing that, they are in fact reinforcing the undesirable behaviors of getting out of bed, intruding on the parents' room, whining and crying. This is true because they are immediately paying off the child, in the cur-

rency of attention—hugs and cookies—by introducing those consequences in direct response to the undesirable behavior. The parents are
ensuring that the child will repeat the late-night bed-begging over and
over again. Why? Because it works. The child gets a huge payoff! If those
parents want their children to stay in their own beds, the currency should
be paid out during and immediately after that behavior is seen and with-
held. So hug the little darlings while they are *in* their own beds and while
they are being tucked in. Do not wait until they are up at 4:00 A.M. trying
to get into bed with you.

Currency can also motivate a child in the negative. What that means
is that children are willing to perform Behavior A in order to escape
Consequence B. An example would be that children will study (Behavior
A) in order to escape a bad grade (Consequence B). Children will speak
to their parents with respect (Behavior A) to avoid getting grounded
(Consequence B). I personally prefer positive consequences in exchange
for positive behaviors, but in the real world children will perform to escape the negative consequences or to avoid losing privileges. You have to
be prepared to embrace motivation where you find it.

1. Categories of Potential Positive Currency
- *Tangible/Extrinsic Reinforcers:* Materials, money, food, token
  economies. External rewards are derived from the world and
  the people in it—as opposed to self-rewards. But, be careful not
  to overdo the external material rewards. To the extent that extrinsic rewards such as toys, privileges and money go up in
  value, internal motivation goes down. A parent who wants to
  boast about his child's grades and gives twenty dollars for each
  A is offering extrinsic reinforcement that is unlikely to inspire
  the child to take pride in the grades or to develop a healthy
  thirst for knowledge. A major mistake parents make is over-
  rewarding their kids to the point that it becomes bribery. Too
  much reward may defeat the self-motivation that most parents
  seek to instill in their children.
- *Token Economies:* Many times a parent can give token rewards
  that can later be redeemed for other values. These economies
  help in maintaining a system of accounting for behaviors and
  serve as an easy way to create credit systems. Tokens can be
  anything—poker chips, tickets, wooden sticks, gold stars or

even play money. The parent can set the value for each token, such as one token equal a cookie; two tokens equal an ice-cream cone; five tokens equal a movie at home; ten tokens equal a small toy; fifteen tokens equal a trip to an arcade; twenty tokens equal a stayover at a friend's house.

- *Social Reinforcers:* Attention, affection, affirmations.
- *Implied Reinforcers:* Certificates, privileges, titles.
- *Natural/Intrinsic Reinforcers:* The good feelings the child gets inside for making progress toward goals, the satisfaction of performance and self-concept changes.

2. Identifying the Child's Potential Currencies

In order to help you empirically determine your child's favorite currencies, answer these questions. You should be able to identify several possibilities.

- What things does your child like to use? Buy? Eat?
- What is your child's favorite pastime?
- What are your child's favorite television programs?
- Who do they most like to spend time with?
- What things, such as dolls or toys, do they like to collect?
- How much do they value their privacy?
- What is their favorite place to be?
- How do they like their accomplishments to be recognized?
- What are they good at?
- What time do they like to get up and what time do they like to go to bed?
- How important are their clothes? Do they have favorite items of clothing?
- Do they have a routine they value throughout their day?

To stimulate your thinking further, here are some suggestions of activities children tend to value. These are potential currencies you might withhold:

Attending an event, like a concert or party	Cooking
	Dancing
Being alone	Dating
Being with one or both parents	Doing artwork
Compliments or praising	Doing volunteer work

Driving

Eating out

Eating snacks

E-mailing

Exercising

Getting dressed up

Getting a massage or back rub

Going on vacation

Going to the mall

Helping someone

Listening to the radio

Playing video games

Playing a sport

Playing music

Playing with a pet

Playing with toys

Reading

Riding a bike

Shopping

Sleeping late

Staying up late

Surfing the Internet

Taking a nap

Taking a shower

Taking a walk

Talking on the telephone

Telling stories

Watching television

Watching a video

Writing letters

Step 3: Administration of Currencies

It is true that a child's currency works best and most efficiently when it is given consistently and immediately. Still, there is a science to scheduling the administration of currencies in an efficient way. There are two basic schedules I want you to understand: *continuous* and *intermittent*.

Continuous reinforcements are given every time a target behavior is performed.

Intermittent reinforcement is when you give the currency during and immediately after some but not every performance of the target behavior.

As a strategy, it is recommended that you offer continuous reinforcement during the learning phase. Once stability is established, you should switch to an intermittent schedule of reinforcement. This is recommended because learning occurs more rapidly during continuous reinforcement, yet will be maintained at a greater strength with intermittent reinforcement. Also, a child will have the tendency to resist efforts to move to the next level of behavior or into a new area of behavior if a schedule of continuous reinforcement is maintained. For example, a child may quickly learn the multiplication tables and work hard for both intrinsic and extrinsic currency, but will resist adventures into the unknown when a continuous reinforcement schedule has been maintained.

It's not so hard to understand really. It falls under the philosophy of "If it ain't broke, don't fix it." Why try something new if the current and comfortable behavior pays you off every time? How many times have you praised a child for drawing an object only to have the child return again and again with basically the same rendering? They know that drawing brought praise, so why try a new one? Children who are reinforced on a 100 percent schedule are also very fragile. If as challenges get more difficult, they begin to experience mistakes and therefore not receive reinforcement, they tend to panic and regress to more infantile behavior. Children who have learned on an intermittent reinforcement schedule are much more stable and durable in their behavior and emotions. They are much more adventurous and willing to try new things in hope of finding a new way to get paid off, perhaps more frequently.

Intermittent scheduling can be based on two strategies. The first is *time based:* Currencies are given based on a time frame, such as giving Cheerios at every five-minute interval during which a child has continuously played well with others. This schedule is highly effective in shaping target behaviors. The second is based on the *number of times* a specified target behavior is performed: For example, every fifth time a child is ready for school on time, an allowance is given.

Shaping Complex Behaviors a Step at a Time

Parents, many times a child's complex behavior will need to be *shaped.* This means that in the beginning of the learning process, behaviors that are close to the target behavior should be reinforced. If the target behavior is to get a child to say a specific word, such as "grand-mommy," you might use Cheerios as the currency (if she likes Cheerios). As you repeat the word and point to her grandmother, the child might say something akin to the word, like "mama." That is close enough for a Cheerio reward. Once "mama" is mastered, however, you would withhold the Cheerio until the child comes up with something closer to the target word, maybe "ur-mommy." After that step, and assuming that the child can actually use the g sound, you would wait and reinforce the next closest approximation to the specific target behavior. That's how it works. Step-by-step you reinforce the shaping until the child masters the desired target behavior. It's important that you be patient here. Your child can be coaxed into the complex behaviors you desire, so long as the child is developmentally ready to perform at that level. This procedure of rewarding successive approximations of a target behavior even works with animals. How do you think animal trainers get a bear to ride a bicycle or a seal to balance a ball on its nose? It is all about well-timed rewards for behaviors that get closer and closer to the target.

Case Study—Potty Training

One of the most frequently asked questions by young mothers concerns the target behavior of potty training. This stubborn and troublesome milestone, if your child is developmentally ready and you have mastered the concepts in this chapter, can be done in less than one day. (I have demonstrated this process on my television show, and you can get a copy of the step-by-step protocol from my website, drphil.com.) However, in the interest of demonstrating the process of behavior change as described in the current chapter, I'll offer a quick review here (at no extra charge!).

1. *Target Behavior:* Urinating and defecating in the potty.
2. *Currency:* Huge social rewards in the form of hugs and kisses, a party, any snack food that's based on results the child values and even a phone call to the child's favorite fantasy character or superhero (aka Grandma or some other willing spirit). I've been doing this so long that I have been through Superman, Batman, the Six Million Dollar Man, Wonder Woman, the Teenage Mutant Ninja Turtles and now Nemo.
3. *Schedule:* Continuous reinforcement to maximize the learning phase.

In order for the child to grasp the target behavior more quickly, I often use a doll that "wets" as both a model and a student for the child to train. It is true that the quickest way to learn is to teach. I allow the doll to urinate in the potty and both of us praise the doll and give it play food, like Cheerios. We make a big deal about how smart and grown-up the doll has become and we give it a special status, such as calling it "Big Girl Sally."

The best time for a child to regularly urinate is about thirty minutes after he or she has taken in a drink, so we wait until there is something to urinate. I have the child sit (or stand) according to what the doll did, and focus on achieving the result. If there is nothing fairly immediate, rather than frustrate everyone, relax and try five minutes later. If there is an attempt but not exactly in the potty, you might shape the target with partial currency.

Usually within just a few hours some urination in the potty will occur, and then all of the rewards will be showered on the child. Balloons will fall, hugs will be given, praise and adoration will be immediate and the doll and child will celebrate their new status and the special phone call is made. Major attention and celebration continues every time for a day or two, and then the schedule of reinforcement is thinned out as the behavior becomes self-perpetuating. I have worked with so many parents that have struggled with this for a year in a battle of wills to no avail. But once they use the important principles of behavioral shaping, it is over in less than a day.

PART II:
IDENTIFYING AND ELIMINATING NEGATIVE BEHAVIOR

The first part of this chapter was devoted to getting your child to behave according to your wishes. The second will be devoted to the other side of the coin—stopping those behaviors you don't want, such as tantrums and breaking the rules at school. In psychological terms, getting rid of unwanted behaviors is referred to as *extinguishing*, much like you'd extinguish a fire. A blaze cannot continue without fuel, such as gasoline or wood. In the case of behavior, actions will not continue to exist without the fuel of currency and reinforcement.

Please note that I'm giving you ways to stop unwanted behavior that will help you avoid conflicts and confrontations with your child. I believe that it is important to avoid confrontation with your children as much as you possibly can. Having head-to-head confrontations, delivering ultimatums and essentially throwing down the gauntlet breed conflict, power struggle and resentment. Therefore, I think it is usually good to try to figure out the best possible alternative and come up with a jointly sponsored plan that both of you buy into and can be excited about. Avoid confrontation as much as possible, but if and when you have one, as a parent, *you must not lose*.

Understand also that all behavior, even bad behavior, serves some purpose. People, including children, only do what works. If you see a behavior being repeated, you can bet that behavior is generating a payoff for the child. Maybe your child wants attention. This isn't necessarily a pathological need, but if he gets the attention as a product of throwing tantrums, whining, crying and manipulating, that *is* a problem.

Another thing you need to be aware of when you use my methods for stopping unwanted behaviors is that when you withdraw reinforcement for a problem behavior, your child may increase that problem behavior at first as a frustration response. A child will turn up the level of intensity of the unwanted behavior out of frustration because you changed the rules of the game and they feel you aren't playing fair anymore. Don't let yourself get upset when that happens because these frustration responses last only a short time before the behavior disappears completely. Then it will very likely spontaneously recur anywhere from one to three weeks later, as the child just checks again to be sure that, in fact, the new rules are still in force.

The principles of currency and reinforcement are the same for reducing undesirable behaviors as they are for increasing desirable actions. Let's look at some specific steps for eliminating problem behaviors.

Step 1: Identify the Problem Behavior

As with identifying positive target behaviors, be as specific as possible in defining the problem behavior. In terms of attitude, be careful to separate the behavior from the child. Here is a brief overview of how to properly define a problem behavior in terms that make its elimination manageable:

1. It must be specifically defined in terms of the observable actions that are targeted for elimination.
2. It must be narrow in scope. For example, if a child is using profanity, specify the exact words targeted for extinction.
3. It must be unambiguously defined. The child and the entire family must have a clear understanding of that which is targeted for elimination.

4. It must be measurable. Whenever possible, the problem
   behavior should be quantified—for example, counting the
   number of unacceptable words spoken.

Step 2: Commit to Withdrawing Currency

The process for diminishing undesirable behaviors can be accomplished
in two ways—*direct extinction* or *substitution of a positive target behavior.*
Remember that when the currency that is maintaining a problem behavior is removed, you can fully expect for the behavior to intensify and get
worse in the short term. Why? Because it has been so successful for such a
long time that your child will not give it up easily. The child will double
his or her efforts to maintain the status quo. It is like putting money in a
Coke machine and expecting the drink to appear. If it doesn't work, you
don't just shrug and walk away. You beat, shake, rattle and roll the machine, call it a few chosen names and consider eternal damnation before
you finally quit. Your child will do the same, but if you are consistent in
your resolve to really stop the flow of currency that has maintained the
problem behavior, things will smooth out. Still, you have to be tough and
you have to be committed, because you will be tested.

  If you hang tough for a while, but then eventually cave, you will just
make the situation worse. All you've done now is teach your child that
she has to be even more maladaptive to get a payoff. When you decide to
change your child's behavior, make a plan and stick to it. I promise you
can win, and your child can win too.

  Isolating and defining the problem behavior is really the easy part.
The harder part is getting real with yourself about what you have been
doing to maintain the problem behavior so that you can stop doing it. The
process of self-examination takes effort. I cannot tell you how many letters
we have received from desperate parents who want to come on the show
because they have lost control of their children. They plead for help, saying they'll do anything. Their kids may be stealing, lashing out violently,
threatening other children or otherwise doing all they can to live up to the
criminal profile of the FBI's Most Wanted. Yet when I ask those parents to
look at themselves by giving them a few penetrating questions that reveal
their legacies and their own reinforcement patterns, they turn white and
run for the hills. As I said in Chapter 1, many parents want me to fix their
children, but they are unwilling to look at their own behaviors and com-

mit to changing them. Remember, the family is a system and a problem child is a symptom, an indication that the family has lost its rhythm.

You have to be willing to change yourself. This is a critical step toward changing your child. You must be courageous enough to stop enabling the very behavior you want to eliminate. Begin by asking yourself in what ways you could possibly be rewarding your child that might elicit, maintain or allow the problem behavior. I'm betting you are, at least in part, giving the currency that keeps alive the behavior that you want to see die.

The second approach to eliminating problem behavior is to substitute a positive target behavior or competing behavior for the undesirable one. Although more complex, this approach is more effective than direct extinction because of the alternative behavior offered to the child. When the direct extinction method is administered, the child's repertoire of behaviors is left with a void, and he or she may choose another undesirable behavior in its place. For example, a child who has been using profanity such as "damn" may give up on that word after a few time-outs and start using the word "sh_t." You can go through a lot of words by the time he finds all of the undesirable ones unusable.

A further complication, called *overcorrection*, can occur with the extinction method. This result can happen when the anxiety of extinguishing the undesirable behavior has repercussions, such as bed-wetting, self-injurious behaviors and excessive eating. The child needs to find a more adaptive method of dealing with these underlying issues.

The process of substitution has three basic requirements. The substitute desired behavior must (1) serve the same function, (2) be more adaptive and (3) be a competing response. For example, if you want to keep your child from using "damn" (since it is usually an expression of frustration or anger), the substitute behavior would be using another word for frustration and anger, such as "darn" or "shoot." The substitute must be more adaptive, meaning that it should not be offensive or create more social problems. And it must be applicable to the same circumstance, such as using "shoot" or "darn" in response to the same frustration. Other examples are:

Problem Behavior	Substitute Behavior
Studying in disturbing environments, such as the television or game room	Studying in the library

Biting fingernails	Keeping hands in pockets
Criticizing others	Praising others
Destructive acts—making fun	Constructive acts—helping people

The Premack Principle

More than thirty years ago, psychology professor David Premack accurately described something mothers have known for generations. He found that high-probability (enjoyable) behaviors can serve as currency for low-probability (unenjoyable) behaviors. Simply put, if they have to, children will do things they don't particularly want to do, such as homework, in order to get to do things they do want to do, such as watch television or play with their toys.

This became known as the Premack principle. It is a simple but powerful truth that your children will perform those need-to-do behaviors with a high degree of consistency and efficiency if you establish and *enforce a consistent rule* that they must follow before they get to do what they want to do. If you think this sounds like nothing more than a fancy version of "eat your vegetables or you don't get any dessert," you are exactly right! The key value is that you can use a desired behavior as reinforcement rather than having to find some other tangible reward, such as money or a toy. Of course, to be effective, you must accurately identify which activities or behaviors your child is willing to work for. If they don't really care whether or not they get to do the activity you are holding hostage, your power is lost. It is also well demonstrated that children value enjoyable activities even more if they have to work in order to get to do them. Again, consistency is key here. When you set up a contingent reward you must administer it with great predictability or power is lost.

Response Costs

On the flip side, children will also refrain from inappropriate behavior if and when they know that that unacceptable conduct will cost them access to something they really enjoy doing. For example, if the child knows that getting a demerit or detention at school for talking in class will cost them the privilege of watching a favorite television program that night, the child will be much less likely to commit the transgression at school. Again, the key is that your kid must be able to predict the consequences of his actions with 100 percent accuracy. That means you have to be totally consistent in enforcing the contingent rule. Children have to know that when they choose the behavior, they choose the consequences—not some of the time, but all of the time. If they can sometimes get away with bad behavior—even when they sometimes don't get away with it—you have lost your power. That means that you have to pay attention. You can't get busy and fail to monitor the situation. I know that I keep repeating this consistency point. I'm doing so because it is critically important.

I recently worked with a mother who was frustrated by her ten-year-old daughter's chronic lying. She told me, "I don't know why she continues to lie, because she gets in trouble every time she does." I immediately had two theories. My first theory was that the little girl didn't get into trouble every time she lied. She got into trouble every time she got *caught* lying. My dad used to say, "For every rat you see, there are fifty you don't see." I suspected that the little girl was probably getting away with lying the vast majority of the time. From her point of view, lying was probably a pretty efficient behavior, because it allowed her to escape accountability for poor performance or misconduct 80 percent of the time. My second theory was that what the mother called "trouble" was anything but. Mom was not *empirically defining* what was trouble and the punishment was not a real punishment for the little girl. As it turned out, on the rare occasions that Mom caught her lying, she was sending her daughter to her room and ground from the telephone. You guessed it, her room was like Disneyland, and she simply talked to her friends online instead of on the phone.

Can you catch your child every time she or he misbehaves? Of course not, but neither do you have to be naïve. And when you do catch them misbehaving, there has to be a consequence that they genuinely find distasteful. It must be there with great consistency. If you have to take extreme measures to make sure they are not getting "bootleg" reinforcement by simply focusing on something else—like getting online instead of being on the telephone—that's when one thing has to be taken away. You may have to take drastic measures. I have recommended to many parents of out-of-control children that they literally strip the child's room of everything except the barest essentials. I tell them to move everything into storage as a sort of bank. I mean everything, including all but essential clothes, the TV, the games, the toys, wall decorations and anything else the child finds entertaining. This becomes the cost of bad behavior, and the child has to earn back the luxuries.

Trust me; your local child protection agency will not come after you for neglect. It sounds harsh, but your child will get over it and come to appreciate those things all the more. Children need to learn that they must earn things rather than feel entitled to them. Sometimes it will be appropriate and necessary to remove a child's stimulation and entertainment for as much as a week or even a month, yet it can be just as effective to remove the child from the stimulating environment for even a few minutes. That is the concept of time-out. And, no matter what you think or what your experience may have been thus far, if properly applied, the procedure can be powerful.

Time-outs

I probably recommend time-outs more often than any other single behavioral management technique because when properly done, they are highly effective. This procedure is readily available to parents in most situations, yet I have had many parents tell me that the time-out procedure is flawed. They say it just doesn't work for their children. Upon closer examination, I generally find that when they use this procedure designed to remove children from positive stimulation, they're doing just the opposite. Sending a child to the bedroom in this day and time is not a time-out from stimulation. It's like going to Disneyland. If my boyhood bedroom had as much outrageous *stuff* as the rooms of most kids these days, I would probably have never left it. I'd have begged to be sent there!

Also, parents, remember that you must empirically define the value of that which you are taking away, as well as that which is taking its place. My room, when I was growing up, was stark. The only furniture I had was a twin bed and a large cardboard box to keep my things in. Even though that might logically look like a negative and a perfect place to be sent for a time-out, that barren room was my safe haven. I loved to retreat to it. So, parents, make your choices about currency based on results. If the child is willing to work hard to have access to a particular activity or thing, then by definition it is positive currency. If they are not willing to work to have access to that particular activity or thing, then, by definition, it is not a reward and you must look for something else.

If the following basic steps are followed, I can assure you that this approach works consistently and effectively.

1. The child should be aware of the reason for the time-out and the duration.
2. The duration should be appropriate for the child's development. A small child would not understand the meaningfulness of being grounded for even a day. For young children 5 minutes can seem like a lifetime.
3. No positive reinforcements should be present or introduced during the time-out. The child should not have any stimulation, not even a window to observe, if possible.
4. Time-out should be terminated at the contracted time.
5. Time-out should only be terminated when the child is behaving appropriately.
6. Time-out should not allow the child to escape or avoid the situation in which time-out might be perceived as preferable to doing the dishes or doing homework.

Contingency Contracts

It's always a good idea for two parties to get an agreement in writing, and that holds true with parents and children too. I've found it to be very effective to put down on paper just what you expect of your child and what the consequences will be if the child does or does not go with the program. These are called *contingency contracts* or *behavioral contracts*. You can call them whatever you like, but I call them a darn good idea. In addition to providing a good record of what has been agreed to, these tend to have a crystallizing or memorializing effect on the child. Once they've seen it in writing, it's hard for them to deny that they understood it. These contracts provide children with early lessons in contractual agreements and the whole concept of what it means to sign a document and agree to its stipulations.

Creating a contract is also good because it is a positive problem-solving communication. It is an active two-party negotiation in which both sides are interested. And it is something that is jointly owned by the two parties involved. This can be used with any child old enough to read and understand what is included in the contract. (If your daughter shows up with a team of New York City attorneys, you might want to reconsider!)

For younger children, it is sometimes helpful to substitute a wall chart that includes a list of duties, chores and responsibilities for the child. I like to break down the day into early-morning chores and responsibilities that the child should do when he first wakes up, such as brushing teeth, combing hair, getting dressed, putting away pajamas, making bed, getting school materials together and being ready at the door to leave at a designated time.

Similar chores and responsibilities can be listed for other parts of the day. Once the child completes a duty or group of duties, Mom or Dad then puts a gold star in the column for those duties for that day. For younger children, it's good to give a gold star for each thing, because they like a lot of reinforcement. For children who are a little bit older, one star for each group of things can be helpful. If the child therefore earns 100 percent of the possible stars, or if you are shaping behavior for 80 percent of the possible stars, for each of the five days of the week, the kid is owed some special privilege on Saturday.

Creating this chart can actually be fun, providing great interaction between parent and child. It doesn't have to look like a Supreme Court document. Have your child design something colorful. Use paint, glitter, markers and cutout images. For younger children, it should be a really fun project for both them and their parents to do together. Make the chart using lots of color and stickers, add rainbows—really cartoon it up so it is something the kids enjoy looking at and working on.

It works fine to do a thirty-day chart, which means you get to repeat the fun of creating a new chart frequently. Again, there are many benefits of parent and child working together, including use of a token economy that teaches the child that when you choose the behavior, you choose the consequences. There is also the opportunity for the child to see real proof that he is making progress throughout the day, week or month.

Here is an example of a behavioral contract. You may also download it at www.drphil.com.

Behavioral Contract

Kid Section

I _____, (the kid) and we _____, (the parents) enter into the following behavioral contract in order to create order and harmony in our home. This contract will be reviewed thirty days from the date of signing, at which time it is subject to either being continued or renegotiated.

By our agreeing to the terms and conditions of this behavioral contract, all parties understand and accept that they are bound by the contract and are not free to vary from the terms and conditions.

I _____, (the kid) agree that I will perform the behaviors listed below in the manner they are set forth and described.

(Insert operationally defined behaviors, such as completing homework in a timely manner, being home on time, addressing my mother and father in a respectful tone, not getting online or on the phone during the homework hours of eight to ten, etc.)

I _____, (the kid) agree that should I violate the contract by failing to perform the behaviors set out above that I will be choosing to suffer the following consequences.

(Insert penalties or loss of privileges associated with poor performance about the specified target behaviors.)

Parent Section

We, _____ (the parents), agree that if _____ (the kid) performs the behaviors as outlined above, that in addition to escaping any of the negative consequences outlined above, he/she will have earned the right to the following privileges.

(Insert privilege to be earned, such as free time to watch television, use of the family car, sleepover, movie, toy, etc.)

Both parties acknowledge that this contract is entered into voluntarily and that the terms and conditions will be respected. If performance is accomplished, parents agree that the child shall not be denied privileges and other consequences.

Kid agrees that if he/she fails to perform that it is him/her and not his/her parents who have chosen to forfeit the consequences, and he/she will not whine, complain or rebel.

_____

_____   _____

The Parents   The Child

_____

Date

• • •

Behavioral contracts should provide very clear and understandable language about such issues as behavior, health, safety, social conduct and academics. They should address expectancies in each of these areas and positive and negative consequences for performance or failure of performance. The contracts should involve language that is age-appropriate and can be clearly understood by the child.

Contracts are good because they take the personality conflicts out of the situation. If something is agreed to in a contract and the child violates the agreement, the child has only to look at the agreement to understand that he failed to comply. It's important that children own up to the consequences of their own choices rather than being frustrated and angry with their parents. There should even be language in the contract that says it is acknowledged that if negative consequences are forthcoming, the child acknowledges that it will be because of his or her choices. That way, the child will have no reason to be upset with or frustrated with the parents. In this way, the child has to live up to the fact that "this is my deal, and it's my responsibility and I fully accept it so I cannot complain about it later."

Without written agreements, discussions often become forgotten, especially when it is to someone's benefit to do so. Other benefits of such agreements:

- It gives the child a sense of justice and control, making him or her more compliant to the agreement and it gives the parent the clear understanding of the plan.
- The essential components of a contingency contract are clear, unambiguous statements of (1) the target or problem behaviors, (2) the consequences and currencies for performing (or failing to perform) them, (3) the contingency between the behavior and consequences and (4) the time frame in which the contract will be enforced.
- By writing the agreements down with specific currencies and behaviors, the contract can be the final authority, which underscores the importance of stating the terms of the plan so there is no confusion or slipping between the cracks. Signing the contract increases the commitment of the parent and child to fulfill their roles as stated.

In some ways, behavioral management is a scientific term for good old commonsense parenting, but it has real science to support its effectiveness. I encourage you to give it a try once you've carefully studied my guidelines. You've got to get it right to get the results you want for your child. I think you will be very glad you did, and my bet is that your child will be grateful too—if not right away, then down the road when he or she is a well-adjusted and authentic adult. Understand that most undesirable behaviors respond to the same principle of reinforcement— whether it is lying, hitting, whining, being overdramatic, clinging, thumb sucking, failure to follow directions, not picking up toys, cussing, etc. The reason I can generalize these behaviors is because all behavior has a purpose, and when you change this underlying purpose the behavior will change. So if any of my working examples in this chapter don't address the issue you face take heart because they all follow the same law of behavior.

Before we move on, I want to talk to you about the child that may be uncommonly stubborn and resistant to change. If you have been a good student and closely followed the principles and guidelines set forth in this chapter and your child either does not respond or despite significant changes in behavior continues to appear unhappy, anguished or emotionally confused and suffering, you must be sensitive to these circumstances and look deeper. You know your child and their medical, mental and emotional histories better than anyone. If your child has experienced life events that may have created debilitating pain, fear or loneliness, it may be that their maladaptive behavior has become a coping mechanism and therefore serves a meaningful and needed purpose in their lives. If, for example, your child has experienced the death of a family member, a painful divorce or a serious or prolonged illness (their own or a family member's), the very behaviors you are targeting may be generating a protective payoff that goes beyond the apparent.

If that is the case, providing them with new behaviors for coping with that internal pain will be essential to their willingness to give up the maladaptive behaviors. You must be patient and may need to simultaneously seek professional help to resolve the pain and conflicts. Hopefully, implementing the five factors for a phenomenal family, overcoming any negative parental legacy and being more sensitive in your parenting style will be curative and healing and act to create a greater sense of safety and security to additionally help your child get past his or her internal issues.

Be careful not to hide behind some exaggerated or imagined trauma to excuse your child's accountability or your own. In most cases, children will respond to these behavioral change techniques and feel a whole lot better for it.

11

Tool 5: Parenting Through Change

Shake It Up to Break It Up

When my kids become wild and unruly, I use a nice safe playpen.
When they're finished, I climb out.
—ERMA BOMBECK

You have to shake it up to break it up. I know it might sound crazy to talk about *creating disequilibrium* in your family as a tool for creating positive change, but that is exactly what I mean. Shaking up dysfunctional behavior patterns and family relationships can be a great tool. In fact it's a power tool. Creating disequilibrium in an unhealthy family structure can be extremely useful and appropriate if the patterns and alliances that define it are causing problems and are deeply entrenched. That's what I mean when I say: You have to *shake it up to break it up.* By creating a major shift in how things are working around your house you can clear the way to getting your family back on track. When old habits and patterns all of the sudden no longer work your child will be vulnerable to your efforts to redefine things.

This is a tool that is loosely based on the concept of disequilibrium used by family therapists who practice structural family therapy. You aren't a therapist but you're embedded in your family's system and you can use what I'm about to lay out for you when you feel really bogged down but want to create positive change from the inside out. For example, creating disequilibrium is very helpful if you're in a family where it just seems that the tail is waggin' the dog. That is, the kids seem to have gained the power or it's become the girls against the guys or the guys against the girls. Maybe you have a child who constantly whines and plays the victim, and it works! An imbalance of power and unhealthy factionalism can feed the ego and tyranny of a child or an insecure parent. And it can destroy a family in a hurry.

For more than a year sixteen-year-old Jasmine had been coming home after school each day in an angry and rebellious mood. She would come through the door like a storm blast, demanding to be fed and throwing the household into turmoil. She'd plop down in front of the television with the volume cranked to ear-splitting levels and scream orders at her mother: "Mom, I told you I was hungry. If you can't get me something, I'm going to McDonald's. I'm starving. Give me some money and the car keys."

Jasmine's mother let her run roughshod, complying to her every demand, which only made the teenager more contemptuous and more demanding.

Every day this tempestuous scenario played out with Jasmine raging and her mother trying to placate her. But there was no making Jasmine happy and no one around her was allowed peace or happiness either.

Then, one day, Jasmine comes home in her usual fury only to discover that the television has disappeared, and so has her mother. A note on the refrigerator door says only: "I will return at six and we will eat dinner. Love, Mom." Quickly she dials her mother's cell phone. When her mother answers, Jasmine rips into her: "Mom, why aren't you home? I'm hungry. What am I supposed to do?"

Her mother remains calm. "Jasmine, I decided to go shopping, and if you are hungry, there is plenty to make a snack. We will have dinner at six, and you will be there."

The tone in her mother's voice shocks her. It sounds so confident and in control. "Mom, where is the television? Is it in the shop?"

"No," replied her mother, "we put it in storage until we can see our family life has calmed down."

"What? Nobody asked me about this. After all, I am a member of the family."

"No, dear, we didn't ask because this is not your choice, it is ours."

The conversation did not help Jasmine's feelings. She felt as if she was losing control, and she was more than a little shocked when her mother kept using the pronoun "we." After all, she had been able to get by with almost anything with her father. She called him to make her case directly. "Dad, Mom said that you put the television in storage. Why are you letting her be so mean?"

Her father also sounded different. "Yes, we did. Your mother and I made the decision together. We need to redo the family agenda. So from now on you need to decide how we are going to work together to make ourselves happier instead of making us all so miserable."

Things did change. The television was out, the use of the car was out, and Jasmine did come for dinner that night and every night following. She was terrified, confused and angry at first. The changes this new united front presented and failure to respond or even engage when she tried to whine and complain were very unsettling. She felt like a stranger. But gradually she began to adapt and calm down. The new family structure actually gave her a greater sense of safety and security than she'd had in a long time. She started to respect rather than abuse her parents and saw her family unified for the first time. The strength of the unified leadership was calming.

Drastic problems call for drastic solutions. In a family that has become dysfunctional or self-destructive, patterns need to change in a dramatic fashion. Using the tool I'm about to present to you in a committed and responsible manner can really stir things up so that you can regroup and restructure in a healthy and balanced way. I call it creating *disequilibrium* because it results in a redefinition of roles and a major shift of power that can be temporarily very unsettling to those who were running the show and having their way. It forces them to adopt a more mature level of behavior to regain privileges and rights lost in the shake-up.

From a psychological perspective, this is a method for redefining your family dynamics and focusing on the priorities that you know in your mind and heart are required to meet your goals of family success. It's like when my mother used to clean our kitchen range after my dad and I had fried up a mess of catfish. Grease was everywhere and just wiping the stove down wouldn't even almost get it clean. First she had to take everything off so she could get it clean and then put it back together bright and sparkling, the right way. (I know, she should have made *us* clean it, but I didn't know how—I was only twenty-eight!) There was no neat or easy way to get it right. Same deal with a family that's way out of balance and control. It takes guts and commitment to pull this off and hopefully you'll have the support of all the adults in the family and extended family. The rewards of a well-run, happy and peaceful family are simply the sweetest life can offer. So yes, it's worth it!

Trouble at Home

Family therapists will tell you that quite often when a dysfunctional family suffers a major breakdown—maybe someone gets thrown out of the house or a teen gets pregnant or runs away or is even taken into custody—the primary problem is that the teenager or teenagers in the house have come to dominate the mentality and the power dynamics of the entire family. As I said, the tail is wagging the dog. I've seen it happen many times and it isn't pretty. It can run a family into emotional ruin and financial bankruptcy.

Again, that child may be the family member presented as the patient to the family therapist, but for this situation to develop other family members have contaminated the situation somewhere along the line. Whether it is the youngest teen or some other family member who is wielding inordinate power, somehow the family power base has been thrown off-balance. Creating disequilibrium can scramble that power base. Shake it up so that the old tricks no longer work. Guilt induction, tantrums, playing the victim and other manipulations must be disabled to create the opportunity for healthy change.

All families have a structure, and if yours is counterproductive, then it's time to make a plan to start over. You can't keep doing what you've been doing and expect to get different results. Things have to change. That change can be accomplished efficiently and dramatically when the adults in the house—I'm talking about you and me—stop playing patsy and start being parents. The idea is for you, the parents, to step up, start running things again and set clear objectives implemented with a strong, shoulder-to-shoulder unified front and a newfound commitment to consistency instead of constant waffling. Self-destructive patterns are put on a hit list to be eliminated, and new patterns are adopted. The child tyrant is overthrown. It's a new day in the kingdom with new rules and a new power distribution. Peace and serenity will be restored. Camelot lives!

The dominant child will naturally be upset and confused about being tossed out of power. Good. That can work in your favor as parents. Again, in this situation, confusion can be constructive. Children in these circumstances, regardless of age, will at first show frustration marked by extreme whining, temper fits and so forth, but will ultimately seek security, predictability and sameness. And you, the adult, can give them exactly that if you give yourself permission to parent with purpose and without guilt.

I don't know for certain how it happened, but many parents today have bought into their children's sense of entitlement. Some operate under the theory that they're better parents if they spare their children *any* difficult times or challenges. Today, many parents feel guilty when they cannot buy their children expensive designer clothes, new cars and the latest high-tech toys that young people demand. The kids don't know any better. But we should.

Young people are inundated by wave after wave from the American marketing machine. After watching hours and hours of television, you can't really blame them for thinking that they "need" every toy, item of clothing and electronic gizmo ever made. And kids are good at playing the victim. "If you loved me you would give me these things." (Tail waggin'!) All too often, parents give in to that. Sometimes it is guilt, insecurity or maybe just plain parental laziness. It's easier for some to cave in than it is to take a stand. So the skinny little tail wags the big dog, time after time.

More Love, Less Money

Here is one piece of advice: Give your children too much love and not enough money. They can handle that. They will adjust. Remember, you teach people how to treat you. If you spoiled your children, then you have to be the one to un-spoil them.

It's essential to remember that the most important things you should feel compelled to give your children are protection, preparation for the world and love. Everything else is a luxury. But you can't expect children to know that. They have no context to assess their status, just as a fish has no concept of what it is like to be outside water. For young people looking at their circumstances, television too often provides the only frame of reference for them. And that is a major cause of many problems in families today.

Creating disequilibrium, resetting the context for a disgruntled, complaining, sourpuss child, might mean taking away everything that is not essential to their welfare. I'm not talking about deprivation here. Your children should still have food, shelter and clothing, but feel free to cut out everything else to shake them up and get their attention. Even the things they may consider as essential as the air they breathe such as MTV, the Internet and Nintendo. I'm talking about even stripping their rooms of anything and everything other than sheets, a blanket and pillow if they are calling you out into a showdown over who is running things. And I'm not talking about Snoopy sheets or Winnie the Pooh covers, I'm talking about the plain-Jane essentials. Your children do not need to have posters, toys and other luxuries and forms of distraction. They take these things for granted and will appreciate them only if you create the disequilibrium of taking them all away one day. Misbehaving and ill-mannered children should not enjoy a rich and luxurious lifestyle. If you allow that imbalance, if you continue to reward bad behavior, you might as well teach them to go on red and stop on green and then pitch them the car keys. That's not how the world works, and you must remember that your job is to socialize them and prepare them for the world. Research is very clear: Children who are overindulged are typically unhappy. They're unhappy because they appreciate nothing. You have to have some bad times, some down times, some lean times, to appreciate the good times. If you cheat your child out of the experience of the contrast, you're not doing them a favor. Their screams will be heard across the land when you pull those plugs. But I've guided more than a few families through this process of disequilibrium, and it has worked beautifully.

> **Survey Fact:** The number one issue for parents of teenagers is peer pressure—what teenagers do when away from supervision.

Parental Power Failure

Joan and Jerry appeared to be a picture-perfect couple when they got married. He was an up-and-coming attorney, hired by his father-in-law as the possible heir to a major law firm. Joan was dedicated to being an all-American wife and mother. She wanted to raise two children, just as her parents had done. This couple had very good intentions, but they were several tools short in the parenting department.

Twelve years into their marriage, their dream family was in dire need of a shake-up. Their eleven-year-old daughter Sara was staging a reign of terror. The family was slave to her daily demands and a schedule that included ballet dancing, cheerleading, softball practice, voice lessons and two girls' clubs. But she wasn't just a social-climbing overachiever, she was over the edge and off the cliff. On two occasions, Joan found marijuana in Sara's underwear drawer while restocking the laundry. When asked about these troubling finds, Sara dismissed the joints and claimed she had no idea where they came from. Joan accepted her contention that it was probably just one of her girlfriends playing a practical joke.

Then there was Gerald III, son of Joan and Jerry. His primary occupation was tearing up whatever he could get his hands on. If he wasn't trying to set the neighbor's cat on fire, he was out bullying the other children. He was overweight from eating cartloads of candy in his room while watching television. His response to parental directives was to throw a tantrum. Joan gave up trying.

She'd dedicated her life to her children but she had no plan and no power to enforce it. Jerry was living his dream of success as a partner in the law firm, but he put in twelve-hour days at the office. Joan had the title of parent and all the trappings, but no real clout or control over her children. In Texas, this situation is disparagingly known as "all hat, no cattle." Her parenting tools were limited to screams of anger and frustration.

This upper-income, educated family was rapidly sliding toward the abyss. Sara was bound for drug rehab, Gerald for juvenile hall. Joan was on track for some stress-related health calamity, and her marriage was destined for divorce court. It was not a pretty picture, and it's all too typical. When parents give up their power and responsibilities, children take over by default. Joan and Jerry are just one example of parents who've let this happen. My research turned up parents whose questionnaire responses indicated they are having problems of one sort or another.

Change Agents

Change can be very painful, but it's worth the effort. Although children may resist, the shake-up is in their best interest in the long term. The key is to get these techniques consistently in play. Another technique for creating disequilibrium is forming new alliances within the family. For example, if there's a child who's the underdog among the siblings or if the children perceive one to be the parent's favorite, disequilibrium can be achieved by making a conscious effort to focus on the underdog child. Raising awareness of how individual family members are seen by others is also a powerful disequilibrium technique. Role-playing on a repetitive basis and giving honest feedback to various family members without the drama of yelling and screaming can be extremely powerful.

I often have parents play different roles and then observe how the children react to them. The kids may fully understand that the parent is just role-playing, but children will react to the roles as if they were real. In other cases, I will have the child act out what he or she perceives the parent's role to be. Sometimes the parent is amazed at the result: "Do I act like that?" The parent acts out the child's part and gets an equally astonished reaction: "Boy, you look silly being me."

When you and another member of the family exchange roles, this is called role reversal. It can be enlightening for everyone to see how they are perceived by other family members. Children can be very adept in portraying their parents, and vice versa. Try exchanging roles and acting out a typical family scenario such as a teen asking for the use of the family car or a grade school child wanting to have a sleepover. But have the parent make the request as if they were the child, and have the child play the role of the parent who denies the request. The role-playing will demonstrate not only how each side perceives the other, but it will also make new approaches and compromises more obvious. It can be fun, and it is always helpful.

Remember, if you have a dysfunctional family you're likely going to be facing very strong negative structures with deep foundations that have to be torn apart and reassembled in a healthier manner. That's what creating disequilibrium is all about. I know that has been achieved when I hear a child say, "What's going on around here? Why aren't you letting me do what I've always been able to do?" Once that happens, you can begin rebuilding because you've reopened the dialogue with that child. Now you can talk and be heard. Now the child will engage because they have have a dog in this fight—they want something. You've shaken things up and created disequilibrium to overcome the dysfunctional system that has defined your family.

What's It Worth?

To create disequilibrium in a dysfunctional family where the children have seized control or are behaving in immature and unproductive ways, there are techniques that can be very effective. Parents must first declare the house a guilt-free zone for all adults with the title Mother and Father.

You must free yourselves to set boundaries, redefine rules, renew mother and father alliances and generally rock the house. Give yourself permission because it's your job to raise your children responsibly. It's not your job to win some popularity contest with your children. They may like you for it and they may not; either way it's your job. They didn't give you that responsibility and they cannot excuse you from it. Chaos may ensue for a time and there may be a great gnashing of teeth in frustration, but out of that chaos, your children will start to communicate with you once again to get what they want. Remember, children can be selfish when they are not socialized properly because they are working with the base survival instinct. They reach for what they think they need, but they will come around. It won't be a warm and loving dialogue at first, but I promise you, things will get better. And again, remember, your job is not for your children to like you, your job is for them to respect you and be guided by you.

If you have a manipulative child who's succeeded in dividing and conquering Mom and Dad, a united parental front will necessitate a change in the child's approach. Children are smart; they may be the smartest people in the family. They know how to divide and conquer and they know how to raise their game to the next level if it's required, but only if it is required. It is this reality of getting from your children only what you require that causes me to be so critical of parents who baby talk to their children. I know it's cute when the child says "waa waa" instead of water, but when that mispronunciation is modeled back to the child, it retards his development of an age-appropriate vocabulary. When the child is required to begin to say the word more correctly, he will rise to the challenge because of thirst. Same deal here, when the child is made aware that he has to earn certain rights and privileges, rather than finagle them with insidious and underhanded behaviors, he will improve his behavior. What I want children to see is that all of a sudden Mom and Dad, who used to argue, fight, oppose and blame each other are now strangely allied. I want them to be scratching their heads, saying, "What happened here? I used to be able to turn them against each other. I used to be able to get them to tell me what I wanted to hear, so they could get a leg up on the other one. Now all of a sudden they're shoulder to shoulder, they're even comparing notes, and they seem to have agreed on standards and rules. I think I've got a problem here, a big problem!" This is a child who has become accustomed to ruling the roost and will not give up the throne easily, so be prepared for some major and creative manipulation. It's going to get very stormy. Are you prepared and committed to deal with it? Before you answer that, be aware that I've heard all the excuses from parents who don't have the strength to do their jobs. Some are compelling, but none are convincing.

Read these excuses carefully because you need to be honest about whether or not you hide behind them. I want you to drop all of these excuses. Your children need to know that you're fully committed to winning this battle for the family's future and that they cannot wear you down in this battle of wills because you're overworked or just plain emotionally tired. If you say to yourself any of the following things at least once a week, it's likely you've surrendered to the children at your house:

Top Ten Most Common Excuses for Not Shaking Things Up

1. I can't do it alone and my spouse either won't help or will undercut me.
2. There is no point, my child just doesn't respond to parenting like other kids.
3. It is just a phase; kids will be kids and I don't want them to just hate me.
4. I just can't deal with this right now; I have too much going on in my own life.
5. I'm so tired of hearing complaints. I just want some peace.
6. They have shut me out and couldn't care less what I say.
7. They don't love or respect me so I just don't care anymore.
8. I have my own problems and I have to fix me first.
9. I tried and I failed. It's too late now.
10. I know me and I'm just not tough enough to pull it off.

If any or all of these excuses have been repeatedly spoken even in just your mind, it's time to declare that a new day has come. You have to get a second wind and stand up for the long-term health of your family. You will pay a price for shaking things up, but to continue down this path is just not an option. Let's get real about your children and what makes them tick.

The True Nature of Children

We like to think of our own children as angels filled with love and good intentions. In many respects, I think you can explain the unsocialized nature of children very succinctly: Children can be selfish and power-seeking. Like many adults, they seek pleasure and avoid pain. That may sound pessimistic, but it is not. Your children aren't evil or bad if they behave this way, they're just waiting for you to do your job and socialize them properly. If you don't, your children can become tyrannical and demanding because they're not mature enough to handle the power surrendered to them inside a complex family. You also need to realize that your child is capable of lying, cheating, bullying and stealing. That doesn't mean they do or even will do those things, but they're capable of them. If you don't establish a clear connection between their behavior and the consequences that are generated from that behavior, they'll be crippled in a world that, unlike an indulgent parent, will not reward them for bad behavior.

Parents, you have to teach and model love, empathy, selflessness, fairness and many other positive qualities so your children will learn those traits. Your behaviors speak so very much louder than your words. And trust me, your children are watching you like a hawk. The old saying "Do as I say, not as I do" is a dog that won't hunt in this day and time. If you haven't been holding your children accountable for their behaviors and modeling what you want them to do, you've contributed mightily to the formation of the little monsters now running the family fun house.

The quickest way for a child to learn socialization skills is through experience, consequences, modeling and your taking the time to explain the logic behind the directions. But you need to keep in mind that your children have been studying you all of their lives and they won't give up their perceptions of you overnight. They know you better than you know yourself. They can tell in a split second if you're tired, angry or happy. And they're experts at figuring out what they can get by with. They know you better than you know them. Somebody is definitely going to run the show. If you don't take control, I guarantee you they will. If they think they can wear you down, shout you down or break you down, they'll do it.

Blurring the Boundaries

The very frightening fact is that every time your children win a battle with you, they lose more of what they really want and need—trust in your guidance. Children aren't equipped to be the leaders of the family. When you allow them to dominate, you blur the boundaries of parental authority. That confuses them. As much as they may fight for control, they really don't want it because they instinctively know they're too young to be in that position. Being in control confuses and conflicts them. When parents abdicate control, their guilt is shared by the children who've won out. It's a psychological minefield.

Kids are shrewd about timing their assaults. Think of the potty-trained child who wets his pants just as his parents are preparing to leave him with a babysitter so they can attend a dinner party. Ninety-nine times out of a hundred, that's not a kidney problem. It's a power move. He thinks you can't do anything about it, because you're all dressed up and ready to head out the door. So you have to toughen up and always be prepared to call his bluff.

Mom 'n' Pop Tag Team

I can't stress enough the importance of you moms and dads out there working as partners and presenting a unified front as you begin the family shake-up. This is important, whether one or both of you are in the home. It's *all for one and one for all* time for you two musketeers. No more bickering, backbiting or team dissension. If you're a single parent and you use child care, babysitters or family members to supervise the children, then you must meet with those other guardians to make sure they're signed on to the plan too.

Shaking up a family requires thoughtful planning. Sit down and work out an approach that all parental parties can get excited about and fully commit to. Get pumped up about this; it's not some grim task you're about to undertake. It's an exciting mission to finally create the family that you've dreamed about. And your children are going to be happier, healthier and more loving. They'll appreciate for the rest of their lives that you cared enough to step up and take control.

This will bring you and your spouse closer as partners because it demands emotional integrity. Each of you has to trust in the other. Each of you has to be trust*worthy*. You have to know that your partner can and will carry out the directives and adhere to the values and the guidelines you two have agreed to. No caving in. No cutting deals with the kids when the other parent isn't paying attention. No trying to come across as the good cop to your bad cop spouse. You must commit to this shake-up and to each other with all of your time, effort, energy and resources.

Once you've committed to the parental team, I want you also to dedicate yourselves to consistency in your shake-up of the family. You can't waffle. Your children's behavior is shaped by the consequences it generates. So those consequences that you lay out and administer have to be consistent each and every time. If you're inconsistent in punishing a child's misbehavior, you invite rebellion and manipulation from the child. Inconsistency equates to an intermittent reinforcement schedule, meaning sometimes the unwanted behavior is punished and sometimes it isn't. This kind of parenting creates child behavior patterns that are absolutely the most resistant to change. Children instinctively know if their parents aren't committed. They can be relentless in wearing down a weak-willed parent.

You've got to be there to confront your child's unacceptable behavior and let him know it's a new day indeed. When you say, "You're grounded for a week," that had darn well better mean 6 days 23 hours 59 minutes and 59 seconds of punishment. It had better mean that you will do whatever it takes to enforce that punishment even if it means staying home from work, following the child to school, canceling a vacation and skipping a dinner party at the boss's house.

If your child has gotten used to your not enforcing punishments consistently, once you become a determined parent he'll do everything he can to fight the shift. If you stand your ground it will cause the tremendous amount of planned disequilibrium you need to redesign your family system. It will get ugly, but don't confuse that with being unhealthy. As long as you and your spouse stand united and don't break and run, good things will begin to happen.

Commando Commitment

You must be willing to adopt what I call commando parenting. If you don't commit to totally immersing yourself in the plan you'll sabotage your child's chance to change, which may, in turn, sabotage your family's future. This isn't something you can play at. If there are two of you in-volved on a daily basis you must both have a whatever-it-takes mentality. This is akin to an intervention, so Dad may have to take two weeks of his vacation time and stay home with the children 24/7 to create a unified front with Mom. It could even mean that one of you has to quit working or downgrade to a part-time job to spend more time at home. You might have to drive a less expensive car, live in a smaller house, cut down on restaurant meals and vacation closer to home, but shaking up this family is more important than all of those extraneous things combined. The fu-tures of you and your children are at stake.

This may well be the most important mission of your life. Your child must be shown with 100 percent certainty that forbidden behavior will meet with the consequences you've laid out. If you don't enforce those consequences, I can assure you that you'll sabotage your child's develop-ment. You will confuse him. You will create anxiety and encourage mal-adaptive behavior. You will dig your own grave and bury your dreams of a happy, healthy family future. Consider this scenario: Jerry comes home from the office. He takes that tie from around his neck, turns it back-wards and puts it on as a headband, because it's time for some commando parenting!

Jerry and Joan showed a high level of commitment to the family shake-up that I helped them plan and carry out. I prepared them to get in the trenches with their children, particularly their daughter Sara, who was deeply committed to maintaining power over her family. She resisted everything her parents tried. She threw stuffed animals. She threw tantrums. She yelled. Screamed. She made herself throw up. She an-nounced that she hated her parents and all of their ancestors. She pro-claimed that they had hated her from the minute she was born. She threatened to quit school, run away and join the French Foreign Legion, if it was still accepting women volunteers.

It was an all-out war and it raged intensely for an extended period. But Joan and Jerry stood their ground and it paid off. They dropped out of their social circle and instead circled the wagons around their children. I helped them give their children the structure they sorely needed. It was no picnic. It was painful. But at the price of temporary peace, we built this family a future. Remember, peace at any price is no peace at all. I'm proud to report that Sara is now a much happier child because the pres-sure of running this family is finally off her. She does not have to mother her brother or her parents. Gerald III has become one of his school's top achievers because now he can focus on school. He has learned to trust that his parents will shoulder their responsibilities and be his guardians and guides.

Action Steps

Before we start the action steps, understand that my basic rule is that you have to be accountable. I devised this brief questionnaire to assess your present state of control. In the following scenarios, mark the response that you would most likely have. BE HONEST!

1. You have planned a one-week vacation and your adolescent breaks a rule of curfew, which has a consequence of grounding for a week.

    A. You would suspend the discipline until you get home from the vacation.

    B. You would try to show how upset you were and make the adolescent see the problems caused by the behavior. Once you could see that the child felt guilt, you would forgive and you would go on your vacation.

    C. You would cancel the vacation and monitor the child until the consequential result was completed.

2. You hired a babysitter for your two children so you could join friends for dinner. However, just as you are about to leave, one of your children starts throwing a tantrum to get a cookie.

    A. You would give the child a cookie and leave.

    B. You would offer a hug and explain that you could not deal with this now, but you would when you returned.

    C. You would deal with the situation at that time, even if it meant canceling the evening.

3. You're in a department store, shopping for something, and your child throws a tantrum because she wants an ice-cream cone.

    A. You go find an ice-cream cone.

    B. You're too embarrassed to be a mean parent, so you hold her in your arms and keep shopping.

      C. You immediately stop shopping and enforce a time-out consequence.

4. You are with your in-laws and your child breaks a rule deliberately because he knows that Grandmother will let him get by.

      A. You let it pass because this situation with Grandma is different, and it has become a typical thing, especially if Grandma thinks it is cute.

      B. You threaten your child with consequences when you get away from Grandma.

      C. You immediately handle the consequences as you would whether Grandma was there or not.

5. You are very tired from an exhausting day, and your child breaks a rule with known consequences.

      A. It will take effort to reinforce the consequence, so you let it go because the child knows that next time there will be consequences.

      B. You yell at your child and threaten consequences. Because the child appears to understand the violation, you drop the issue.

      C. Although it takes every ounce of your strength, you enforce the consequence and level the discipline.

Scoring: If you checked off any responses other than the Cs, you're guilty of forfeiting control of your family and failing to live up to your responsibilities as a parent. It's tool time for you!

Ways to Create Constructive Disequilibrium

Simply deciding to change destructive behavior doesn't get the job done. You've got to have a battle plan. Here are some of my basic suggestions for doing that successfully:

1. Gather the army. Your army is the parent team. Your mission is to recognize that you've lost control of your kids and then to take steps to reclaim it. Make a commitment to each other that you'll be mutually supportive throughout this campaign and beyond it. You may not agree on some of the tactics or specific target behaviors, but you must agree that your first obligation is to present a united front. If you're divided, both of you are doomed.

• **Create a timetable to implement the steps.** It takes some planning. Rehearse your approaches so that both of you are clear on the plan. Create a game plan with a plan B. For example, you might use the following tactics:

- Hold a family meeting.
- Explain some of the concerns and potential future consequences if you continue as before. You might mention a recent newspaper article or a meeting with someone you respect.
- Explain that many of the plans will create a change in the normal routine and that not everyone is going to be happy, but this is a position you're taking for the benefit of all concerned.
- Present the changes on a drawing board so that everyone can follow the plan. Discuss the consequences in the present form.
- Consider questions and answers.
- Set the date for implementation, such as immediately or tomorrow.
- To begin your plan, on the first day, put all television sets in storage; take out all telephone lines except one. On the second day, put the stereo in storage and play the first family game. On the third day, begin behavior change program toward goals.

• **Write an expression of commitment.** Much like the Declaration of Independence, only in this case you can write a letter of declaration so you can refer to the higher ideas you began with. Too often, children break our resolve by inventing distractions. There are good reasons why all religions have a bible of principles so that everyone can understand the overriding values and the implications. This may seem daunting at first, but if you work together and don't try to cover every possible incident, it will become a source for further amendments. Remember, you don't have to be perfect. Just make a beginning and you can always change it later.

2. Anticipated animated resistance. Once you begin a committed commando restructuring, your children will often revert to primitive behaviors, such as stomping around, wetting the bed, crying, throwing tantrums and other disruptive behaviors. Think ahead and make a list of your child's most probable power plays and plan a reaction to each. If your spouse is in the home or if your child can reach out to them over the phone, it is critically important that you are both up to speed and fully and completely support each other.

3. Develop a communication system. It will be important to develop a communication system between the parents so that the children will quickly understand that they cannot divide you. There may be unexpected issues not anticipated in the rehearsal and some immediate discussion is needed. For example, suppose your child comes in angry because a bully picked on him and he is throwing things around his room. A tug on one's right ear might signal to the other parent that it's time for joint action. Or a wink would signify that the parent would rather be alone to handle the situation. A hand signal might signify that an immediate conference needs to be held. You will want to have discrete signals for at least the following:

"I need help":

"I want to be alone with the child now":

"I am disagreeing with you":

"I want to say something now":

"I need your support now":

"Let's have a quick conference before this gets out of hand":

"Let's not give in":

4. Hold a consultative and support session. It is highly recommended that parents schedule a consultative session every night if possible, at least during the first month of the change. The sessions should have a consistent agenda, such as the one recommended below:

- Share with each other the feelings you have about the ordeals of the day, without blame or insinuations of responsibilities of the other parent. This should be limited to ten minutes in order not to make it a griping session.

- Tell each other what positive behavior each observed of the other. Give each a positive feedback and explain why you thought the other's behavior was so good. This should take about ten minutes.
- Assess how effective the change of responsibility is going. Are there adjustments that need to be made?
- Discuss new developments and possible approaches that could be addressed.
- Agree to commit to the change and support each other, especially when asked.

Stay Positive and Look Ahead

When you commit to shaking up your dysfunctional family, it can seem like a daunting and dreary task, so you need to keep in mind that you're doing an important, honorable and exciting thing. This is an opportunity to create the family environment you've always wanted. It is, by far, the most important work you'll ever do. It will have long-lasting rewards in the form of children who grow up to be better parents themselves. Think of it this way: In shaking up your own children and creating a stronger family, you're contributing to the richness of the lives of your grandchildren and great-grandchildren. You're breaking a cycle that otherwise might well make their lives very difficult. The ripple effect of your decision will impact generations to come. Feel good about it. Throw everything you've got into it. And know that your children will be forever grateful that you care enough to stand up and do what needs to be done for their sake and the future of your family.

12

Tool 6:
Parenting in Harmony

Put Your House in Order

*The best way to keep children at home is to make the home
atmosphere pleasant—and let the air out of the tires.*
— DOROTHY PARKER

The Sweeper: Two of the tools that I handed you earlier were for setting goals and changing your family power structure. This one is for
cleaning up your family's environment to make it easier to focus on that
restructuring for a more successful future together. As a psychologist and
as a father I know the challenges of dealing with important family matters against a backdrop of a household ten-ring circus. I know what it's
like trying to have a serious conversation with a teenager when his cell
phone is ringing every two minutes, his stereo is blasting in sonic booms
that register ten on the Richter scale, and Britney Spears is doing a simulated striptease on MTV. Many households today are chaotic beyond belief, not only with all of the multimedia distractions but with dogs
barking, cats yowling, sinks overflowing, neighborhood kids running
around, telemarketers calling, door-to-door salespeople ringing the doorbell, microwaves beeping and the general mayhem that makes modern-
day life so maddening.

Parents, your voice is simply drowned out by the cacophonous multimedia monster that floods the senses of teens and preteens. And you
can't blame the kids, since we pay for most of the cultural distractions.
Our homes are no longer castles that provide sanctuary. Tragically, most
parents don't even try to fight it. They surrender to it. And this chaotic
lifestyle and external bombardment has contributed greatly to the current crisis in families. It's time for a clean sweep.

In the cycle of one generation, rituals around the dinner table have all but disappeared in a flurry of fast food, Big Gulps and hasty good-byes. *See ya, wouldn't want to be ya!* Instead of talking to each other and reinforcing behaviors we want our children to develop, we shoot for snippets of shared information while channel surfing. We own the remote control, but because of the Internet we have absolutely no control over the material our children have access to or even the people they talk to. Cell phones are a decidedly mixed blessing. They enable us to stay in contact with our children like never before, but they also create relentless interruptions, drug conduits for dealers and party planners for teens in perpetual motion.

Then there's the daily forced march to ballet classes, gymnastics lessons, soccer practice, voice training, volleyball camps and baseball clinics. Each activity may be well intentioned and designed to help our children develop their talents, but I wonder what all of this spoon-fed instruction is doing to kids' attitudes about life and their ability to entertain themselves. What a radical idea? Kids and parents shuttling back and forth seven days a week at all hours of the day is a higher form of insanity.

Any pragmatic person has to ask if our family lives are really enhanced by the wear and tear of tournaments, recitals, lessons and leagues. The statistical evidence is strikingly clear. We're striking out as families. Adolescent depression is at an all-time high. Teen suicides have increased in every category except gun-assisted attempts. Drug abuse is rampant in schools. Virtually every other statistic demonstrates that we're paying a high cost for our peripatetic lifestyles.

Thousands of parents have written me about their struggles to stay connected. This woman, Mary, offered a typical story:

> Dr. Phil,
> I am at my wits' end with trying to raise a good, loving family, but I am failing every day. My two daughters, ages thirteen and fifteen, are never at home, and when they are, we hardly speak more than two sentences. I realize that this is typical for teenagers, but it has been this way from the beginning. There is always something more important or more interesting than listening to me. Trying to discipline them is a joke because there is nothing I can use as reinforcement. They are both interested in cheerleading and softball leagues. And they show their good intentions by going to a social club

with a mission of helping the elderly. They are really good girls, but I probably know my next-door neighbor better than I know my own children. If they ever got into trouble, I would be the last to know. I feel so guilty because I am not the mother I should be. Help me learn to talk to my daughters.

The future doesn't look good for the next generation if this madness marches on. As parents we have got to step up and take control of our own families. Where is it all headed? What could possibly be next? Whatever it is it cannot be good if we continue to surrender to nonfamily influences or allow what I call net-sitting instead of parental supervision or even babysitting. It is true that a kid glued to a computer screen is convenient and he or she doesn't bug you with questions and comments while you are watching some mindless sitcom, but trust me, convenient is not a good thing in this context. Your child being disconnected and out of control is not a good thing either.

This madness doesn't have to continue. Families can be fixed one by one if parents set goals for success at home and commit to accomplishing them by shaking things up and restructuring in a healthier environment. I'm excited at the potential for doing that because I believe more and more parents understand the urgency of taking action. Let's look at three distinct areas in which you as a parent control your home environment:

- Allocating time for priorities
- Controlling external stimulation
- Setting the schedule at home

Time Allocation

Make a list of the distractions that disrupt parent-child and family communication at your house. I've provided some examples but feel free to add your own. Include even those that may have some redeeming value. The intent isn't to be critical of these distractions, but rather to show the magnitude of their disruptive influences on family development. For example, from ninth grade until the time he's a senior in high school, the average kid spends a total of 3,600 hours on school work. During the same period, he's watched approximately 6,000 hours of television. Six thousand hours! That is absurdly out of control.

Time Distractions from Family Connections

Check off those activities that have cut into family time, even if there are some positive aspects to them.

1. Watching television
2. "Talking" on Internet chat rooms
3. Surfing the web
4. Downloading music
5. Video games
6. Instant messaging
7. Cell phone calls
8. Watching DVDs
9. Lessons
10. Touring teams
11. Competitive clubs
12. Tournaments
13. Tutoring
14. Going to movies
15. Shopping
16. Field trips
17. Parties
18. Staying in the bedroom with the door closed
19. Church or spiritual meetings
20. Going to the mall
21. Cruising around in a car
22. _____
23. _____
24. _____

When you write down your entries, note the number of hours or minutes dedicated to the family's simply relating to one another or just hanging out—as opposed to watching TV or doing something else. When I say dedicated, I mean nothing else is a priority at that time. The family is expected to be there with the expectation of connecting, even at a modest level. How does the time stack up?

Environmental Control of Stimulation—Lifestyle

This tool comes with a special message: You do not have to compete with all of these distractions. The best way to accomplish your mission for family control is to insist on an environmental cleanup. It's your legal right to protect your home environment so that it reflects your family values. Regardless of what Madison Avenue would have you believe, there are benefits to living without the television on all the time and not plugging into the Internet every hour of the day. If you parents are going to reclaim the hearts and minds of your children, you must clean up the external distractions that dominate their lives. The sooner you start this process and the younger your children are when you change the rhythm of your life, the easier it will be and more profound will be the impact.

We have become much too reactive. We allow our environments to control us instead of the other way around. As a result, our kids are often overstimulated. We've given in to the myth that children must be constantly entertained or engaged in structured activities. Every house has multiple televisions, typically all turned on at the same time, along with radios, stereos, computers and other bombardments. I'm not suggesting your kids should live in sensory deprivation or soundproof rooms devoid of all distractions. But there has to be some balance. Children don't need to be electronically bombarded every waking minute, and they don't need to be involved in structured activities every minute of the day. They're not going to turn into puddles of flesh because they're not taking lessons, practicing a sport or honing a talent. Don't be scared to death that your child might fall behind all the other kids. Stop trying to keep up with the Joneses by having your child participate in every extracurricular activity and private lesson known to man. So what if the kid on the corner can perform a dance move better than your child? Maybe by staying home and having to entertain themselves, your children will become better adapted to getting along with one another or being by themselves. We need to calm down and come together. We need to simplify our family lives. Children should have quiet time for reflection and creative flow, and they need to learn how to entertain themselves. Human beings are designed to follow life rhythms. Our minds require tranquillity to foster creativity and focus on success goals such as those you conceived for your family's return to health. If there's never a quiet waking moment in your children's lives, they will never hear themselves. That could be a problem because they just might have some important things to say to themselves.

That's why it's so important to de-stress your family environment. From the results of the following action step, determine what you can do to simplify things in your home. Then look at what you can do to take the pressure off your children so they no longer feel overscheduled and overtaxed. If, for example, your mornings are chaotic because everyone is scrambling in different directions on different schedules, resolve to wake everyone up thirty minutes earlier—and maybe get them to bed thirty minutes earlier at night. Call a meeting and call for more cooperation and greater calm. Will your children resist? Of course. Will they roll their eyes and complain? You'd better believe it. But leaders have to lead and as a parent you have to step up. It's not always a democracy, and it's not anarchy. It's your family. You can decide when your family needs to start their day and how they need to start it. In a quid pro quo world it's very simple to say, "If it's chaotic on Monday, everybody is getting up thirty minutes earlier on Tuesday." It's very possible to make everyone agree to prepare for the next day before going to bed at night. Yes, as stunning as this may seem, there are actual recorded cases of children laying out their clothes, getting their book bags packed and finding essential items like shoes *before* they go to bed. As the guys at Ripley's say: *Believe it or not!*

Explain to everyone that the goal is to bring the family closer together, to make it healthier and happier. Parents can and should control the family's living environment as one step in taking responsibility for its welfare. If you want to calm down your household so that everyone living in it is less irritable, frustrated, overstimulated and overscheduled, you have the power to do that. It's also important to make certain you're not a source of the stress because you lack organization or because *you* are trying to multitask too much. It's well documented that children will reflect the mood and personality of their parents. If your house is chaotic, if your children are stressed, look in the mirror. You may be the source of, or at least a contributor to, the chaos that interferes with their mental, emotional and intellectual efficiencies. A child who lives in a chaotic environment at home will not do as well out in the world.

To stop dysfunction of any kind, you must stop the behavior that supports it. Whether it's a disconnected and overstressed family, the problem of being overweight or a shattered relationship, you've got to change the lifestyle to change the unwanted results. In this case, it means cleaning up the family environment instead of clearing the fat out of the stove. The shredded family fabric at your house is not going to be stitched together until you clear out the chaos, stress and counterproductive communications such as fussing, fighting, blaming and backstabbing. To begin the healing process, parents have to establish rules and boundaries. Good behavior should be rewarded. Bad behavior should be penalized.

Take a few minutes and use the brief questionnaire below to measure the lifestyle you created, and determine what you would do differently.

Your Family's Priorities vs. Your Family's Time Commitments

Families who find themselves struggling to find or recapture their rhythm never planned on allowing their relationships and environments to erode and become dysfunctional. It just seems to slip away a little at a time. Parents may start with the firm conviction to have a daily family dinner or maybe even regular family meetings yet without realizing it they begin to give in to schedule conflicts and competing priorities. No one ever makes a conscious decision to stop the rituals, they just slowly get crowded out. You may not have consciously decided to eliminate important family functions but you can certainly consciously decide to reinstitute them.

Let's begin by taking a look at your top ten family priorities. Being completely candid and honest, use the space below to list in descending order of importance the top family priorities or values you would pursue in a perfect world. For example, if being a God-centered family is your top priority, list that as number one, and then list your second most important priority and so on. Please note, I'm not saying that you necessarily live consistently with these priorities—just that they are at least philosophically important to you. The first few will be easy, but you may have to think a bit to come up with the rest.

Top Ten Priorities

1.
2.
3.
4.
5.

6.
7.
8.
9.
10.

Now shift gears and think carefully about how you as a family spend your time. In the space below, list the top ten activities which absorb the most time for family members. For example, if work or school is your family's number one time absorption, list it in the first position. If sleep is number two, put it there and so on through number ten.

Top Ten Time Expenditures

1.
2.
3.
4.
5.
6.
7.
8.
9.
10.

You should now compare the two lists to determine whether or not the way your family is living and investing their time in the real day-to-day world is congruent or incongruent with what you listed in the first list and know in your heart to be important. I fully understand that in the real world it is not possible to ever live 100 percent consistently with idealistic priorities. However, life is about striving for excellence—if not perfection. If you find the priorities and values at the top of your first list reside at the bottom of your time allocation list, you must consciously commit to reordering your time and energy commitments in such a way as to put what you know to be important back on center stage. How to do that is what this book in general and this chapter in particular is all about.

Scheduling in the Environment

Time management is critical for all families. Most now live in the Laser Lane, hurtling down life's highway at the speed of light. Seventy percent of families now have double incomes. That may mean double the earnings, but it also means double the stress. That's why we have kids booked with activities up the wazoo. Even single-income families get sucked into the competition because they fear their kids won't be able to match up with the obsessively trained double-income kids. Parents are scared to death that if their daughter isn't in dance lessons before she stops crawling, she'll never get into the neighborhood Bolshoi Ballet. For boys, there's intense pressure to specialize in one sport and make it a focus from toddlerhood through the teen years. Fun no longer seems to be a factor, and the all-around athlete is going the way of the dodo and the eight-track tape.

A friend told me that he was confronted one day by another father after his son's junior high basketball practice.

"Your son is the future of this team," said the other father, who stood about six-eight with an athletic build. "I don't know if you have the financial resources or not, but your boy needs to be getting private coaching and he needs to be playing in summer leagues and going to all the camps. I played college ball [the guy mentioned this at least three times during the short speech], and I know the dedication it takes."

My friend thanked the other father for his interest, then ignored his advice. He wanted his son to play basketball for the love of the game, and he wanted him to enjoy other sports too. He'd also seen the other father's son play. The boy was fully grown by the age of thirteen and he was only five-seven. He'd told his teammates that he was totally burned out on basketball and hated being pressured to play it. At least twice, the son of that college ball father had fainted in class, either from exhaustion or stress or to get out of practice or a game. This kid was headed for serious trouble.

Common sense is no longer common. Sure, it takes dedication to excel at anything whether it's sports, art or a job. But our lives require balance, and parents have to understand that children, and teens in particular, are tuned to nature's clock, not the clock on the wall at the gym or dance studio. You can't ignore the biorhythms that control humans' natural energy levels. In most people—except teenagers, whose brains are still growing and who follow a later cycle that keeps them up at night and sleeping later in the day—the mornings are the most productive at the cognitive level. The body and brain have restored themselves and the toxic levels from the activities of the day before have subsided. Physical abilities tend to build in the afternoon, and there is a natural relaxing pace as the evening comes. But adults tend to run schedules according to their own body clocks or their own time constraints. This forces kids into unnatural rhythms that can mess them up.

> **Survey Fact:**
> The three greatest parenting fears for raising a family are explaining sex, instilling values and co-parenting.

When parents clean up the family environment, they should be sensitive to the natural rhythms of their children. You don't play tag and dodgeball or wrestle roughhouse on the floor and then expect kids to transition instantly to eyes closed in bed. Scale the day down so your kids have quiet-time activities that prepare them to go to sleep. Use that quiet time to strengthen family connections by reading to your children, talking to them about the day or making plans for the next day's activities.

With that natural scheduling in mind, do this simple audit. On the form below, write in the activities that best fit. Include those family activities that create the best outcome yet are consistent with the energy flow. I have some suggestions in the parentheses.

Daily Biorhythms and Scheduling

Morning (cognitive activities, such as problem-solving)

_____

_____

Early afternoon (cognitive and physical activities, such as work duties):

_____

_____

Late afternoon (physical activities, such as games):

_____

_____

Evening (meditative activities, such as contemplation and quiet talk, stories):

_____

_____

Connecting the Dots

Remember Mary's letter earlier in this chapter, in which she detailed her concern that she was losing touch with her overscheduled teenage daughters? I provided to her the audit you just did and she responded after taking it. She said that she and her husband sat down one evening and planned their decision to take control of their family environment. They evaluated what they'd been doing and the unsatisfactory results that had followed. They realized that they were only spending about thirty minutes a week connecting as a family. They and their daughters agreed to schedule more time together. They set up family council meetings in which everyone discussed their plans and frustrations (not with one another) once a week, and at least four dinner meetings in which they would eat together with no phone calls and no TV. They also decided to go out to dinner together or have some friends—the daughters' or the parents'—over for a meal at least once a week so that they'd get to know one another's closest pals. At first the daughters expressed frustration because many of their favorite activities did not fit into the family's priority list. They felt that was unfair. But they agreed to go with the plan. Both the parents and the daughters came together in a weekly session so they could organize and share all scheduled activities to help reduce conflicts and chaos. Everyone in the family was happy to relieve the stress. As it turned out, the girls found an orderly way of getting most of what they wanted anyway, but it was done within a family context. The time-scheduling then came naturally because of the new daily process.

You will feel de-stressed once you've cleaned up your family environment. If some of the suggestions seem corny or old-fashioned, that's okay.

The stranger they feel, the more they need to be done. If it feels weird or unnatural to do what you know is healthy and productive, that should give you a clue as to how far off the mark your current reactive lifestyle truly is. I encourage you, for the sake of your family's future, to overcome those feelings and commit to cutting out the noise, turning down the volume, slowing the pace and coming together for your family's mutual benefit. The rewards will be substantial, I promise you.

13

Tool 7:
Parenting by Example

Walk the Talk

Don't worry that children never listen to you;
worry that they are always watching you.
—ROBERT FULGHUM

The most powerful role model in any child's life is the same-sex parent. (If you are the opposite-sex parent, don't despair; you are likely
a very close second.) Daughters primarily look to their mothers and sons
to their fathers. And believe me, they are watching you every minute.
You can run, but you can't hide. Children are very perceptive. The dis-
claimer of "do as I say, not as I do" doesn't give you a free pass either. You
didn't buy that baloney when you were a kid and your kids won't buy it
now. Your children watch and learn from you from the time they come
into this world. For better or worse, they observe, learn and imitate your
behaviors, your actions, your values, your beliefs and even your expressions. It's a fact that children learn vicariously by observing the behavior
of others and noting the consequences of their actions. They watch what
happens to family members when they succeed or fail and those experiences become part of their reference files for how they live their own
lives.

In psychology, this is known simply as modeling. Children are the
products of their learning histories and those histories are in no small
part comprised of what they observe in you.

The good news is that you are in a position of tremendous power in
regard to influencing the development of your child. The bad news is that
you are in a position of tremendous power in regard to influencing the development of your child. Your children assign you such power as their

model of adulthood because you protect and nurture them and you spend the greatest amount of time with them. The question is, How are you using this opportunity? I'm betting that you may not be consciously aware of even a fraction of that power. How many ways is your conduct writing on the slate of who your child will become? You are your child's first teacher and this is a school that never lets out. You serve in that role throughout their lives. In the early years, at least, your kids look up to you as though you're ten feet tall. They follow your lead to see what they're supposed to be and do. That is a good thing because they do need someone to look up to, to guide them and to help them see around corners.

Research tells us that children who do not have role models have far more behavioral problems than those who do. Modeling is important because it is the primary way that children learn the values they will carry for life. It is true that actions speak louder than words. Your actions teach them how to take personal responsibility for their own behavior, choices, actions, thoughts and feelings. Observing that you live with passion gives them a passion for living. Such power cannot be ignored or neglected, not if you dream of building an extraordinary life for your child, not if you want your family to thrive at phenomenal levels.

Raising perfect children is simple enough if you, as their role model, happen to be perfect yourself. Unfortunately, as parents, we are far from perfect, so we just have to do the best we can with a keen sensitivity to the fact that we are being watched in all we do. If you want your child to be neat, with a perfectly tidy room every day, then you must be neat. If you want your kids to read, then they must see you cracking open and enjoying good books. If you want your children to learn how to express themselves, then you must engage your family in discussions. If you want your kids to be healthy and fit, then they must see you eating healthy food and creating a lifestyle for yourself and for them that includes regular exercise and family recreation. If you want them to handle anger appropriately, then you can't cuss out the guy who took "your" parking space. If you want your children to be honest, you must exhibit honesty in your everyday life. If you want your children to have joyful, well-adjusted dispositions, then they've got to see you acting, feeling and living that way too.

Model Parenting

Through your actions, your words, your behavior and your love, you can direct your children toward where you want them to go. You show them how to be happy, well-balanced and fulfilled adults. But since you aren't perfect, your children are going to pick up on your imperfections too. Our children can also mirror our dark sides, our vulnerabilities and our weaknesses. A renowned psychologist named Albert Bandura, who was the architect of what is known as social learning theory, observed that children develop through learning from the people around them. One of Dr. Bandura's famous experiments was to have an adult punch and kick a Bobo doll while a young child watched. A Bobo doll is one of those plastic blow-up toys with a weighted bottom that bounce back after you hit it. Bandura would then put the child all alone in the room with the doll. I will bet you can guess what happened next. Sure enough, the child started kicking and punching the daylights out of ol' Bobo just like the adult had. Bandura's point in this particular experiment was that even a violent personality can be learned by watching and learning from those around us.

You don't need a Ph.D. in behavioral sciences to know that too many parents in this day of fast-paced living and double-income families are failing as role models. One of the results of that is self-destructive behavior. Take me seriously here: Children are three times more likely to smoke if their parents smoke. Overweight adolescents have a 70 percent chance of becoming overweight or obese adults—and that increases to 80 percent if a parent is heavy or obese. An estimated 78 million people have been exposed to alcoholism (or other drug abuse) in their own families, and children of alcoholics have four times greater risk of developing alcoholism than children of nonalcoholics. I should point out that although alcohol abuse may be a disease to which some people are genetically predisposed, alcoholism, or at least its treatment, does involve an element of personal choice.

Debilitating depression runs in families too, and it is not always due to inherited biological makeup. Parents who suffer from depression are not good role models. They have poor coping skills and weak problem-solving skills and tend to express negative beliefs about themselves and life in general. When children are exposed to this level of maladaptive behavior, they internalize it, increasing their own risk of depression. In fact, children of depressed parents are three times more likely to suffer from depression at some point in their development. It's also true that suicide is escalating at an exponential rate. People with a family history of suicide are two and a half times more likely to take their own life than those without such a history.

The ripple effect of home violence witnessed by children is staggering. Children who grow up in abusive households begin to think that Daddy hitting Mommy is somehow normal. Abuse is a learned behavior. Its violent lessons get passed on from parent to child.

Although the most powerful role model for most young people is the same-sex parent, children still watch very closely how their opposite-sex parent treats the other parent. Daughters, for example, will watch very closely how their fathers treat their wives. If a daughter observes her father being condescending to her mother, she will come to expect this from the men in her life. If she sees her father treating women in general and her mother in particular as sex objects, she is likely to fill that role in her own life. If she witnesses mental, physical or emotional abuse, she will set that low standard in her own life. Dad, you can also model for your daughter how reasonable and decent guys should treat her. If you treat her with dignity and respect, if you treat her like a lady, you are not only enhancing your relationship with her and making her feel special and valued, you are setting a high standard to which she will hold the boys in her life. Understand that if you model coldness and emotional unavailability and generally ignore her, she will not only set a low standard, but she will also be hungry for male attention and male validation. That hunger could easily make her vulnerable to exploitation from predatory men.

Fathers need to help daughters understand that good men are supportive and respectful and not abusive. That may mean also opening your daughter's eyes to the darker nature of certain men. If a father sees that his daughter is putting herself in a position to be easy prey, he needs to step up and help her understand what that could mean for her reputation and her ability to attract responsible and supportive men. Words are heard, actions are experienced.

How are you doing as a role model? When it comes to managing your own behavior and emotions, are you training your children to manage theirs? You have to be brutally honest with yourself about what you are putting on display. So many parents tell me, "I just have a bad kid." If that's your attitude, you've given up before you've begun and you are ignoring your own ability to be a powerful influence. Part of the challenge here is accepting the truth that there are things that you've done or not done to contribute and shape them into being bad.

I'm not trying to drag you down; I'm trying to get you to be real because you cannot change what you do not acknowledge.

Circular Causality

Let's begin to get real by recognizing that, even in direct one-on-one interactions you model for your child how to handle such things as stress, emotional upset and pressure. The modeling is so powerful in these one-on-one interactions that your child will actually mirror back to you exactly the same demeanor and actions you are displaying. Behavioral scientists commonly refer to this as circular causality. Circular causality is a what-goes-around-comes-around sequence. You tell your toddler that it's time for bed, and he doesn't want to go, so he resists and fails to obey your directions. So you dig in your heels, ready for a showdown. He senses the tension and pressure and screams "No!" You become frustrated since you have already had a hard day, so you turn up the volume. He sees what's happening and the fact that he's not getting his way. So just like you, he gets frustrated and moody and throws a tantrum, maybe even kicking or breaking toys. Out of frustration and anger, you escalate as well and begin to scream, yell or spank your child. This frustrates your child even more, the tantrum worsens and he further resists you. By this time, you're hysterical. Your yelling and screaming intensify—with the unfortunate effect of further escalating your toddler's bad behavior. He has taken your lead, reflected your tone and conduct, and not only has the immediate situation worsened but he has filed away in his mind exactly how these situations are to be handled.

Circular causality scenarios like this are described as *auto-exacerbating*, meaning that the situation and everyone in it make things worse. By not

> **Survey Fact:**
> **The top three behavioral problems parents face with their children are:**
>
> **not paying attention**
> **losing control/ tantrums**
> **talking back**

being able to control yourself in front of an out-of-control toddler, you model, escalate and reinforce unacceptable behavior. In effect, you're modeling the very same behavior you want to stop, and you're making each other angrier in the process. You may not have known that you were eliciting, maintaining and escalating maladaptive behavior, but you were.

The good news is, if you can begin to stop modeling unacceptable behavior—and model acceptable behavior instead—you will begin to de-escalate situations rather than escalate them. Remember, you are one of the top two most powerful influences in your child's life. If you have modeled bad behavior, you have done so powerfully. If you begin to model healthy, productive behavior you will do so powerfully. What would happen, for instance, if your initial reaction to your child's misbehavior was to be a model of self-composure and self-control instead of a hothead? I invite you to drop your end of the tug-of-war rope.

Trust me, your children will pick up your calmer response pattern and graft it onto their own conduct. You must be the one who models calmness, or whatever behavior or emotion is required, in order to change the interaction. Once you start engaging in more positive and controlled behavior, you will literally alter the nature of your interactions with your children.

With this new pattern of response, you create a calmer atmosphere where you can reopen negotiations that promote cooperation. I promise you, this shift of attitude will fundamentally change the environment and the spirit in which you interact with your children. It will also make it much better for handling disciplinary issues because you will now be focusing on the right target. I'm not saying it will be easy. But you have to decide whether it is worth it. (Hint: It is!)

Assignment

Based on what we've discussed so far, what kind of marks do you give yourself as a role model for your family? What are you modeling to your children through your own behavior? The following list of questions may help you consider your standard of conduct as a role model. Be really honest here, even if it is scary to admit certain things about yourself.

1. Do you model a life of passion and purpose, where you feel vibrant and alive, or does your life include things, such as

your job, that you constantly complain about and profess
to hate?

2. Do you model taking good care of yourself physically, or do
you eat junk food, continue to be overweight, smoke
cigarettes or not exercise?

3. Do you effectively resolve conflicts with other people, or do
you withdraw, stomp your feet, slam doors, get mad or do
everything you can to avoid confrontations?

4. Does your family see you handling life's disappointments
with a rational, positive strategy, or do you medicate the
problems with food, alcohol, drugs, gambling or other
addictive behaviors?

5. Do you model financial responsibility with regard to your
bills and dealings, or do you overindulge and live beyond
your means?

6. Do you model high morals by avoiding such behaviors as
gossiping, lying to employers, cursing and taking unfair
advantage?

7. Do you model social responsibility by volunteering at your
church, school or local shelters and hospitals?

8. Do you model properly defined self-worth and -esteem based
on character traits, or do you pursue worth and value
through material things such as designer clothes, fancy cars
and other status symbols?

9. Does your family see you reaching for something more, or
have you gotten too comfortable in the nonthreatening
sameness of your life?

10. Do you model mastery and competency in situations, or does
fear slip into your interactions and keep you from doing
many things?

11. Do you approach problems and setbacks as opportunities, or
do you label every problem a crisis?

12. Do you model relationships with other people that are
loving, affirming and supportive, or do you criticize other
people, tear them down or talk behind their backs?

13. Do you go through the day with energy, feeling totally alive,
or are you constantly tired, stressed, emotionally flat or even
depressed, worried and unhappy?

14. Do you spend genuine time with your family, including being involved in and supporting their activities, or do you beg off because you've "got too much on your plate"?

If you haven't been doing a very good job, it is not too late to get on the ball. Being a worthy role model may mean you've got to *ramp up*. You've simply got to require more of yourself in every category, even the mundane things like grooming, health, self-control, emotional management, relationships, social interaction, work performance, dealing with fears and every other category of daily life. If you begin to do things with more energy and thoughtfulness and love, believe me, your new level of performance will inspire your entire family to live with more passion and exuberance.

I am not advocating a contrived, going-through-the-motions existence. I'm challenging you to take responsibility. Clean up your own act first so that you really are the adult that you want your children to become. It begins with you. You cannot expect your children to be better than you teach them to be. If you are solid here, great. If not, you need to clean up your own messy life before you demand that they clean up their room, let alone their life. Shed any negative attitudes. Dump any self-destructive behavior patterns. Turn up the positive attitude and get out there and shine the light so they can follow you.

Maybe you aren't motivated enough to get your act together for your own welfare, but what about theirs? Do it for them so that they have a positive role model to follow into adulthood. Sure, it's going to take work and commitment to get your life on a positive track. You're going to have to take a deep look, maybe for the first time, into the influences on your life and why you've become who you've become. Don't just think about what it might mean for you; think of what it will mean for those adults in progress who look to you for leadership and inspiration. This is something you can and must do. Children need their parents to blaze the trail. You've got what it takes to be a great role model for your family. You don't need anything that you don't already have within you.

Modeling and Mastery

I've made the point that when you model behavior, you get a certain result. But there's a second, very powerful aspect to being a role model that helps your children relate more positively and constructively, not only to you but also to themselves. If your child chooses to adopt behavior that they have observed in you, there is a higher degree of ownership of that behavior on their part, because it was chosen. In the negotiation chapter I talked about how it's important that children perceive a healthy degree of self-determination and mastery over their life and environment. If you constantly preach to your children about what they should do, and therefore assign them behaviors, they are less likely to own that behavior than if they had chosen to emulate it based on their experience with you. It is extremely important that your child perceive that their personality is their own, arrived at naturally through their own life experiences. I'm not saying that you shouldn't coach, direct, counsel and instruct your children, because you definitely should. But it is important that you recognize that your behavior can also speak volumes and does not have some of the side effects that attempting to tell a child what to do does have. Thus, with the right modeling, you don't have to light a fire under them so often, because modeling lights a fire *within* them.

Modeling Values

I'm sure you, and most parents, want your children to develop into people of character who live with values such as honesty, empathy, kindness, compassion, respect and responsibility. But you can't teach values the same way you teach your child to ride a bike, swing a baseball bat or tie his shoes—not even close. It comes back to *you* again, and I hope by now you know that you must be the example of what you want to see in your children. *The secret to raising a child of character is being a person of character yourself.* This is a tall order, no doubt about it. Every time you take a step, it's as if you are carrying your child on your shoulders. Modeling values is all about your kids' riding piggyback on you.

My father used to say, "If you don't stand for something, you'll fall for anything." That is especially true when applied to raising children. You make the choices for your children early in their lives, during their critical years of growth and learning. Questions about what to eat, what to wear, what your living environment will be like, and which schools they go to are handled by you with little or no input from your children. You work these things out for your family, and you do so with their best interests in mind.

But there will come a time in your children's lives when they will be faced with critical decisions—and they will have to make their own choices. What you do now powerfully prepares your children for making those choices later. You teach them how to live by showing them how to make choices. Will your child learn from you so that she won't be lured into a car by a stranger? Will your son watch his father and learn to refuse alcohol and drugs? Will your daughter watch you and see that she has a choice to abstain from sex or to practice safe sex when she is old enough to handle the emotional aspects of it?

If you've done your job, your child will have the courage and conscience to make the right choices when you aren't around. The lessons you model for them are so important, if you don't get a sense of urgency from reading this, I beg you to walk up to your child right now and stare into her or his eyes. The reflection you see is the adult your child will become.

I learned how powerful parental role models are at a young age, though the lesson came at a very high price. When I was thirteen, all of my friends owned motorcycles. I wanted one too. But the truth was, we didn't have money for food half of the time, so we sure didn't have money for some motorcycle. My only hope was to earn enough money on my paper route to buy a moped, which was nothing more than a bicycle with a motor stuck on it—pedals and all. When I raised that prospect with my father, he shot it down. But much to my surprise, he offered a deal: "If you're going to ride a motorcycle, I want you riding something reasonable with enough power to get out of the way if you need to, not some moped. I'll cosign a loan at the bank for a motorcycle. If you can find a way to pay twenty-five dollars a month, I'll find a way to pay twenty-five dollars a month."

I was thrilled, to say the least. Now I could ride with my buddies. My dad gave me two restrictions, however: "Don't ride outside the boundaries of our neighborhood and don't let anyone else ride your motorcycle, because we can't afford the insurance."

Not three weeks after I got my motorcycle, I was at my girlfriend's house, way out of our neighborhood, just hanging out in the front yard. A buddy of mine came by and asked if he could take my motorcycle for a spin. I pitched him the keys, provided he just rode up the street and back. Off he went, not just down the street but a whole five blocks away. Doing over 70 miles per hour, he broadsided a Buick Riviera and was flung 300 feet in the air, landing on his stomach and smashing his face into the curb. Even five blocks away I could hear the crash. I knew it was him and

I got this horrible feeling in my stomach. Amazingly he was alive but barely conscious when we got to him. He was rushed by ambulance to the hospital. That night my friends and I stayed at his bedside, thanking God that our friend was alive. That's when my dad walked in. I was petrified. After he checked on my friend and made sure he was going to make it, his thoughts turned to me and the situation. He looked down at me and I fully expected him to fly into a rage. Instead he calmly said, "Son, I hope and pray that he took that motorcycle without your permission, or you're in a lot of trouble and our family is in a lot of trouble."

Here my dad had stretched the family finances beyond all reason to try to give me some light in my life and I had irresponsibly thrown it all away and put us in great peril. I so very much wanted to be able to say "Yeah, that's what happened, Dad." But I knew better because he had always told me that two wrongs didn't make a right. Lying to save my hide wouldn't help the situation. I said, "Dad, I wish it were so, but yes, I let him take the motorcycle, and I know it doesn't help but I am sorry."

My dad stared out the window for what seemed like forever and a day. I remember thinking I had never seen him look so tired or so old. I sat there on what I thought was the judgment seat, awaiting some dire punishment. His words to me I will never forget. My dad took a deep breath, put his hand on my shoulder and told me, "Well, son, we will just have to work it out." For all of the times he had been emotionally unavailable, he sure came present in that time of crisis in a young boy's life.

I know my father remembered this incident too, because a few weeks before his death in 1995, he told his Sunday school class about it, and how proud he was that I had told the truth when it would have been so much easier to lie. He made no mention of his own strength or sacrifice, only mine.

I've come to learn that for most of us, the events that mold our character are typically events that, but for our personal stake, are of little interest and of little drama. But once you add that element of personal involvement and personal impact, once you add that relevancy, events that barely hit the rest of the world's radar screen take on considerable power. That singular event, that lesson learned from disobeying my father and choosing not to rely on my internal compass of values, would prove to shape me and change me. It is no exaggeration to say that it was a pretty good wake-up call, certainly not one I would wish on any thirteen-year-old kid, but I know I created personal value from it. That character-building experience, however trivial it might seem to others, altered how I approach life to this very day. I recognize the consequences of not relying on that internal compass, how if I don't, I may step blindly into disaster, with potentially life-altering results. At the same time, I am fortunate that my dad valued honesty. He modeled honesty, and I learned it too. He also modeled that fathers stand by their sons and that the loyalty of a father's love is not there only when it is convenient. He modeled a depth of commitment to family. Life just goes better when you have the heart to be forthright and the commitment to be loyal.

My point is this: Do not underestimate the significance of what values and beliefs you model on a day-to-day basis. A daily event may not be some big crisis, it may just seem like some routine event to you, but it may very well be the tipping point in your child's development of character.

By the way, the motorcycle was totaled in that accident, but it still had to be paid for. Dad didn't match the payments, because he reasoned that his payments were for the part of the motorcycle that no one else was supposed to ride.

Here is the bottom line: Through your modeling you can teach your children values that will serve as a framework for handling life even when it turns into a raging storm.

Live What You Teach and Preach

I subscribe to the old saying "It's better to see a sermon than hear one." Be careful not to say one thing and model another. You might tell your family that it is important to volunteer for good causes, but if you rarely do it yourself you aren't walking your talk. It's a fact that your kids will generally choose the lesser standard of behavior. So live up to your own exhortations.

I still think fondly of our former neighbors, the Conways, because they were such a fine bunch of people. John Conway, the father, pastored a local church and had a terrific sense of humor. He could make a stuffed bird smile. John had a good pastor's gift for presenting a moral lesson disguised as a funny tale. Here's one he told me:

> I usually come home at noon every day to have lunch with my wife and little boy. It is during that one hour of the day that I can be with

my family, and I can leave behind the issues and the stresses that so often go along with being a pastor. On this particular day, I had had to deal with budget problems, mutiny in the choir and a Sunday school teacher threatening to quit. About five minutes after I got home, the phone rang. It was the church calling. My wife answered it, cupped her hand over the phone and whispered, "Are you home?" "No," I mouthed, so she told the caller, "He's not here." As I sat down to lunch with my family, my six-year-old son very quickly volunteered to say the blessing. "Dear God," he began, "Please forgive Daddy for telling a lie, and please forgive Mommy for helping him." My wife and I looked up at each other, shocked. It was one of those "gotcha!" moments. I could not have been more embarrassed than if my fly had been open in front of the congregation. Yet it sure taught us a life lesson we will never forget.

When your actions and values conflict like this, it confuses your child. The result is that he doesn't really accept or believe in any of the values you're trying to teach him because none of it makes sense. As Pastor John's story shows, you can't just give sermons, you've got to live them too.

Exercise: Values for Your Family to Live By

Your child will be forced to learn values by trial and error unless you make it your goal to teach them through your example. So prepare yourself to be the value master. Get down on paper what values are important in your family—values you need to model for your children—so that they will be equipped to make good decisions and choices. Not all families value the same qualities and attributes, so this is a good opportunity for you to define your family's values with distinct and unmistakable clarity.

As you prepare to do this exercise, ask yourself the following questions, then write your answers in your journal:

- What do you believe in?
- What principles have guided your life?
- What do you stand for?
- What makes life meaningful for you?
- What do you need in your life to make it complete?

1. From the list below, circle the top ten words or phrases that best describe how you want your family to be:

> supportive   talkative   affectionate   respectful   disciplined
> meaningful   caring   accepting   controlled   well-behaved   free
> humorous   creative   soft-spoken   energetic   easygoing
> engaging   productive   loving   gentle   religious   spiritual
> charitable   fun   playful   successful   winning   flourishing
> lucrative   unbeaten   prosperous   conquering   cooperative
> helpful   obliging   collaborative   sharing   just   fair   adequate
> passable   average   reasonable   polite   decent   civilized
> honest   well-mannered   proper   correct   moral   wholesome
> venturesome   healthy   natural   significant   strong   reverent
> polite   civil   gracious   autonomous   independent   self-sufficient
> self-reliant   responsible   compassionate   devoted   warm
> likable   tolerant   patient   uncomplaining   accommodating
> long-suffering   indistinguishable   unnoticeable   disregarded
> empathetic   generous   kind   liberal   conservative   thrifty
> courageous   trustworthy

2. Now choose three of those ten words that are the most important to you. Take those three words and use them to write three sentences that describe the underlying value in the form of a statement. For example, if one of the words you selected was *respectful*, then you might write: *Our family will treat themselves, one another and other people with dignity and respect.*

Value 1: _____

Value 2: _____

Value 3: _____

3. For each of the three values you described above, write three ways you will behave to model these values. By acknowledging and articulating

how you will live these values, you will help incorporate them into the heart of your family's value system.

Behaviors Required to Model That Value

Value 1: _____

_____

_____

Value 2: _____

_____

_____

Value 3: _____

_____

_____

As a parting shot, let me emphasize that you are accountable for what you are modeling to your family. You have always been accountable, and you always will be. That is how it is. That may not be how you want it to be, but that is how it is. I encourage you to hold yourself to a higher standard. Be aware of the influence that your actions, emotions, and behavior have on your children, both internally and externally.

Let me remind you that although you are the most important role model in your child's life, you are not the only one. There are many people in the world who will step in your shoes and become models for your child, good or bad: your family and friends; your child's sitters, teachers and coaches; and the people who your child watches on TV.

Never lose sight of the stakes involved here. Your children are profoundly shaped by you, and your actions will resonate, for good or ill, throughout the rest of their lives. Be a parent who lives the qualities, characteristics and values you would like your family to emulate. Let your life be a living example of what you want to see in your children.

Epilogue

I believe that in every life and in the life of every family, there are a precious few moments in time when all things wrong can be made right, when all good things possible can be claimed. Moments when opportunities are either seized or missed and begin a chain of events and consequences that become the essence of our time in this world. There are critical choices and decisions that, when looked back upon as you stand at the end of your life, will be seen with great clarity as having been so pivotal as to have determined who and what you became and, just as important, what became of your children. Those events are unfolding in your life even as you are reading this very page. Some occur in the blink of an eye, while others accumulate a little at a time as days turn into weeks and weeks turn into months and then years. A great gift of life would be the ability to recognize those important moments, opportunities, decisions and choices for what they are at the time they are happening. *A great gift of life would be to know what to choose, what to do and how to do it at that critical time.*

My goal in writing *Family First* was to create a book that had the potential to become or at least contribute to one of those moments, one of those opportunities to know what you need to know, when you need to know it. My hope was to plant the seed for that ability to recognize those important moments by raising your sensitivities to certain critical elements for the healthy development of your family and children so you can respond in a positive manner that will have a lasting impact on those you love so dearly. I believe that if you can increase your knowledge about these important issues you cannot help but be a better parent.

My further hope is that this book will be a call to arms ignited by what I personally and professionally believe are meaningful insights—insights decisively stated in action-oriented terms so that you can translate them into behaviors that will create positive results in your family. These behavioral prescriptions are not intended to be one-size-fits-all solutions. But when you add your personal knowledge of your particular family and the personalities, strengths and weaknesses of your children you will achieve the customization of the plan needed for maximum impact.

As you seek to grow as a parent, a question you must answer is this: What is good information and what is not? These days you are likely being bombarded by an endless stream of theories and advice about parenting and family dynamics. How much is enough direction for your children? Who should run the family and how? To spank or not to spank? Co-sleeping, good bonding or bad karma? Potty training, when and how? Everybody has an opinion and many times those opinions are conflicting.

And what about me and *Family First*? Is the information I'm giving you right and correct and therefore worthy of being embraced? The answer to that question is up to you. I never ask anyone to substitute my judgment for their own. I ask only that you weigh carefully that which I have suggested here. If it will not withstand vigorous challenge, then you should reject it. I believe that *Family First* will withstand the challenge, and I believe in you and your ability to make a difference by using the concepts and action plans in your own family. But if you do disagree, then please seek answers elsewhere. If you totally reject everything I have said to you in this book but it causes you to have a heightened sensitivity and awareness and to find better-fitting answers elsewhere, answers that improve your family life, then I have been successful. This is all about results.

Assuming you believe there is value in these pages, your challenge is to consistently reorder or reemphasize your priorities and get excited about taking the steps to ensure that being a member of your family is a phenomenal experience for every individual. You cannot allow yourself to take the line of least resistance and live in a comfort zone of sameness. The difference between winners and losers is that winners do things losers don't want to do. Winners take action and take the risk of reaching for more. All the good intentions in the world will not change the course of your family without action. Winners are willing to tell themselves the truth about themselves as well as about their family and circumstances. You cannot change what you do not acknowledge. You can be a champion in your family with the tools we have focused on here. You can and you must.

I have intentionally been very forthcoming about my experiences in my own family, because coming from a flawed background is not something to be ashamed of, but it is something to overcome. I have shared with you the necessary factors of a phenomenal family comprised of phenomenal people, and included specific behavioral prescriptions for creating that reality. We have examined your family legacy acknowledging the good things and actively working to eliminate the bad. You have taken a careful look at how your children most likely see you and learned how to shift gears to bring about the best possible results in your interactions with them.

You have strapped on a tool belt holding the power tools of parenting. These are the tools you need whether you are in a traditional, single-parent or blended family. Beginning with a purposeful guidance system for pursuing your definition of success, you have learned to make communication a meaningful skill set instead of just an overused term. You have honed your negotiation skills to help you and your child to come up with important life plans that you can both be excited about. You have been vested with a powerful technology for creating behavioral change that prepares you to eliminate problem behaviors and establish desirable ones. You have been given the plan and challenged to have the courage to create a constructive disequilibrium in your home when the balance of power has gone askew.

You now have a plan for fashioning the environment in which your family exists in a way that pulls for success, peace and harmony. You have even identified specific action plans for creating their authentic personhood to ensure that they have a chance to become every bit of the unique individual they are meant to be. You have acknowledged the fact that as a powerful role model in your child's life your actions speak louder than words, and you have only to look at your children to see a reflection of who you are and how you live your life.

All of this work, learning and preparation for leading your family should be at the core of your mission in this life. The time for action, the time for leadership, is now. As you create the rhythm of your family, treat it with a reverence that sets it above all else. The thing about family—particularly the relationship between parent and child—is that there does exist this rare purity of identification, the ability to revel without envy in our child's success. Oscar Wilde, commenting on the small side of humans, made the observation that we all die a little inside at a friend's success or good fortune. But this is not true of parents and their child. In a truly phenomenal family, each family member views every other's interests as overlapping—in particular, our child's success is *our* success. Family is the purest form of love and must be preserved and nurtured like no other.

Someone once said to me: "When you look back at the scrapbook of your life, you will not see in it people you worked with. That scrapbook will be filled with *family* photos." She was right. Family takes precedence over all. Think of two people: One is a fabulously successful artist or CEO or athlete but a remote father to his children, a stranger to them; the second is an average guy, a plumber perhaps or a bus driver, who never wrote himself into the history books but who went the extra mile for his kids, always showed up, earned from them fierce love and respect. Which person would you want to be? To me the answer is obvious and this is not just a philosophical musing. It is an everyday choice.

Your children go out into the world every day. Whether it's their first day in kindergarten or at a new school after you've moved, their first time to compete in a spelling bee or a dance contest, they take their experiences of home with them. Maybe it is a Little League baseball game that challenges them or a mean and cruel bully at school; what will they say to themselves when life makes its certain demands? Have they been parented in a way that will cause them to go into the world feeling confident, worthy, special, safe and secure? Will they go forth with calm self-assurance and an expectation of success, because they have been valued, loved and nurtured every day of their lives? Or will they go into the world with self-doubt, feelings of inferiority and guilt or shame because their private reality, their home, is flawed and ugly. Will they worry about disappointing you and being judged when they experience the inevitable failures in life, or will they look inside themselves for the strength and ability you have worked to implant so they can draw upon it when you are not around to help? You have within your grasp the ability to make sure that every one of those questions is answered in the right way. As I said as we started this journey through *Family First*, the love in your heart has given you the energy and now you have the plan.

Never forget that it is an energy and a plan that you need, because there is a tug-of-war going on and as a parent you must never surrender. You must be willing to stand in the gap and be the anchor and the strength in your family. Your strong leadership will be your family's compass for their exciting journey through life. To this day, although he is long deceased, I still hear my father's voice in times of trial: "Son, be the man God intended. To whom much is given, much is expected and you have been blessed immensely." You can be that compass; I know you can and it's not too late. My father's positive influence in my life was immeasurably greater in the later and sober years of his life even when I was already grown and had gone on to my own life. It truly is not too late. Beginning today you must step up and without fear or guilt have the courage to say no when you must. You must have the courage to say yes when the risk-to-reward ratio supports it. Step up and make the plans and lead the way. I believe that the things in life that you will regret most are the things you don't do. Don't let this parenting initiative be one of the things you don't do. You can make your family proud, I know it—I absolutely know it.

It has been said that our children are messages that we are sending to a future we may never see. That may be, but our children will see it, our children will live it. Create for them a chance by leading your family with passion and commitment. And when you do, God will smile.

Appendix

Brief Description of
Survey Methods

In the fall of 2003, a questionnaire was administered to the audiences in the studio before the *Dr. Phil* show, as well as on the Dr. Phil website. The results between the two data collection sites were not significantly different. More than 17,000 subjects volunteered to participate in either the web-based study or the questionnaire administered during the *Dr. Phil* show. Many of the topics learned from the survey mirrored the subject matter of this book. The results of the responses were represented by the demographic categories of gender, age group, residence address, number of children raised in family, parenting time demands and type of family structure. Volunteers were treated in accordance with the Ethical Principles of Psychologists and Code of Conduct (American Psychological Association, 1992). The results cited in this book have been drawn from some of the analyses of the survey to be published in peer-reviewed journals. For more information about the survey, go to www.drphil.com.

Bibliographic References

CHAPTER REFERENCES

Chapter 1: Family Matters

Belsky, J., et al. 1984. *The Child and the Family*. Reading, MA: Addison-Wesley.

Gladding, S. T. 2001. *Family Therapy: History, Theory, and Practice*, 3rd ed. New York: Pearson Education.

Napier, A. Y., and C. A. Whitaker. 1978. *The Family Crucible*. New York: Harper & Row.

Chapter 2: Special Strategies for Divorced and Blended Families

American Academy of Pediatrics. 1999. *Caring for Your Baby and Young Child: Birth to Age Five*, 4th ed. New York: Bantam.

American Academy of Pediatrics. 1999. *Caring for Your School-Age Child: Ages Five to Twelve*. New York: Bantam.

Chapter 3: The Five Factors for a Phenomenal Family

Belsky, J., et al. 1984. *The Child and the Family*. Reading, MA: Addison-Wesley.

Bifulco, A., et al. 2002. Childhood adversity, parental vulnerability and disorder: examining intergenerational transmission of risk. *Journal of Child Psychology and Psychiatry* 43: 1075–1086.

Brook, J. S., et al. 1999. Transmissions of risk factors across three generations. *Psychological Reports* 85: 227–241.

McGraw, J. 2001. *Closing the Gap: A Strategy for Bringing Parents and Teens Together*. New York: Fireside Books.

———. 2000. *Life Strategies for Teens*. New York: Fireside Books.

Chapter 4: Your Family Legacy

Belsky, J., et al. 1995. Maternal personality, marital quality, social support and infant temperament: their significance for infant-mother attachment in human families. In R. R. Pryce and R. D. Martin (Eds.), *Motherhood in Human and Nonhuman Primates: Biosocial Determinants* (pp. 115–124). Basel, Switzerland: Karger.

Bifulco, A., et al. 2002. Childhood adversity, parental vulnerability and disorder: examining intergenerational transmission of risk. *Journal of Child Psychology and Psychiatry* 43: 1075–1086.

Brook, J. S., et al. 1999. Transmissions of risk factors across three generations. *Psychological Reports* 85: 227–241.

Chen, Z. Y., and H. B. Kaplan. 2001. Intergenerational transmission of constructive parenting. *Journal of Marriage and Family* 63: 17–31.

Freud, S. 1957. *Civilization and Its Discontents*. London: Hogarth Press. (Original work published 1929.)

McGraw, P. 1999. *Life Strategies: Doing What Works, Doing What Matters*. New York: Hyperion.

———. 2000. *Relationship Rescue: A Seven-Step Strategy for Reconnecting with Your Partner*. New York: Hyperion.

———. 2001. *Self Matters: Creating Your Life from the Inside Out*. New York: Simon & Schuster.

Simons, R. L., et al. 1992. Gender differences in the intergenerational transmission of parenting beliefs. *Journal of Marriage and Family* 54: 823–836.

———. 1991. Intergenerational transmission of harsh parenting. *Developmental Psychology* 27: 159–171.

Chapter 5: Your Parenting Style

Simons, R. L., et al. 1991. Intergenerational transmission of harsh parenting. *Developmental Psychology* 27: 159–171.

Sweney, A. 1981. *Leadership: Management of Power and Obligation, Part 1*. Wichita, KS: Test Systems, Inc.

Chapter 6: Powering Up

Beck, J. 1999. *How to Raise a Brighter Child: The Case for Early Learning*. New York: Pocket Books.

Berk, L. E. 2001. *Awakening Children's Minds: How Parents and Teachers Can Make a Difference*. New York: Oxford University Press.

Calkins, L. 1998. *Raising Lifelong Learners*. New York: Perseus.

Caruana, V. 2004. *Giving Your Child the Excellence Edge: 10 Traits Your Child Needs to Achieve Lifelong Success*. Carol Stream, IL: Tyndale House Publishers.

Christensen, L., et al. 1993. Effect of meal composition on mood. *Behavioral Neuroscience* 107: 346–353.

Dye, L., et al. 2000. Macronutrients and mental performance. *Nutrition* 16: 1021–1034.

Editor, 1994. Smart glue: brain research. *The Economist*, October 15, pp. 114–115.

Eliot, L. 1999. *What's Going On in There: How the Brain and Mind Develop in the First Five Years*. New York: Bantam Books.

Eysenck, H., et al. 1998. *Know Your Child's IQ*. New York: Penguin.

Friedman, D. 1997. Drumming to the rhythms of life. *U.S. News & World Report*, June 9, p. 17.

Golinkoff, R. M., et al. 2004. *Einstein Never Used Flashcards*. Emmaus, PA: Rodale Books.

Gordon, N. 2003. Iron deficiency and the intellect. *Brain Development* 25: 3–8.

Healy, J. M. 2004. *Your Child's Growing Mind: Brain Development and Learning from Birth to Adolescence,* 3rd ed. New York: Broadway Books.

International Society of Sport Psychology Position Statement. 1992. Physical activity and psychological benefits. *The Physician and Sportsmedicine* 20: 179–184.

Kanarek, R. B., et al. 1990. Effects of food snacks on cognitive performance in male college students. *Appetite* 14: 15–27.

Lawlis, G. F., and G. Palumbo. 2004. *Upping the IQ.* Mindbodyseries.com.

Levine, M. 2002. *A Mind at a Time: America's Top Learning Expert Shows How Every Child Can Succeed.* New York: Simon & Schuster.

Lloyd, H. M. 1996. Acute effects on mood and cognitive performance of breakfasts differing in fat and carbohydrate content. *Appetite* 27: 151–164.

———. 1994. Mood and cognitive performance effects of isocaloric lunches differing in fat and carbohydrate content. *Physiology and Behavior* 56: 51–57.

Schoenthaler, S. J., et al. 2000. The effect of vitamin-mineral supplementation on the intelligence of American schoolchildren: a randomized, double-blind placebo-controlled trial. *Journal of Alternative and Complementary Medicine* 6: 31–35.

———. 1991. *Improve Your Child's IQ and Behavior.* London: BBC Books.

———. 1999. Vitamin-mineral intake and intelligence: a macrolevel analysis of randomized controlled trials. *Journal of Alternative and Complementary Medicine* 5: 125–134.

Scrimshaw, N. S. 1991. Iron deficiency. *Scientific American,* October, p. 48.

Sizer, F., and E. Whitney. 1997. *Nutrition concepts and controversies,* 7th ed. Belmont. CA: West/Wadsworth.

Snyder, M., et al. 1999. Music therapy. *Annual Review of Nursing Research* 17: 3–25.

Stipeck, D. 2001. *Motivated Minds: Raising Children to Love Learning.* New York: Owl Books.

Wesnes, K. A., et al. 2003. Breakfast reduces declines in attention and memory over the morning in schoolchildren. *Appetite* 41: 329–331.

Zeisel, S. H. 2000. Choline: needed for normal development of memory. *Journal of the American College of Nutrition* 19: 528S–531S.

———. 1997. Choline: essential for brain development and function. *Advances in Pediatrics* 44: 263–295.

Chapter 8: Parenting with Clarity

Egeland, B., et al. 1987. International continuity of abuse. In R. J. Gelles and R. Lancaster (Eds.), *Child Abuse and Neglect: Biosocial Dimensions* (pp. 255–276). New York: Aldine de Gruyter.

Chapter 10: Parenting with Currency

Gladding, S. T. 2001. *Family Therapy: History, Theory, and Practice*, 3rd ed. Pearson Education.

Speigler, M. D., and D. C. Geuvremont. 2002. *Contemporary Behavior Therapy*, 4th ed. Wadsworth Publishing.

Chapter 13: Parenting in Harmony

Boszormenyi-Nagi, I., and J. IL. Framo. 1962. Family concept of hospital treatment of schizophrenia. In J. H. Masserman (Ed.), *Current Psychiatric Therapies*, Vol. 2. (pp. 159–166). New York: Grune & Stratton.

Boyle, M. H., et al. 1992. Predicting substance use in late adolescence: results from the Ontario Child Study follow-up. *American Journal of Psychiatry* 149: 761–767.

Gosling, S. D., et al. 2004. Should we trust web-based studies? *American Psychologist* 59: 93–104.

Speigler, M. D., and D. C. Geuvremont. 2002. *Contemporary Behavior Therapy*, 4th ed. Wadsworth Publishing.

Straus, M. A., and R. J. Gelles. 1988. How violent are American families? Estimates from the National Family Violence Resurvey and other studies. In G. T. Hotaling et al. (Eds.), *Family Abuse and Its Consequences: New Directions in Research* (pp. 14–37). Newbury, CA: Sage.

GENERAL PARENTING SOURCES

American Academy of Pediatrics. 1999. *Caring for Your Baby and Young Child: Birth to Age Five*. New York: Bantam.

Brazelton, T. B. 2001. *Touchpoints: Three to Six: Your Child's Emotional and Behavioral Development*. Cambridge, MA: Perseus Publishing.

———. 1992. *Touchpoints: The Essential Reference: Your Child's Emotional and Behavioral Development*. New York: Addison-Wesley Publishing Company.

Brazelton, T. B., and J. D. Sparrow. 2003. *The Brazelton Way*. Cambridge, MA: Perseus Publishing.

Chapman, G., and R. Campbell. 1997. *The Five Love Languages of Children*. Chicago: Northfield Publishing.

Clinton, H. R. 1996. *It Takes a Village: And Other Lessons Children Teach Us*. New York: Simon & Schuster.

Covey, S. R. 1997. *The Seven Habits of Highly Effective Families*. New York: Golden Books.

Eisenberg, A. 1994. *What to Expect: The Toddler Years*. New York: Workman Publishing.

Eyre, L., and R. Lyre. 2003. *The Book of Nurturing*. New York: McGraw Hill.

Faber, A., and E. Mazlish. 2002. *How to Talk So Kids Will Listen and Listen So Kids Will Talk.* New York: Quill/HarperCollins.

Forehand, R., and N. Long. 2002. *Parenting a Strong-willed Child.* New York: McGraw Hill.

Guthrie, E., and K. Matthews. 2002. *No More Push Parenting: How to Find Success and Balance in a Hypercompetitive World.* New York: Broadway Books.

————. 2002. *The Trouble with Perfect.* New York: Broadway Books.

Latham, G. J. 1994. *The Power of Positive Parenting: A Wonderful Way to Raise Children.* P & T Inc.

Lawlis, G. F. 2004. *The ADD Answer.* New York: Viking Press.

MacArthur, J. 2000. *What the Bible Says About Parenting: God's Plan for Rearing Your Child.* Nashville, TN: W Publishing Group.

Shaw, R., and S. Wood. 2003. *The Epidemic: The Rot of American Culture, Absentee and Permissive Parenting, and the Resulting Plague of Joyless, Selfish Children.* New York: Regan Books.

Siegel, D. J., and M. Hartzell. 2003. *Parenting from the Inside Out: How a Deeper Self-Understanding Can Help You Raise Children Who Thrive.* New York: Penguin Putnam.

Snyderman, N., and P. Street. 2002. *Girl in the Mirror: Mothers and Daughters in the Years of Adolescence.* New York: Hyperion.

CO-SLEEPING

Blair, P. S., et al. 1999. Babies sleeping with parents: case-control study of factors influencing the risk of the sudden infant death syndrome. *British Medical Journal* 319: 1457–1462.

Crawford, M. 1994. Parenting practices in the Basque country: Implications of infant and childhood sleeping location for personality development. *Ethos* 22: 42–82.

Farooqi, S. 1994. Ethnic differences in infant care practices and in the incidence of sudden infant death syndrome. *Early Human Development* 38: 215–220.

Forbes, J. F., et al. 1992. The co-sleeping habits of military children. *Military Medicine* 157: 196–200.

Granju, K. A. 1999. *Attachment Parenting: Instinctive Care for Your Baby and Young Child.* New York: Atria Books.

Hauck, F. R., et al. 1998. Bedsharing promotes breastfeeding and AAP Task Force on Infant Positioning and SIDS. *Pediatrics* 102 Part 1: 662–664.

Hayes, M. J., et al. 1996. Early childhood co-sleeping: Parent-child and parent-infant nighttime interactions. *Infant Mental Health Journal* 17: 348–357.

Heron, P. 1994. Nonreactive Co-sleeping and Child Behavior: Getting a Good Night's Sleep All Night Every Night. Master's thesis, University of Bristol, Bristol, UK.

Lewis, R. J., et al. 1988. The relationship between adult sexual adjustment and childhood experience regarding exposure to nudity, sleeping in the parental bed, and parental attitudes toward sexuality. *Archives of Sexual Behavior* 17: 349–363.

McKenna, J. J. 1990. Evolution and sudden infant death syndrome: Infant responsivity to parental contact. *Human Nature* 1: 145–177. (See all his references at www.nd.edu/~alfac/mckenna.)

Mitchell, E. A., et al. 1997. Risk factors for sudden infant death syndrome following the prevention campaign in New Zealand: A prospective study. *Pediatrics* 100: 835–840.

Mosenkis, J. 1998. The Effects of Childhood Co-sleeping on Later Life Development. Master's thesis. University of Chicago. Department of Human Development.

Mosko, S., et al. 1997. Maternal sleep and arousals during bedsharing with infants. *Sleep* 20: 142–150.

Nelson, E. A., et al. 1996. Child care practices and cot death in Hong Kong. *New Zealand Medical Journal* 109: 144–146.

Oppenheim, D. 1998. Perspectives on infant mental health from Israel: The case of changes in collective sleeping on the kibbutz. *Infant Mental Health Journal* 19: 76–86.

Richard, C., et al. 1998. Apnea and periodic breathing in bed-sharing and solitary sleeping infants. *Journal of Applied Physiology* 84: 1374–1380.

———. 1996. Sleeping position, orientation and proximity in bedsharing infants and mothers. *Sleep* 19: 685–690.

Sears, W. 1995. *SIDS: A Parent's Guide to Understanding and Preventing Sudden Infant Death Syndrome*. New York: Little, Brown & Co.

Sears, W., and M. Sears. 2001. *The Attachment Parenting Book*. New York: Little, Brown & Co.

Skragg, R. K., et al. 1996. Infant room-sharing and prone sleep position in sudden infant death syndrome. New Zealand Cot Death Study Group. *The Lancet* 347: 7–12.

Thevenin, T. 1987. *The Family Bed*. New York: Perigee Books.

SPANKING RESEARCH

Bean, A. W., et al. 1981. The effect of time-out release contingencies on changes in child noncompliance. *Journal of Abnormal Child Psychology* 9: 95–105.

Bernal, M. E., et al. 1968. Behavior modification and the brat syndrome. *Journal of Consulting and Clinical Psychology* 32:447–455.

Day, D. E., et al. 1983. An analysis of the physical punishment component of a parent training program. *Journal of Abnormal Child Psychology* 11: 141–152.

Larzelere, R. E. 2001. Combining love and limits in authoritative parenting. In J. C. Westman, *Parenthood in America* (pp. 81–89). Madison: University of Wisconsin Press.

————. Child outcomes of nonabusive and customary physical punishment by parents: An updated literature review. *Clinical Child and Family Psychology Review* 3: 199–221.

Larzelere, R. E., et al. 1998. Punishment enhances reasoning's effectiveness as a disciplinary response to toddlers. *Journal of Marriage and the Family* 60: 388–403.

————. 1996. The effects of discipline responses in delaying toddler misbehavior recurrences. *Child & Family Behavior Therapy* 18: 35–57.

LaVoie, J. C. 1973. Punishment and adolescent self-control. *Developmental Psychology* 8: 16–24.

McCord, J. 1988. Parental behavior in the cycle of aggression. *Psychiatry* 51: 14–23.

Roberts, M. W., et al. 1990. Adjusting chair timeout enforcement procedures for oppositional children. *Behavior Therapy* 21: 257–271.

————. 1988. Enforcing chair timeouts with room timeouts. *Behavior Modification* 12: 353–370.

————. 1982. Resistance to timeout: Some normative data. *Behavioral Assessment* 4: 239–248.

Sears, R. R. 1961. Relation of early socialization experiences to aggression in middle childhood. *Journal of Abnormal and Social Psychology* 63: 466–492.

Straus, M. A., and V. A. Mouradian. 1998. Impulsive corporal punishment by mothers and antisocial behavior and impulsiveness of children. *Behavioral Sciences and the Law* 16: 353–374.

Yarrow, M. R., et al. 1968. *Child Rearing: An Inquiry into Research and Methods*. San Francisco: Jossey-Bass.

Pro-Spanking Resources

http://www.geocities.com/spankwithlove3/

To Spank or Not to Spank? http://www.rtnfc.org/fs/fs0072.html

http://www.religioustolerance.org/spanking.htm

C. I. Scofield, *Scofield Reference Bible*, new and improved edition, p. 672.

R. C. Dentan, "The Proverbs," in C. M. Layon, 1991. *The Interpreter's One-Volume Commentary on the Bible*, Abingdon Press, p. 304.

The Family Research Council, a fundamentalist Christian organization, has an article "Spare the Rod? New Research Challenges Spanking Critics" at http://www.frc.org/frc/fampol/fp96ipa.html. They have materials available on this and other social matters that are written from a fundamentalist Christian perspective. They are located at 801 G Street NW, Washington, DC 20001. Toll-free number is 1-800-225-4008.

The Christian Family Foundation has a section on their website devoted to this topic: http://www.family.2b4.com/children/100Children.htm; http://www.family.2b4.com/letters/Q&A-hm.htm; and http://www.family.2b4.com/chidren/TheRod.htm.

Mack and Brenda Timberlake, "The Spanking Dilemma," at http://www.strang
.com/cm/stories/ct197111.htm.

Fundamental Baptist News Service, "Study Says Spanking Is Destructive," at
http://wayoflife.org/~dcloud/fbns/study.htm.

Mark Benedict, "Ann Landers Advises Against Spanking, But What Does God's
Word Teach," at http://www.family.2b4.com/children/ann-land.htm.

Christian Answers Network, "When Is a Child Old Enough to Be Spanked and
How Should It Be Done?" at http://www.christiananswers.net/q-flc/flc-f001
.html.

It's in the Bible, "Child Training/Parenting," at http://www.wolfe.net/-bibline/
info/childtraining.html.

Murray Straus, "Demystifying the Defenses of Corporal Punishment," at
http://pubpages.unh.edu/~mas2/CP64E.pdf. You need software to read these
files. It can be obtained free from: http://www.adobe.com/prodindex/acrobat/
readstep.html.

James Dobson, 2002. Complete Marriage and Family Reference Guide. Carol
Stream, IL: Tyndale House Publishers, pp. 114–115.

PHILLIP C. MCGRAW, PH.D., is the #1 *New York Times* bestselling author of *The Ultimate Weight Solution*, *Self Matters*, *Relationship Rescue*, and *Life Strategies*. He is the host of the nationally syndicated, daily one-hour series *Dr. Phil*. Dr. McGraw is one of the world's foremost experts in the field of human functioning. He and his family currently live in Los Angeles, California.